A modern course in
by

Oxford University Press 1976

EVERYTHING

EVERYWHERE

EVERYONE

Book 1

Oxford University Press, Walton Street, Oxford OX2 6DP

Oxford London Glasgow New York Toronto Melbourne
Wellington Cape Town Ibadan Nairobi Dar es Salaam Lusaka
Addis Ababa Kuala Lumpur Singapore Jakarta Hong Kong
Tokyo Delhi Bombay Calcutta Madras Karachi

© Oxford University Press 1976

Filmset by Thomson Litho Ltd., East Kilbride, Scotland
and printed in Great Britain at the University Press, Oxford
by Vivian Ridler, Printer to the University

Preface

This is a new course in Integrated Science for 11–14 year olds. It consists of two pupils' books and one teacher's book. It is based on the official Scottish syllabus in Integrated Science which has been used so successfully both in Britain and overseas for several years.

Each of the two pupils' books is divided into approximately 30 one-week teaching units, assuming 4–6 periods per week. Each of these teaching units is further divided into an initial three (sometimes six) pages of practical activities, followed by one page of text summarizing the basic ideas in the unit, and concluding with two pages of background enrichment material which draw out the human and social side of the ideas in the unit. A few of the units are preceded by a double-page pictorial essay containing additional introductory and resource material. The teacher's book contains suggestions about introductory activities, equipment requirements, teaching strategies, and extension work.

The books have been written for children (and teachers) to use, to read, and above all to enjoy. The books try to show that science questions everything, reaches everywhere, and is an intensely human activity—rich and exciting, amusing and bizarre—involving everyone. Science touches *everything, everywhere, everyone.*

About the authors

Bill Buckie BSc (Edinburgh) taught Science at Falkirk High School from 1963 to 1972, becoming Head of Biology in 1967. He joined Jordanhill College of Education in 1972 and is now Science Adviser for the Lothian Region.

Robin Sinton BSc (Edinburgh) began teaching Science at Falkirk High School in 1965 and in 1967 became Head of Biology at Galashiels Academy. He joined Hamilton College of Education in 1971 and is now teaching and living in New Zealand.

Les Young BSc, PhD (Glasgow) began teaching Science in Glasgow in 1964 and in 1967 became Head of Chemistry at Douglas Academy, Milngavie. In 1974 he became Deputy Headteacher at Clydebank High School and is now Headmaster of Hermitage Academy, Helensburgh.

Contents

Starting science
1. Trying, thinking, looking, taking care   2
2. Looking and listening   10
3. Measuring   16

Looking at living things
1. What are we?   24
2. How are we?   30

Exploring energy
1. Energy is   36
2. Energy converters   42

Explaining matter
1. Matter is   48
2. Examinations and explanations   54
3. A particle catalogue   62

Water
1. A very common substance   68
2. Stopper and shake   74
3. What's in the mixture?   80
4. A matter of life or death   86
5. Food and water   92

Growing and developing
1. From cells   100
2. Into a baby   106
3. Into boys and girls   112
4. Into men and women   118

Electricity
1. Electrons standing still   126
2. Electrons moving   132
3. Electrons pushing   138
4. Counting electrons   144
5. Electrons working   150

An ocean of air
1. Three gases   156
2. What's in the air?   162
3. Taking a breath   168
4. What happens in the lungs?   174
5. How do plants breathe?   180

Puzzles and problems   186

Starting science 1

Trying, thinking, looking, taking care

A laboratory is a new kind of classroom for you. You will want to know what happens in it. You can begin to find out by doing the work laid out.

At each station you will do something. Write down what you notice. Ask a question.

Trying

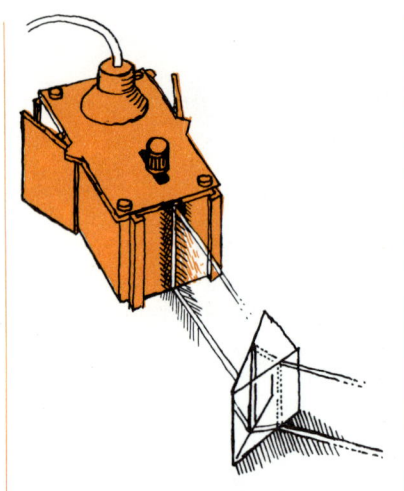

Try to bend the ray of light with the plastic block.

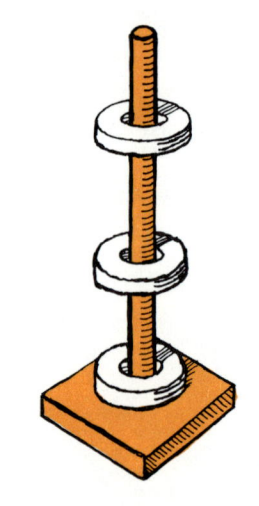

Try to float the metal rings. Try to stick them together.

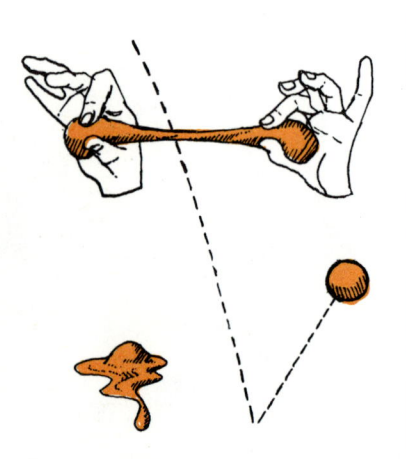

Try the potty putty.

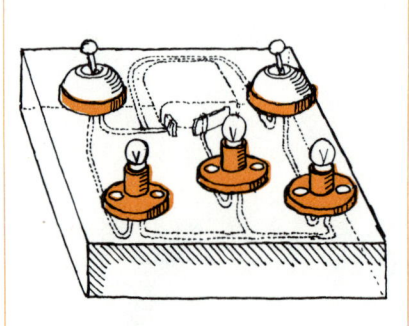

Try to switch all the lights on at the same time.

Try to pull the suckers apart.

Trying

Try whistling different notes into the microphone.

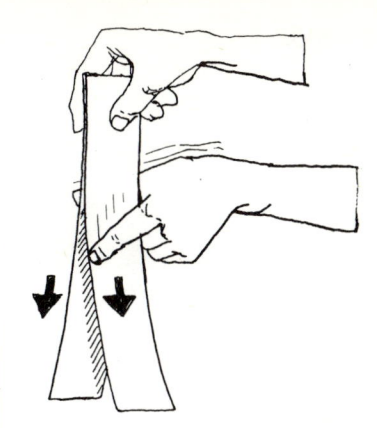

Try stroking the folded strip of newspaper with your thumb and forefinger.

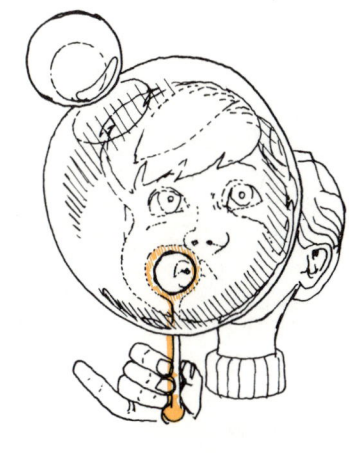

Try to blow a bubble.

Try pressing the cork down.

Try to make the slinky walk downstairs.

Try to stick the balloon to the wall.

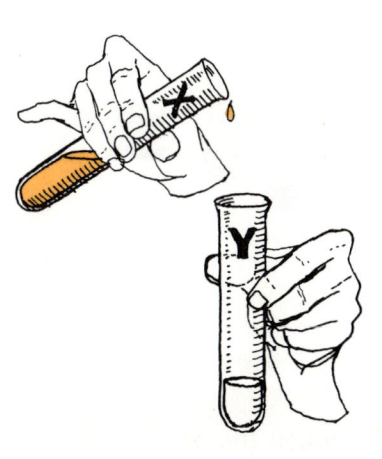

Try pouring one liquid into the other.

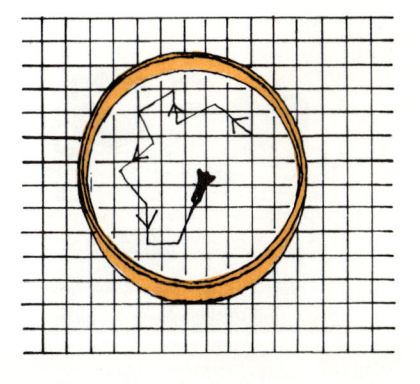

Try drawing the path followed by the animal.

Thinking

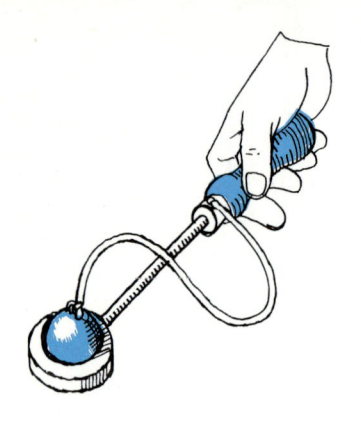

How can you pass the ball through the ring?

How does the toy balance?

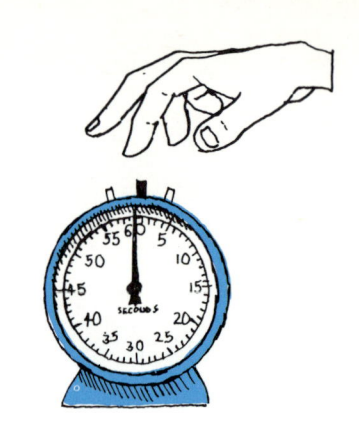

How do you work the stop clock?

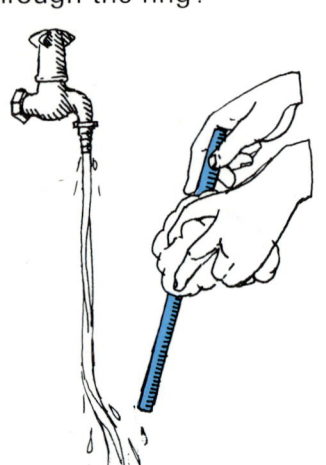

How does the piece of rubbed plastic bend the running water?

How do you know what the animal feeds on?

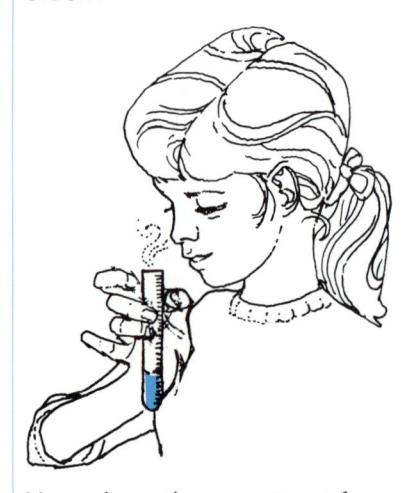

How does the scent get from the bottle to your nose?

How can metal cubes of the same size have different weights?

How can the police tell whose fingerprints these are?

How can you find out what someone is thinking?

Looking

Look at the stone.

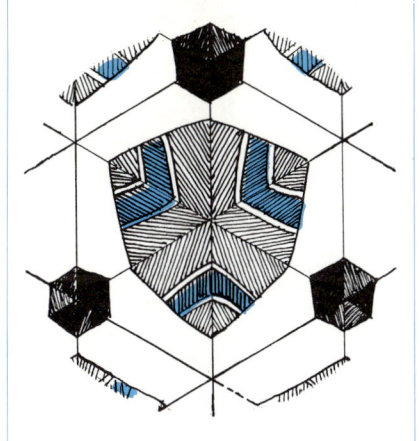

Look into the tube.

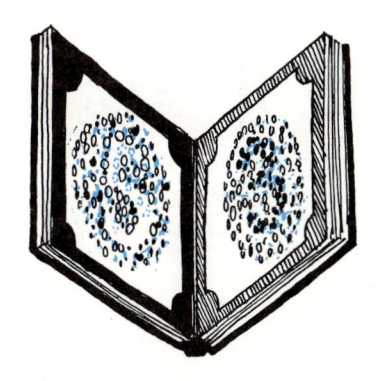

Look through the book.

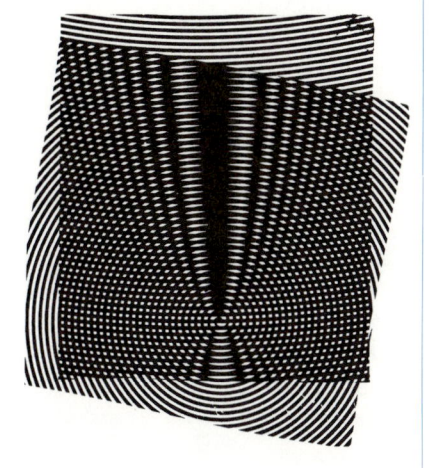

Look through the plastic.

Look at the plant.

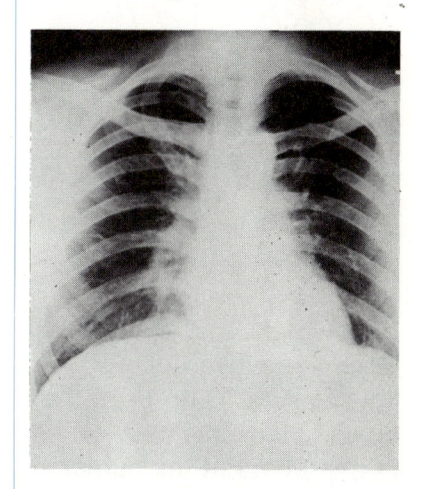

Look at the X-ray photograph.

Look at the scientist in the spoon.

Look at the aquarium.

Look at the photograph.

Taking care

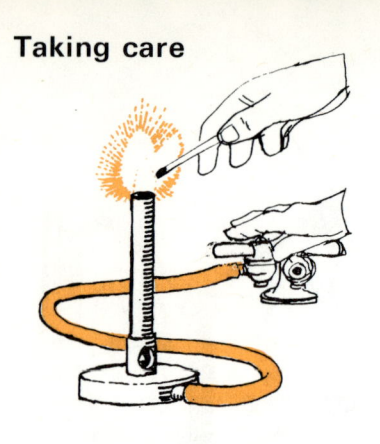

Take care when working with gas. Light the burner.

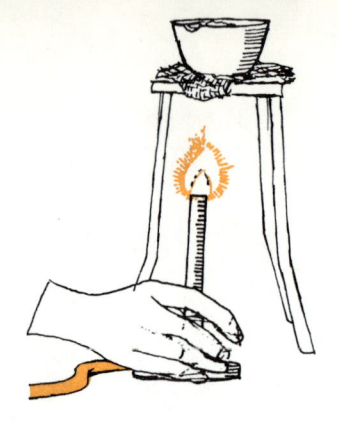

Take care when heating materials. Put the burner under the dish.

Take care when adding liquids. Add a drop of brown liquid to the clear liquid.

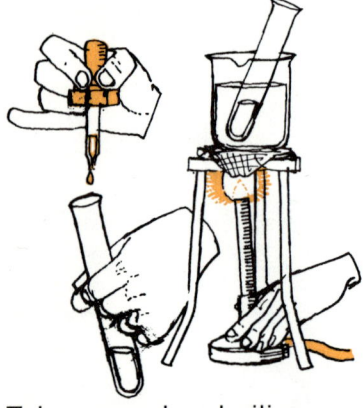

Take care when boiling liquids. Add 10 drops of the blue liquid to the clear liquid in the tube. Put the burner under the container.

Take care when handling acids. Add one drop of acid to the stone.

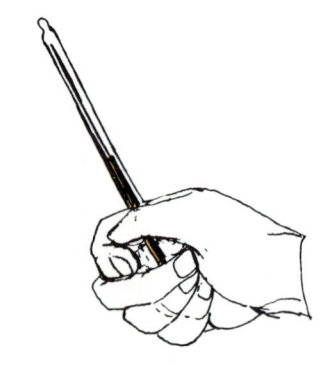

Take care when handling glass. Take the temperature of your hand.

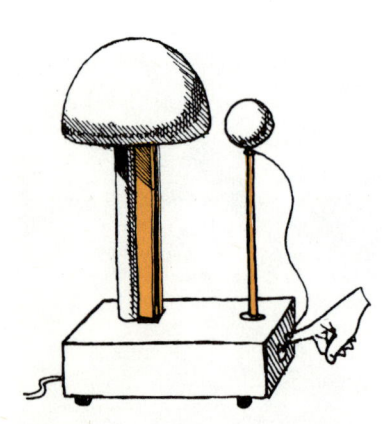

Take care when working with electricity. Switch on the machine.

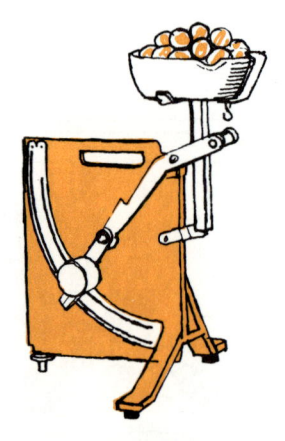

Take care when measuring out materials. Weigh out 50 g marbles.

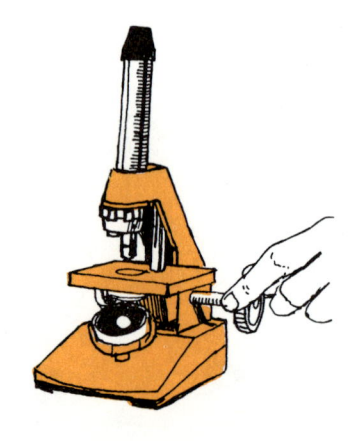

Take care when handling instruments. Use the knobs to get a clear picture.

What is science?

You are reading about science in a science room during science time. What is science?

Science is about the things around us

There was little that was new in the work you did in the laboratory. You thought about thinking. You tried to pull two suckers apart. You heated a liquid and took care when you did so. You looked at a photograph. You asked questions. You answered questions. That is what science is about. It is about the things and the events around us.

Scientists look at the things around us

And that begins to tell us what scientists do. They look at things and happenings. They look at everyday and at unusual things. They look at the rare, and at the common events. They will look at anything: big or small, living or never alive, useful or useless. No matter what it is some scientist, somewhere, somehow, will be prepared to look.

They ask questions about these things

Scientists do more than look. They notice. They look and ask a wondering question. That is noticing. What are wondering questions? These are the questions that come into your head when you are about to fall asleep. 'Wonder what makes me sleepy?' 'Wonder if the world will ever come to an end?' 'Wonder if budgies can really speak?' These are good questions; they are wondering questions.

They try to get the answer from the thing itself

Scientists start by looking. Then they ask questions. In that way there is no difference between a scientist and any of us. The differences begin with the answers. Answers from other people are not good enough. Answers from books are not good enough. Scientists try to get the thing itself to answer. That is tricky, but that is what science is about.

Starting science 1

Leonardo da Vinci

If a list of great artists is made, Leonardo's name will be on it. Look and you can see why.
If a list of great scientists is made, his name will be on that too. Look and you will see why.

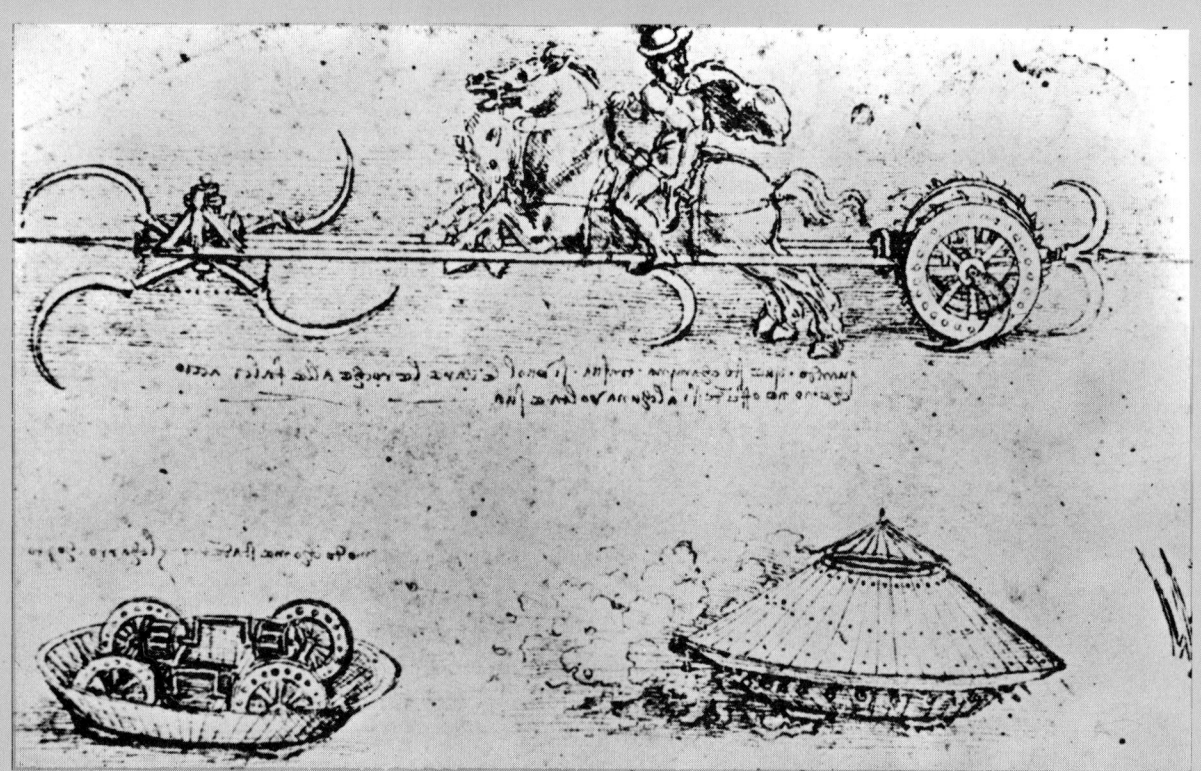

Make a list of great inventors and Leonardo will be on that too. 500 years ago he designed tanks, ball bearings, submarines, helicopters, and one or two other machines.

He was a very good engineer, although many of his devices were never built. Why not? To make many of these machines special materials are needed. It is only in the last 100 years that these materials have become available.

Starting science 1

An interested man.   An interesting man.

Looking at the sky, Leonardo realized that the moon did not shine by itself, that stars are very much bigger than our Earth, and that stars are very far away.

Leonardo was a great artist, a great engineer, a great astronomer, a great anatomist, and a great inventor. More than all these, he was an interested man. He was interested in the things and the happenings around him. Being interested is what he thought was important.

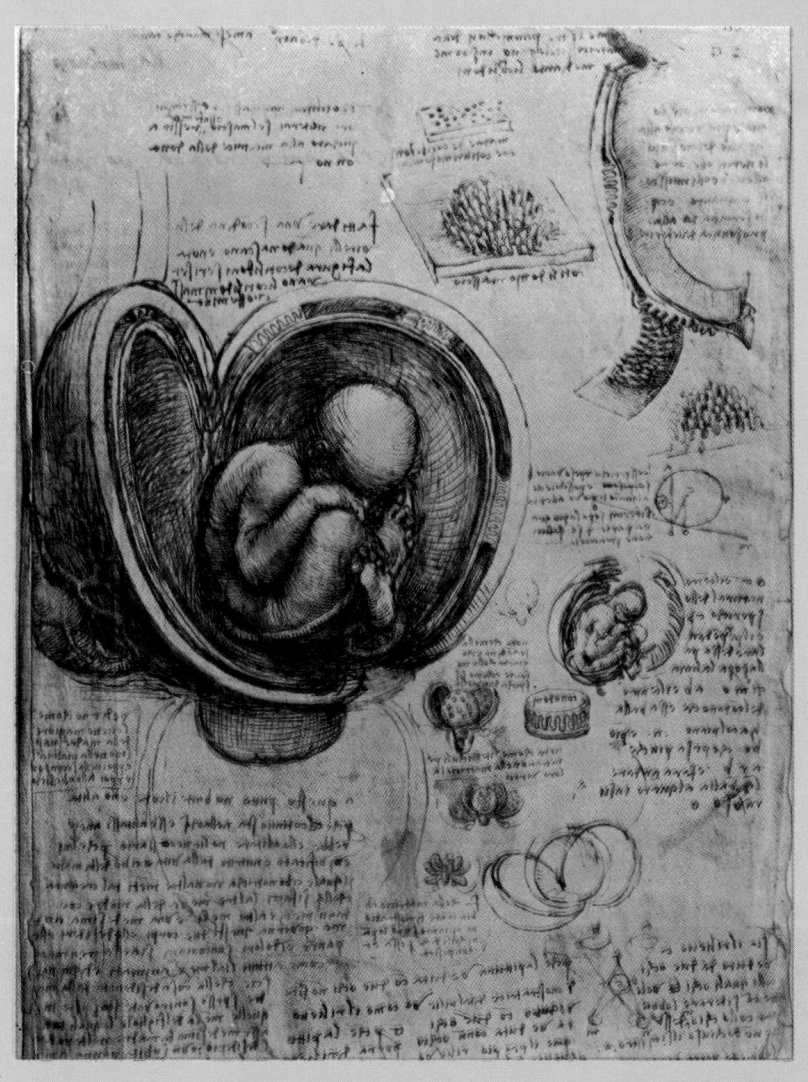

Hands are very difficult to draw well. Leonardo thought that he could draw hands better if he knew more about them. So he examined how they were built. What would you call that? Art or science? Or both?

In Leonardo's day people read books to find out how bodies were built. Leonardo thought it was better to look at bodies than at books. The answers the bodies gave were better. In his day that way of finding answers took courage as well as sense.

Starting science 2   # Looking and listening

If scientists start by looking, then we must start by looking. We must look at looking, and at our other senses. Then we must look at asking. And answering.

What do you hear?

Your teacher has a sound-making machine. It can make sounds of different loudness. It can make high and low notes. These are sounds of different pitch.

What is the highest note you can hear? Is this the same for everyone in the class? What is the highest note anyone in the class can hear?
What is the lowest note you can hear? Is this the same for everyone in the class? What is the lowest note anyone in the class can hear?

Notes of different pitch will be made. Each note will have the same loudness. Which sound appears to be loudest?

What is the quietest sound you can hear? How do you know the machine is working?

Your teacher will make two sounds, one after the other. Are these notes the same or not?

Starting science 2

What do you see?

Look at the pictures. Write down what you see. Then find a way of checking to see if that is right. Look at each picture again very carefully. Try to find out how the trick has been done.

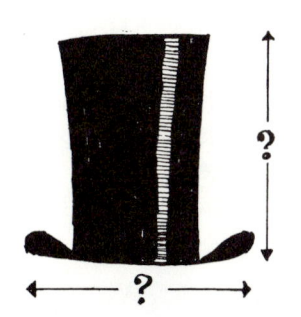

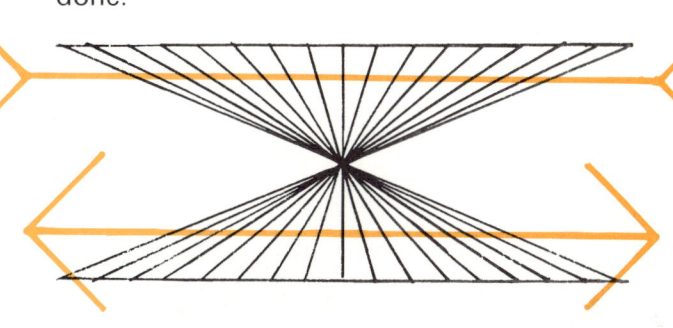

PARIS IN THE THE SPRING

11

What do you think?

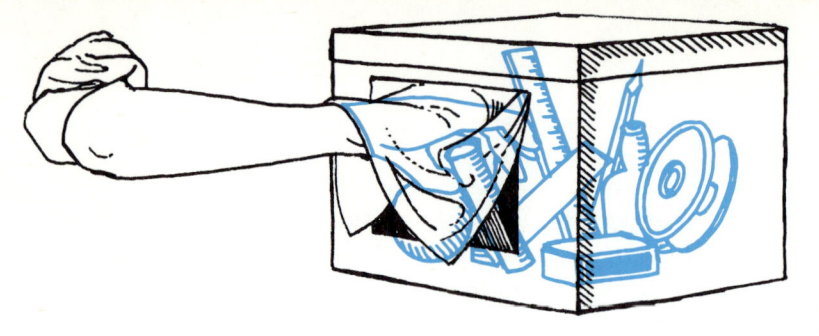

There are different things in this box. How many can you feel? What are these objects? What clues told you about these items? Check to see if you were right, but tell no one else in the class. Did you really need to check?

What is in this box? How can you find out without opening it? When you have decided what is in the box open it and check.

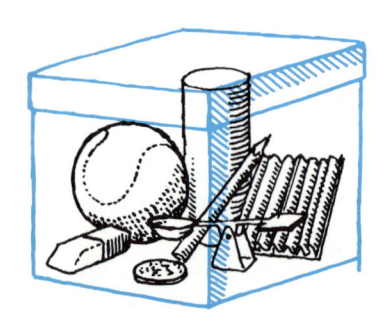

There is more than one object in this box. How many objects are there? How do you know?

Some cigarettes have been removed from this packet. How can you tell how many are left without looking? How could you check, still without opening the packet?

Say as much as you can about what is in this box. Then open the box. Can you now think of anything you might have tried before opening to check?

There is something in this box. It appears that there is nothing. How would you know there is something present? What is it?

What is the inside shape of this box?

How do we know what goes on in these boxes?

Starting science 2

Scientists notice

What we know depends on what our senses tell us. We must find out what our senses can and cannot do.

Our senses detect change

All around us are changes. It is the job of our senses to tell us about these changes in our world. To do this well we have several senses. Each detects special kinds of changes. At this moment your ears are sensing changes in sound in the classroom. Your eyes are detecting differences in the light from this page. But your ears do not hear and your eyes do not see. Your senses detect differences in the world. Your brain sorts out what these mean.

Our senses are good

Your senses are very sensitive. They keep you well informed about your world. You can see markings on the moon thousands of kilometres away. This photo is made up of thousands of tiny dots. Look carefully. Your senses can pick one change out of many. You can hear your name called out in a noisy room. Your senses can detect many changes. You can see. You can hear. You can taste and smell and feel. You have other senses and you are not sure what they do. You even have senses you do not know about.

We cannot sense everything

Even so there are changes which are beyond our senses. We cannot hear sounds above or below a certain pitch. But we know sounds are being made. Instruments have been invented to show us that there are changes. We can get confused about the meaning of some changes. We can sort out that confusion. The simplest way to do this is to measure. Scientists spend a lot of time finding out whether there is a change or not. They spend a lot of time trying to measure these changes.

Starting science 2

The illusion industry

It seems that illusions are things we can do without. But then, things are not always what they seem. We get a lot of pleasure from illusions.

This film print is just one of many that make up any shot.

Even a short action is made up of hundreds of photos. It appears to be one action.

Photos cannot speak. The sound is fitted at the side of the film.

Actors are never shot. But why do they bleed?

A giant? No, a normal man and a toy ship.

14

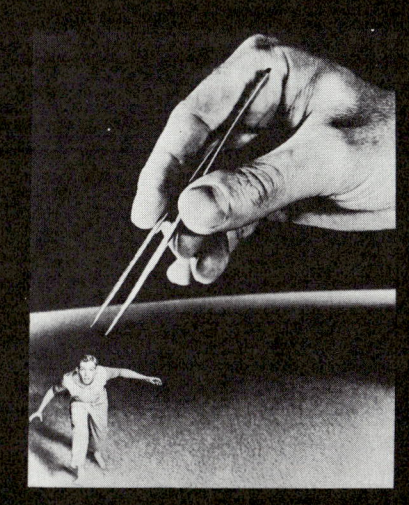

A giant hand? Or an incredible shrinking man?

A dinosaur? No, a magnified lizard.

You see the driver's terrified face. Then you see the car go over the cliff.
Add these together and the driver is in the car going over the cliff.

Does this spoil watching films? No. After all seeing is believing. Or is it?

Starting science 3

Measuring

To help our senses we have invented many instruments. Some instruments help to check the accuracy of our senses. Here are a few of these and their uses.

Easy measurements

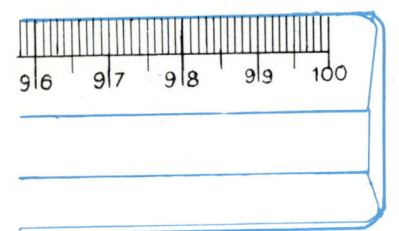

Length is measured in metres m and centimetres cm.
Length is measured with rulers, tapes, metre sticks.
Length is measured when you answer the questions:
'How long, or broad, or deep, or high, or wide is it?'

Measure the length of this page. How wide is it? How long is your hand? How tall are you? How high is this room? How would you measure the width of this dot •? How would you find the length of the edge of this leaf?

Area is measured in square metres m^2 and square centimetres cm^2.
Area is measured by multiplying length by breadth.
Area is measured when you answer the question:
'How big a surface has it?'

Measure the area of this page. How large an area has your bench? What is the surface area of the floor? How would you measure the area of the leaf? How would you measure the area of your body?

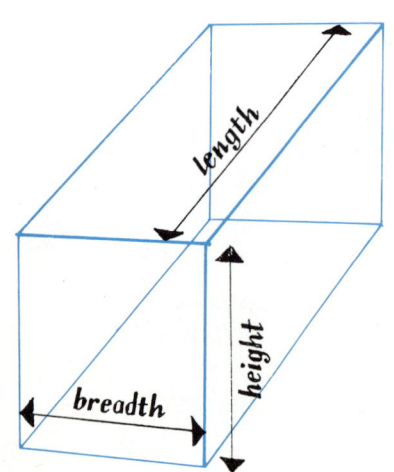

Volume is measured in cubic metres m^3 and cubic centimetres cm^3.
Volume is measured by multiplying length by breadth by height.
Volume is measured when you answer the question:
'How big a space does it take up?'
Measure the volume of this book. What is the volume of this room? What is the volume of a room at home? How would you measure the volume of this page?

Harder measurements

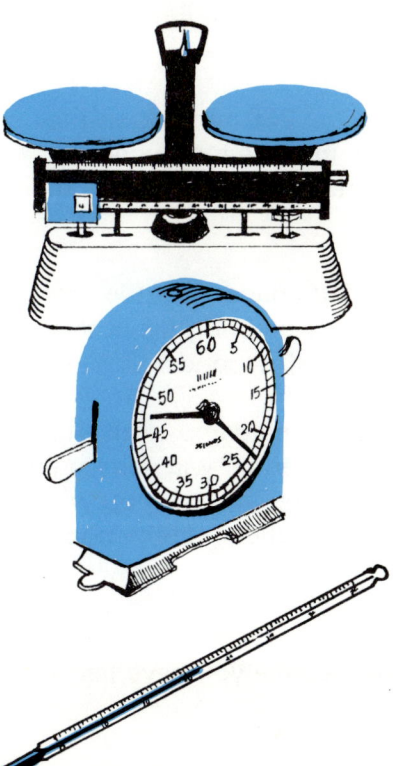

always read the bottom of the meniscus

You cannot easily measure the volume of a liquid by multiplying length by breadth by height.
The volume of liquids is measured in litres l and millilitres ml.
The volume of liquids is measured using syringes, measuring jars, pipettes, and burettes.
Measure the volume of a spoonful of water.
Find the volume of a small bottle.
How would you measure the volume of one drop of water?
How would you find the volume of a pencil; of a ring?

Mass is measured in grams g and kilograms kg.
Mass is measured with scales or balances.
Mass is measured when you answer the question:
'How much stuff is in it?'
Measure the mass of this book.
What is the mass of a penny?
How much stuff is in 50 ml water?
How would you measure the mass of air in a tyre?

Time is measured in seconds s, minutes min, hours, and days.
Time is measured with stop watches and stop clocks.
Time is measured when you answer the questions:
'How long does it take?' 'How long does it last?'
Measure the time it takes you to read page 16.
How long does a fruit gum last?
How long does it take to jump up in surprise?

Temperature is measured in degrees Celsius °C.
Temperature is measured with a thermometer.
Temperature is measured when you answer the question:
'How hot or cold is it?'
Measure the temperature of the air in the room.
How cold is the water from the cold tap?
How would you measure the temperature of a volcano?

17

Many measurements

It is now time for a rest. And with that rest you could have a cup of coffee. Make it this way.

The materials you will need are:
coffee   sugar   milk   water

The instruments you will need are:
balance   measuring jar   thermometer   clock

The containers you will need are:
filter paper   spoon   250 ml flask   paper cup

The safety equipment you will need is:
tripod and gauze   stand and clamp   damp cloth

Hot water is dangerous. Boiling water is very dangerous. They both scald, and scalds are very painful. Follow these instructions and think about them.

Use the stand and clamp to hold the 250 ml flask on the tripod. Measure out 100 ml water into the measuring jar. Put this water into the flask. Light the burner and boil the water. Turn out the burner.

Weigh out 3 g coffee on a clean filter paper. Put this into the paper cup. Weigh out 10 g sugar and put this in the cup. Add to this 20 ml milk. Stir for 30 seconds.

Wrap the flask with the hot water in the damp cloth. Hold the flask firmly in both hands. Your partner will release the screw holding the flask. Pour the water into the cup with the coffee. Stir for 30 seconds. Allow the coffee to cool to 60 °C.

That might not be the best cup of coffee you have tasted. It is probably the most exact.

When you have finished tidy the apparatus away.

Scientists measure

In the past people used their bodies to measure. This seems a simple and sensible thing to do. Why stop?

We must make exact measurements

Your hand is certainly a handy measuring instrument. But is it a good ruler? Measure this page using your hand. Now measure using a ruler. Which is more accurate? Counting too is hard using body units. How many thumb lengths make one hand length? How many hands in an arm? It is easier to count when you know 10 millimetres make 1 centimetre and 100 centimetres make 1 metre.

We must be able to compare measurements

There is something else. Your hand is not the same size as your neighbour's hand. Your measurements are all a bit different from everyone else's measurements. To check on our senses we measure. But that would be useless if everyone used different measurements. One hand means a different thing for everyone. One metre is the same length everywhere. It is a standard measurement.

We can ask many measuring questions

Scientists spend much time asking and answering measuring questions. Is that clock exact enough? Will we need to invent a new kind of clock? What is the speed of light? How long ago did dinosaurs live? When will the next eclipse take place? How often does your heart beat in a minute? They ask and answer these questions when they are noticing.

Starting science 3

Earthquake

The list on this page is a measuring instrument. It is called the Mercalli Scale. It gives inexact but easily made measurements. The measurements described on the next page are more exact. They were not made easily.

The Saada hotel in Morocco before and after an earthquake on 29 February 1960.

Mercalli number

1. Seismographs can detect such a small shock; humans cannot.
2. People in tall buildings might notice this.
3. People can tell where the shock comes from.
4. Teacups rattle and ceilings crack.
5. Everyone notices this. Furniture and beds rattle.
6. People leave their houses in fear.
7. Window panes break. Church bells ring.
8. Church towers and chimneys collapse.
9. Some buildings are totally ruined.
10. Cracks appear in the street. Gas and water mains are broken.
11. All stone buildings are destroyed. Railway lines are twisted.
12. All man-made things are in ruins. The landscape is entirely changed.

Jumping into the oven

There are very strong winds in the centre of a thunderstorm. To measure how strong these winds are planes sometimes fly through the storms. That is like jumping into the oven to find out how hot it is.

The plane was now flying through the storm for the seventh time. Suddenly it was no longer a normal storm flight. Through the loudspeaker in the control room came a message. The voice was loud and frightened. It scared everyone in the room.

'Control. Control. This is 3-5-4. Get me out of this. Get me out.' You could hear the terror in the voice. 'Control. I can't handle the plane. Get me out.'
'3-5-4. This is Control. Steer right. Steer right.'
'Control, this is 3-5-4. I can't turn. I can't turn it.'
'3-5-4. Control here. O.K. Keep your present direction.'

A few seconds passed. No one spoke. There was silence. Everyone was waiting for another call. '3-5-4. This is Control. Do you read me?' No answer. More seconds slipped by. All eyes were on the silver dot on the radar screen. They did not see a dot. They saw a plane in serious trouble. They saw a plane with three men on board. But what was the trouble?

Then suddenly, just as quickly as it had started, it was over. 'Control. 3-5-4 I'm O.K. at 7500 metres.'
'3-5-4. Control. Nice to hear from you. Come on home.'

The pilot told Control what had happened. It was a normal run and then it was like hitting a brick wall. The plane was very badly shaken about and went completely out of control. Pulling on the stick, pushing the rudders made no difference. The plane was moving. The pilot didn't know whether it was going up or down. And he had no say in the matter. It was the storm which was carrying the plane. All the time it was snowing or raining or there were huge hailstones battering the plane. Then, all of a sudden, they were out of the storm.

They asked the meteorologist for an explanation. He thought for some time. His idea was that storms contain huge air bubbles. They had battered and banged through one. It carried the plane up at a speed of 120 km per hour. Now he thought this idea could be checked if they could find another storm. Perhaps the crew would like to find one of these bubbles?

Looking at living things

All creatures great and small

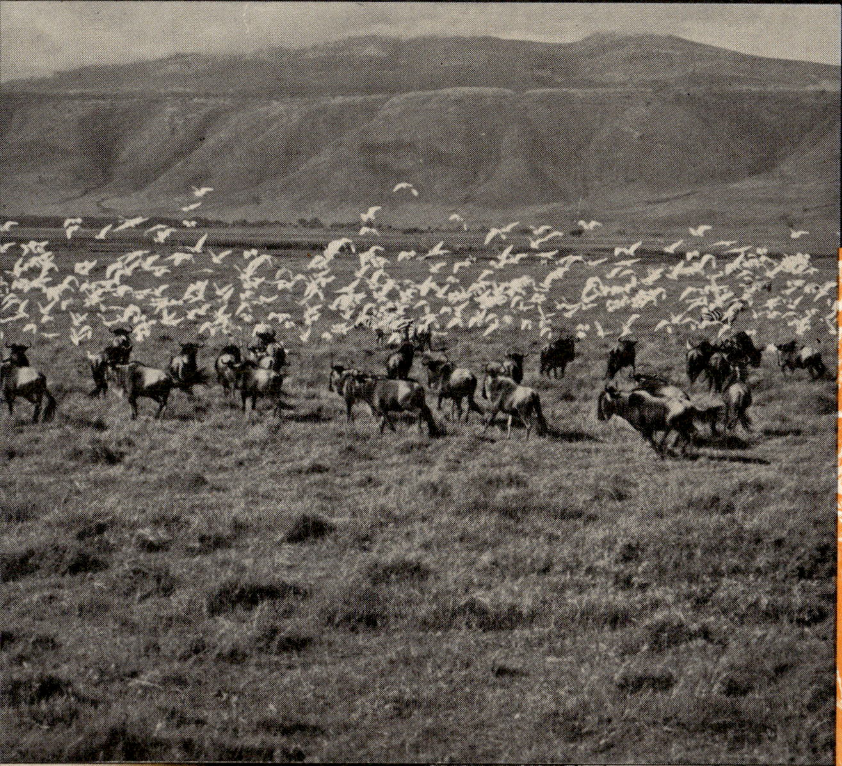
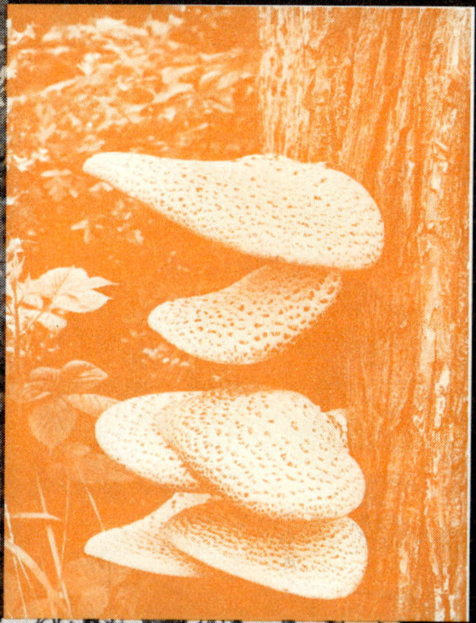
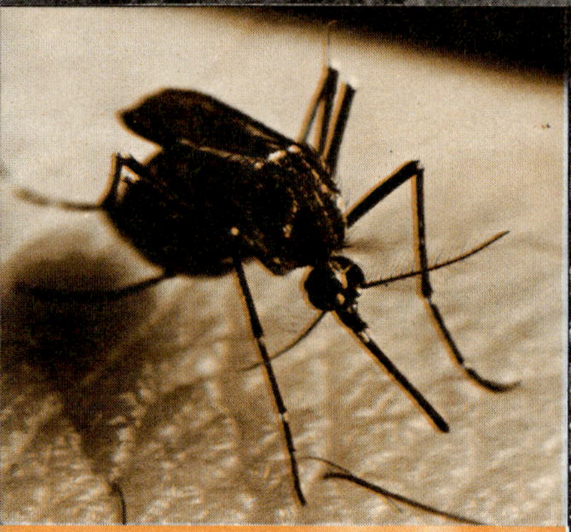
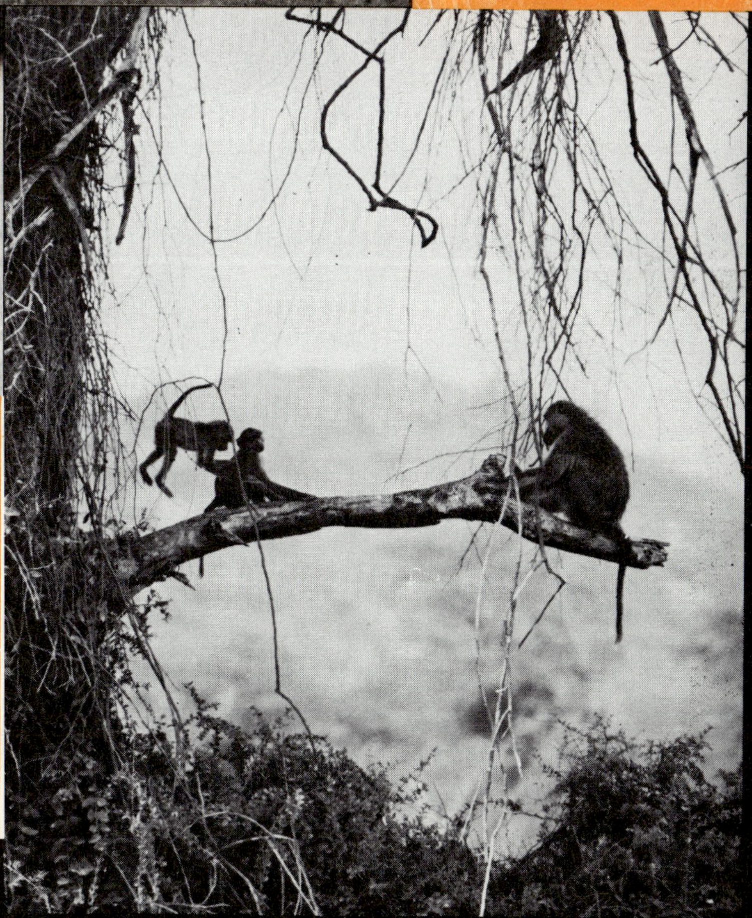
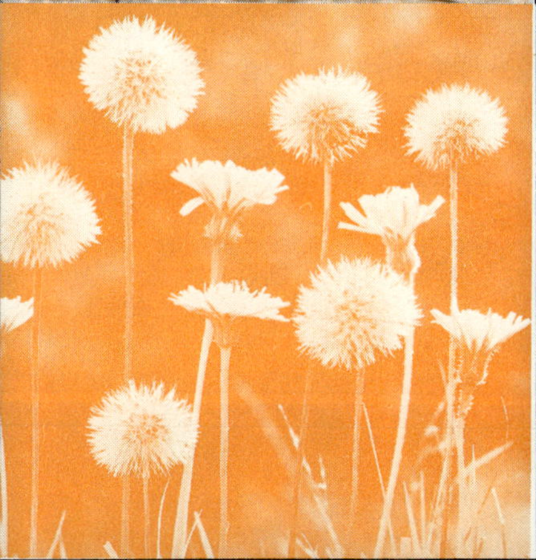

Looking at living things 1

What are we?

Some scientists study big apes. Some examine creatures whose skin is their skeleton. Others look at organisms which never eat. So will you.

Looking at yourself

The most interesting animal is yourself. That is also the animal easiest to get hold of. So start with yourself. How do you start? You make a report (secret of course).

Forename: Surname:

Sex: (male or female)

Birthday: Age:

Brothers: Sisters:

Height: cm   Weight: kg

Temperature: °C

Breaths per minute: Breathing volume: ml

Pulse rate:

Hours spent sleeping: Bedtime:

Hair: straight/wavy/curly/corkscrew/fair/red/brown/black/grey

Skin: pink/olive/dark brown/light brown/yellow/black

Eyes: red/blue/grey/green/light brown/dark brown

Favourite food:

Most hated food:

Past illnesses:

Looking at living things 1

Looking at others

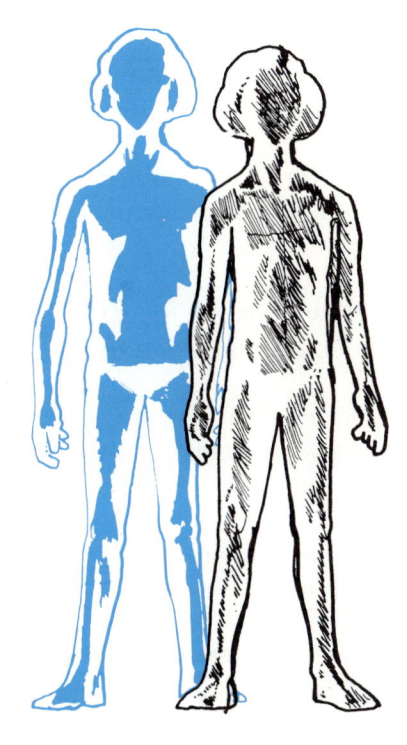

Look at any other human and you see yourself. The other person may be a bit different, but not much. See for yourself.

Look at your partner. Make a list of 5 differences between yourselves.

Look at your partner's face. Make a list of 5 differences between your faces.

Look again. As quickly as you can, make a list of 10 similarities you notice.

Which lists were easier to make: the similarities or the differences? Which lists have the more important features: the similarities or the differences? Are we more like one another than we are different?

Look at the reports. Is it normal for human beings to be different from each other?

You can see how different we can be. Make a bar chart showing the breathing rate of everyone in the class. Which is the most common number of breaths taken in one minute? Which is the least number of breaths taken in one minute? Which is the greatest number of breaths taken in one minute? What is the difference between the lowest and most common breathing rate and between the most common and the highest breathing rate? Are these differences very great?

Write a paragraph of three or four sentences on human beings. Say what you think makes human beings different from all other organisms.

25

Looking at living things 1

Looking at insects

Look at an insect and you do not see yourself. The insect is completely different. It is so different it may remind you of things you had forgotten to notice about yourself.

Write down, in two or three sentences, what you notice first about the locust.

How many legs does a locust have? Try to work out the order in which the legs move. In what ways can locusts move? Are all the legs the same?

Give the locust some fresh grass. How does the locust eat this? How would you find out the locust's favourite food?

Look at a dead locust with the hand lens. In what ways are locusts' faces different from ours? In what ways are they the same?

Look again at the dead locust. How are the wings of a locust different from the wings of a bird?

Look at the report on yourself. How many of the items could you fill in for a locust report? How many of the items do not even apply to locusts?

Make a list of the ways you are different from a locust. Make a list of the ways you are similar to a locust. Are you more different from a locust than you are similar?

Now look and think about a geranium plant. Are you more like a locust or more like a geranium?

Because they are so different, locusts can tell us about ourselves. That is a good reason for studying locusts. Can you think of any other reason for knowing about locusts?

26

Looking at living things 1

What am I?

To know what a human being is, it is not enough to look at human beings. You must look at other things.

I am male, aged 12 years. I have one brother and two sisters. I am 150 cm high and weigh 45 kg. My hair is black and straight. My eyes are blue and my skin white with freckles. I love ice cream and hate cabbage. I speak English and I quite like school.

I am female. I have 6 legs and wings attached to the middle part of my body. On my face there are 5 eyes and two long stalks stick out. These are antennae and are for smelling. My jaws are like a long needle. They are tough because they are part of my skeleton. I stick my jaws into the blood vessels of other animals and suck up blood. That is the only food I eat. I do not go to school because I was born knowing all I need to know.

The word picture of the boy is correct. When you read the word picture of the mosquito you realize something. You realize that the picture of the boy is not complete. It does not tell you how the boy is different from other creatures. By looking at other creatures you can see what is missing. The first word picture tells how someone is different from other people. The insect word picture shows how alike all people are.

I am male and female. I am green and have many leaves. I do not move. What does eating mean?

Looking at living things 1

Wanted for murder

Louse

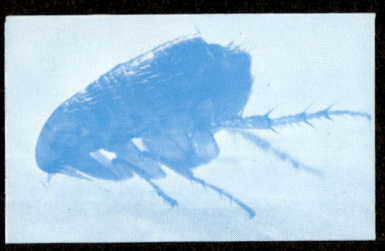

Flea

Tse-tse fly

Housefly

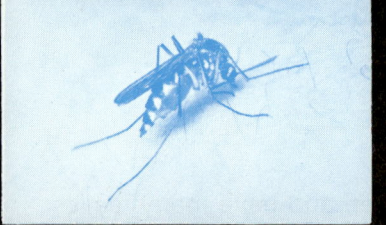

Mosquito

Some insects are our deadliest enemies. To combat an enemy, you must know as much as you can about him. Here is a selection of really dangerous insects, and some of the ways in which they are dangerous.

Lice carry microbes. Lice have a very unpleasant habit. They feed on blood. They feed on our blood—while we are living! To do this they stab a hole in our skin. Into this wound pass microbes. The microbes carried by lice cause typhus fever. Typhus fever is also called jail fever, ship fever, hospital fever, famine fever.

Fleas also bite us. The most important germs carried by fleas are the ones causing bubonic plague. You know this disease better as the Black Death.

The tse-tse fly in Africa feeds on blood. It pierces the skin and sucks out blood. Germs carried by the tse-tse fly cause the disease called sleeping sickness. This disease affects cattle and horses as well as man.

The housefly you know well. It is not as dangerous as the others on this page. That does not make it safe. It sucks up liquids from fresh or rotting foods. Germs from the rotting food are passed onto our fresh food. Sometimes these germs cause food poisoning.

Mosquitoes are the most notorious of all the harmful insects. The male mosquito is not dangerous. He lives his life feeding on fruit juices. The female, however, feeds on blood. The female mosquito can carry the germ that causes malaria. She can also carry the germ that causes yellow fever. Truly, the female of this species is far deadlier than the male!

Yellow fever

In 1900 everyone thought the belongings of yellow fever victims were deadly. They believed the disease passed from one person to another through articles like bedding and clothing. Everyone except Dr. Walter Reed, an American army doctor in Cuba. He was not quite sure that the disease was spread in this way and he wanted to be sure.

So, to be sure, he had two little houses built. The first house was really nasty. It measured only 4 m × 6 m. The doors were arranged so no mosquitoes could get in. The two windows were on the long wall beside the doors, so no breeze could get in. There was a fire to keep the room warm, and buckets of water to keep the air moist. Then there were the boxes.

These boxes held unwashed towels and sheets from the yellow fever wards of the Havana hospitals. They had been brought in by soldiers on the night of 30 November. On that same night, three men came in to spend three weeks in that room. Their first and only job was to open the boxes and to spread the linen around that hot, tiny, sticky room.

Night after night, Dr. Cooke and Privates Fernetan and Fox stayed in that house. They slept on yellow fever blankets and wondered about the men who had last slept on them. They dried with yellow fever towels and wondered about the men who had been dried on them before. On the 21st day they were taken to a clean, airy tent. They were taken to await an attack of yellow fever. It never came.

The second house was really nice. A cool breeze came through the two windows opposite the door. The bed was clean, and cleaner still was the bed linen. Over the windows was netting so fine that no insect could get in—or out.

At noon on 21 December, John Moran, a clerk, walked into that room. He joined 15 she-mosquitoes released there at 11.55 by Dr. Reed. These insects had last fed from the blood of yellow-faced soldiers in the hospitals. Some had fed recently, others not, but all were now hungry. In a minute the buzzing started around his head. In two minutes he was bitten. In the 30 minutes he was in that room he was bitten 7 times (without the satisfaction of destroying even one of the insects). He returned later that day for another session, and he returned the next day for the last time.

On Christmas Day, 1900, he had a fine present. It was in his head. How it thumped. It was in his eyes. How sore they were. It was in his bones. How they ached. He had yellow fever. But he lived.

So Reed was now sure. The dirty pest hole of a house (with no mosquitoes) was safe. The clean house (with infected mosquitoes) was dangerous. The infection was passed by mosquitoes.

Looking at living things 2

How are we?

There are millions of different kinds of living things. Where do they come from? What do they do? How do we sort them out?

Group them together

Which is the odd animal out in this collection? Try to name the other animals. The other animals all belong to one group. What is that group?

The odd animal belongs to another group of animals. What is the name of that group? Name at least four other members of that group.

Both these groups belong to the bigger group called the mammals. We also belong to this group. Mammals can be recognized by their hair, or fur, or wool.

Name: 1 mammal which can fly.
          2 mammals which live in the sea.
          3 mammals which live in Australia.
          4 mammals which have white fur.
          5 mammals which are useful to man.
          6 other mammals you can think of.
          7 animals which are not mammals.

Which statement is correct:

Animals in the same group live in the same place.
Animals in the same group are built in the same way.
Animals in the same group are the same colour.

In what ways is a monkey more like a human than a pig?
In what ways is a pig more like a human than a frog?
In what ways is a frog more like a human than a fish?
In what ways is a fish more like a human than a fly?
In what ways is a fly more like a human than a plant?
In what ways is a plant more like a human than a stone?

Looking at living things 2

Keep them apart

You have brought in a collection of organisms and pictures of organisms. Your job now is to sort them into groups. You will sort them into groups depending on the way they are built.

Sort out all the mammals. Write the names of ten.

You can easily separate out the plants. When you have sorted them out, have a look and decide how they are all alike. Then break this large group of plants into smaller groups.

Another big and important group of animals are those with more than two pairs of legs. Separate from your collection all the animals in this group. Insects are part of this group. Separate out the insects. In what ways are insects built similarly? What other kinds of animals are in this group? In what ways are they similar to insects? In what ways are they different from insects?

There are five groups of animals with backbones. Here are these groups:

> fish
> amphibia
> reptiles
> birds
> mammals

From your collection, separate out the backboned animals. Take each of these animals and put it into its group. Give a reason for putting it into that group.

What kinds of living things are left in your collection? Why are these things included in the one large group: the living things?

Looking at living things 2

The evolution game

Where do all these organisms come from? That's a long story—about two thousand million years long.

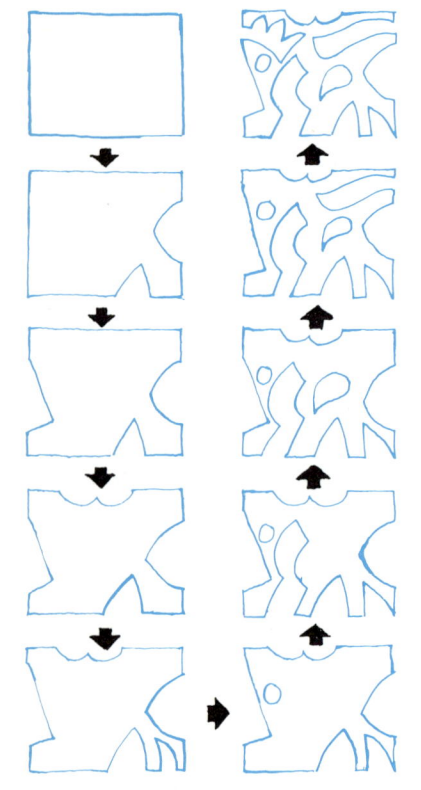

Take 10 identical sheets of paper. Put one aside. Take the next 9 sheets. Cut the same shape from each. Put one of these cut sheets next to sheet 1. Take the next 8 sheets and cut out a different shape from each. Put one to the side with sheets 1 and 2.
Keep on with this game until you have 10 sheets in a row. Now look at that row. Look at the first sheet. Look at the last. See how many small changes can add up. See how you can start with one thing and slowly change it into something different.

Different people in the class have made different series of cuts. Put the first sheet of paper in the centre. Arrange the others in a star coming out from that centre. The sheets at the ends of the arms have a common ancestor.

Mammals have hair and do not lay eggs. Reptiles have a scaly skin and lay eggs. It is very likely that these two groups are related. What might the common ancestor be like? Is such an animal possible?

Birds have wings and beaks; reptiles have legs and teeth. The way both groups are built suggests they are related. What might their common ancestor be like?

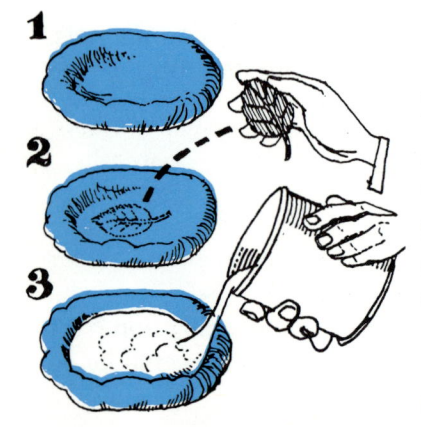

A lot of information about our ancestors comes from fossils. You can make a model fossil in this way. Make a bowl shape from plasticine. Press something—a twig, a shell, a leaf—into the plasticine. Remove it. It leaves a mark. Pour some plaster into the bowl. When the plaster sets you can remove the plasticine. That is a model of how some fossils are made.

Look at a display of fossils. Try to see how each one was made. Is it a print or a flattened organism?

Looking at living things 2

Your animal relatives

There are millions of different kinds of living things. They are sorted into family groups. The family groups are sorted into even bigger groups.

You are one in a family of humans

You have a mother and a father, grandparents, and perhaps brothers and sisters and cousins. When you are older you will probably have children of your own and then later perhaps grandchildren. You, and all these people, are related to each other. You all belong to the same family. Sometimes an outsider can look at you and another member of your family and guess you are related. The guess is made because you look alike.

Humans are one in the family of animals

Different kinds of organisms are also sorted into family groups and are sorted in the same way. You can see this more clearly when you look at the group to which we belong. We are more like chimpanzees and gibbons than we are like cheetahs and tigers. We belong to the ape family. Cheetahs and tigers belong to the cat family. But apes and cats are more like each other than they are like mosquitoes and locusts. Apes and cats belong to the bigger group called the mammals. The mosquitoes and locusts are insects.

Humans are in the ape family

If the human beings, chimpanzees, and gorillas are in the ape family, that means these kinds of organisms are related. You saw how this could come about when you played the evolution game. There are small differences even between organisms of the same kind. Some of these differences can be handed down to their young. Over many generations these small differences can add up to make organisms quite different from their ancestors. If the ancestors separate in the way they live then they can produce two new kinds of organisms. These new kinds are different, but they are related. In the animal world our relatives are the gorillas, the chimpanzees, the gibbons, and the orang-utans.
Do you see any resemblances?

33

Looking at living things 2

Making faces

By now the story of human evolution is perhaps neither fantastic nor ridiculous. Just mysterious. How do we know that our ancestors looked like that? Here are the beginnings of some answers.

Often the only clues we have about how our ancestors looked come from bones, especially bones from the skull. As these bones are very old, they are in pieces with bits missing. The skull on the right has been built up from many pieces found together. Some pieces are still missing.

Experts on skulls can guess what the rest looked like. By looking at the place where the lower jaw hinges on to the skull they might decide the size and shape of that lower jaw. So they draw this part in. The missing parts are drawn in here.

The next stage is to decide what muscles were attached to the skull. This may be fairly easy. For example, big jaws probably needed big muscles to move them. Ridges on the skull can show where the muscles were attached, and how big they were. The muscles are drawn in here.

When there are few clues, what do you decide? For example, how big were the ears, how hairy was the face, what was the colour of the hair? To decide this, the bone expert is joined by an artist. Another artist might have decided on something quite different.

Other items are often found beside the human or man-ape bones. These tell about the life of our ancestors. Other animal bones tell us what meat they ate. Pieces of stone which are oddly shaped and which do not belong to that area are sometimes found. What do you think they were for?

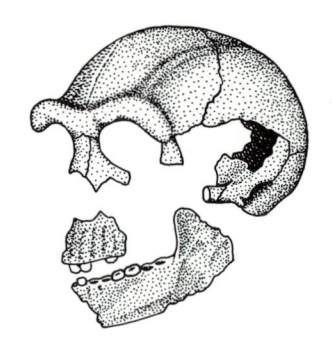

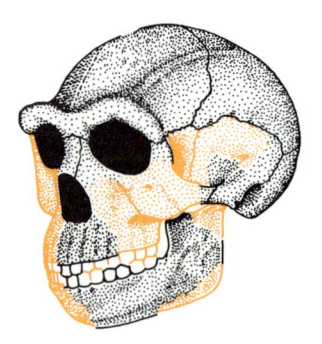

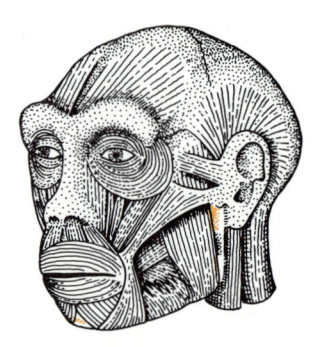

Pekin man

Dr. Davidson Black had an idea that the first men and women might have lived in what we call China. So when he was offered a job in Pekin he jumped at the chance. Only in China could he find out whether his idea was correct.

When he arrived he searched carefully but found neither human nor man-ape fossils. Then one day a friend, Dr. Anderson, came into the office. Dr. Anderson had brought two teeth. Someone had found them sticking from the rocks at Dragon Bone Hill. A chemist bought them to crush down into a magic dragon bone powder. Dr. Anderson saved him the trouble. He bought both teeth—whole. Was Dr. Black interested in them? Dr. Black was very interested. He did not believe in dragons, nor in magic potions. He did believe in fossil men and he believed these teeth came from fossil men. Dragon Bone Hill would have to be searched for more fossils.

At that small hill outside Pekin a search for man's beginnings was started. It was not easy. Explosives were used to separate large pieces of rock. Explosives were being used all around the fossil hunters for other reasons. At the time, 1927, there was civil war in China. In the cities there were riots; in the countryside there were robbers. The diggers kept working, although often they could not reach the city.

Then, three days before the end of the 1927 season one of the diggers, Dr. Bohlin, found an important tooth. He hurried back to Pekin to give it to Dr. Black. Several times he was stopped by bandits. The treasure they wanted was gold, so they ignored the old tooth in Dr. Bohlin's pocket. But for Bohlin and Black that dirty old tooth was the real treasure. Black spent night after night examining it. It was different from anything he had ever seen: so different that he guessed it came from a new kind of fossil man. He called this new kind of man *Sinanthropus pekinensis*—the Chinese Man from Pekin.

He was convinced on one tooth alone. To convince others he had to find more pieces of skull. The digging went on. Through 1928 and 1929 they filled a thousand boxes with fossils of animal bones. There was nothing matching that one tooth until the end of the 1929 season. Dr. Pei, another member of the team, thought he would open up two caves at the end of a long crack. When he entered he found a collection of rocks and dirt.

And there it lay, the top of a skull, almost complete and almost covered. And Pei knew what he was looking at. It was part of the skull of another Pekin Man. Black had guessed right.

Exploring energy 1

Energy is

You need energy. You use energy. You use many words for energy. Can you say what energy is? There are stations round the laboratory. At each station carry out all the instructions. At each station write: what you see; what you hear; what you feel.

Energy changes

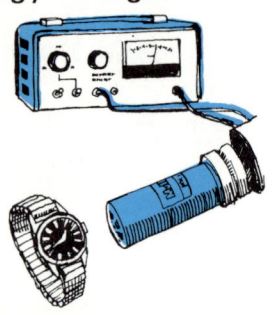

Bring the luminous dial of a watch near to the Geiger-Müller tube.

Swing the pendulum. Watch it swinging.

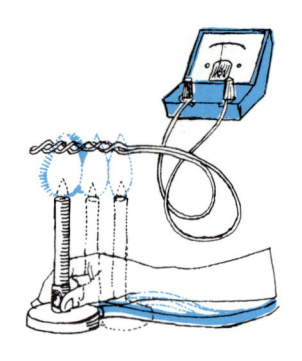

Move the flame under the twisted wires. Remove it before the wires get red-hot. Watch the meter.

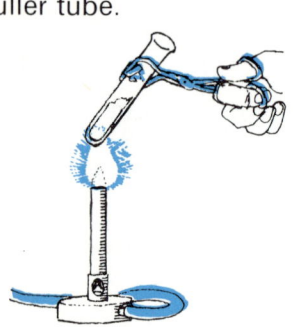

Put 1 cm of the chemical ammonium dichromate into a test-tube. Heat it carefully.

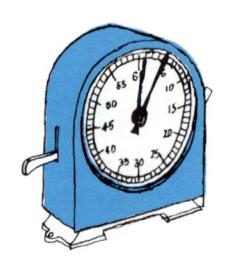

Set the alarm timer for one minute. Watch. Wait. Listen.

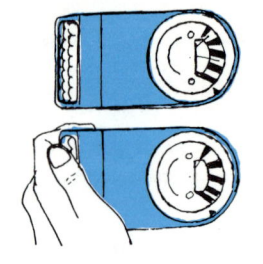

Cover and uncover the photocell. Watch the needle.

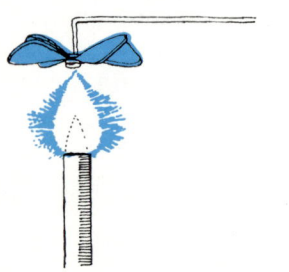

Hold the aluminium propeller above the flame.

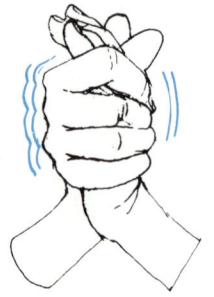

Rub your hands together as fast as you can.

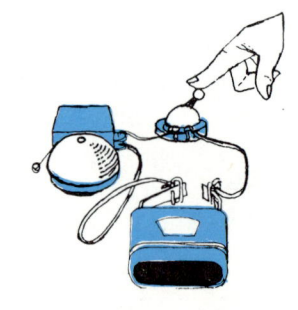

Switch on the circuit with the bell and the battery.

Exploring energy 1

Forms of energy

To identify the forms of energy you must ask yourself questions. The answer will either be yes or no.

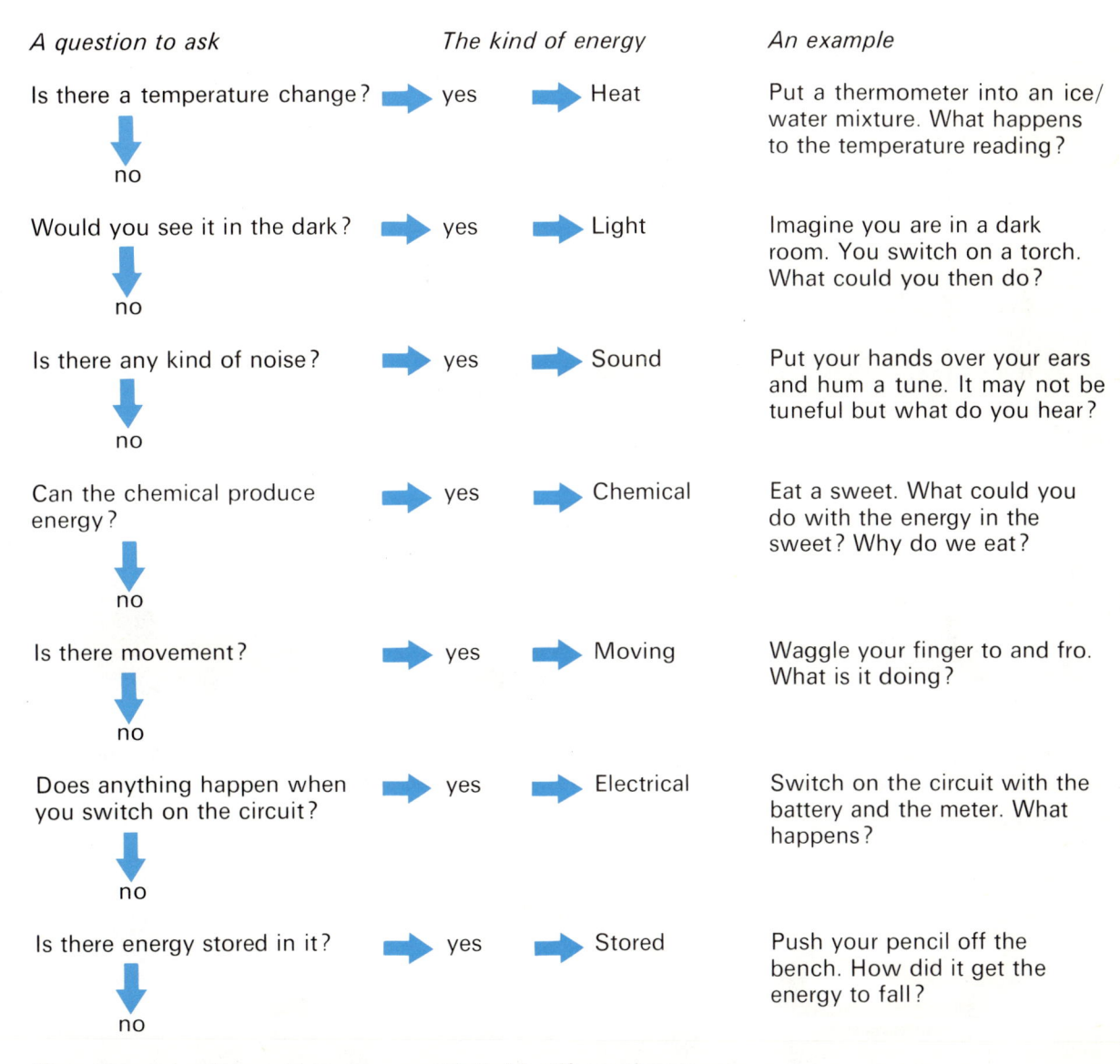

A question to ask		The kind of energy	An example
Is there a temperature change? → yes	→	Heat	Put a thermometer into an ice/water mixture. What happens to the temperature reading?
↓ no			
Would you see it in the dark? → yes	→	Light	Imagine you are in a dark room. You switch on a torch. What could you then do?
↓ no			
Is there any kind of noise? → yes	→	Sound	Put your hands over your ears and hum a tune. It may not be tuneful but what do you hear?
↓ no			
Can the chemical produce energy? → yes	→	Chemical	Eat a sweet. What could you do with the energy in the sweet? Why do we eat?
↓ no			
Is there movement? → yes	→	Moving	Waggle your finger to and fro. What is it doing?
↓ no			
Does anything happen when you switch on the circuit? → yes	→	Electrical	Switch on the circuit with the battery and the meter. What happens?
↓ no			
Is there energy stored in it? → yes	→	Stored	Push your pencil off the bench. How did it get the energy to fall?
↓ no			

There is no simple question you can ask to identify nuclear energy.

Now work out what kinds of energy you were working with on page 36.

Exploring energy 1

Connecting the changes   Energy can change from one form into others.

Chemical energy in a battery → changes to → Electrical energy in the wires → changes to → Moving energy (it moves)
Sound energy (noise)
Heat energy (it gets hot)
Light energy (sparks)

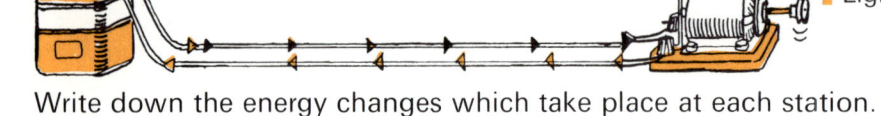

Write down the energy changes which take place at each station.

Make a gun. Wrap a match in foil. Heat the foil.

Put the flame under the tube for a short time. Then remove the tube.

Put the alka seltzer tablet into a beaker of water.

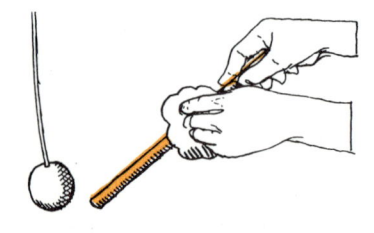

Rub the plastic rod with the cloth. Bring the rod near to the suspended ball.

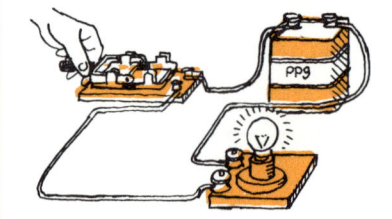

Switch on the electric circuit.

Play with the friction toy.

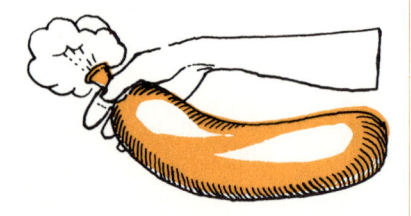

Blow up the balloon. Hold the neck of the balloon slightly open. Let out the air.

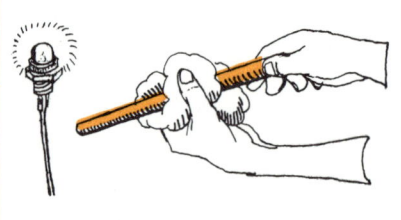

Rub the plastic rod with the dry cloth. Bring the rubbed rod near to the neon bulb.

Light the candle. Watch the candle.

Exploring energy 1

About energy

As you grow up you will hear more about energy problems. These problems can be solved, but only if you know something about energy. The solutions start here.

Everything that happens needs energy

When you opened this book you used some energy. Reading this line uses more. Everything you do needs energy. In fact, everything that happens needs energy, no matter how small the change is. There is no exception to the rule: everything that happens needs energy.

Energy can be stored

There is more than one kind of energy. This book shows what stored energy is. Knock the book off the desk and it will hit the floor with a noise. Noise is sound energy. That sound energy was stored in the book, but not as sound. It was stored in the way the book was placed. Burning the book will give you light and heat energy. This energy is stored in the paper. It is stored in the way the chemicals of the paper are put together.

Energy can be working

Stored energy is one of the two main kinds of energy. The other main kind of energy is working energy. You know when energy is working because things happen. There is more than one kind of working energy. The easiest kind of working energy to recognize is moving energy. You can see things move from one place to another. Other kinds of working energy are heat, light, sound, and electrical energy.

One kind of energy can be changed into another

Energy can change from one kind into another. This is another rule. The change can be controlled or uncontrolled. In our bodies, all energy changes are controlled. Machines are devices we have invented for controlling energy changes. From controlled energy changes we can get useful work.

Exploring energy 1

Energy out of control

We use a lot of energy in our homes. If the rules are followed we are quite safe. If not, we are in danger. The penalty for breaking the rules is fire. Fire is energy out of control.

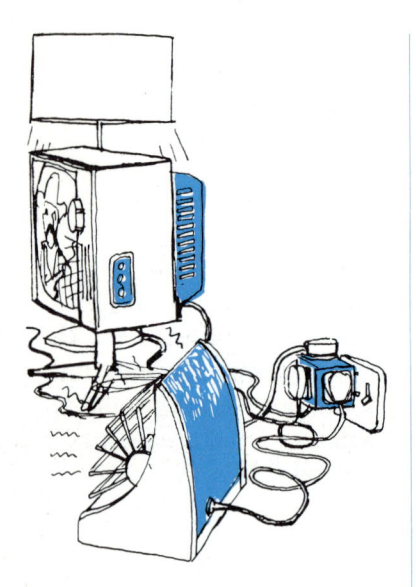

This point is overloaded.
What will happen?
What are the rules?

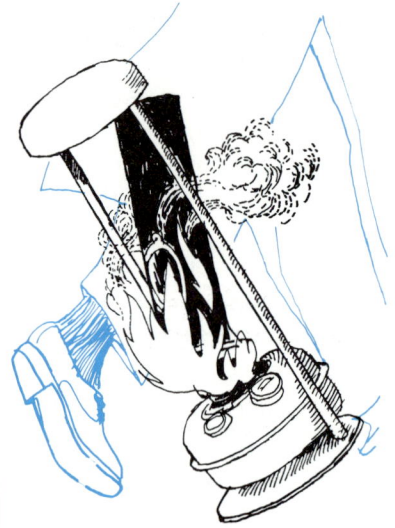

What happens if you trip over a lit oil heater?
What are the rules?

Coal fire: no one there.
Sparks on carpet.
What are the rules?

The gas goes out.
You strike a match. Bang!
What are the rules?

What safety rules are being broken here?

Find out:

What to do
in case of fire.

What to do
if cut off by fire.

The safety rules
for the kitchen.

Find out by talking to
friends and relatives
or ask at your fire station.

Fire!

Fireman Benny has gone into an apartment on the fifth floor. He makes a careful search but the apartment is empty. He opens the hall door and he is hit with a hard wind of heat. He drops to the floor and the heat passes over him. The smoke is thicker than he has ever experienced it; he coughs uncontrollably. His first impulse is to get out to the fire escape and air but he puts his nose to the floor and tries to relax. As his coughing stops he can hear soft moaning. He listens carefully for the direction and it seems to be coming from the landing between the top floor and the roof. He crawls on his stomach. The heat is unbearable and he feels all the energy draining from his body. He reaches the landing and sees an incredible mess of human beings. They are piled on top of one another, perhaps breathing their last breaths.

There are seven people. They tried to flee from the burning building but the roof door was chained shut to keep out prowlers. It was a steel door and the heat from a fire five floors beneath had nowhere to go. Benny can hear the desperate thump of the axehead hitting a wedge as he grabs the nearest body. The links of the chain are tough so the firemen on the roof cannot break them. They work instead on the hinges.

Benny carries a two-year-old girl down to the fifth floor. He wants to give her mouth-to-mouth resuscitation but he has to think of the others. He blows two hard, hopeful breaths into the girl's mouth and returns to the landing. He is close to collapse, and gasping with the heat and smoke. Then, like a miracle, he feels an arm swing round him. Artie Merritt has managed to come down the fire escape from the roof. He and Benny drag a woman down the stairs. She is still breathing but badly burned. They leave her next to the baby and return to the landing to drag a man downstairs. As Benny lifts another child the steel door swings open and hangs down, caught by the chain. The heat and smoke rush out to the midday air and the firemen fight their way downstairs.

Exploring energy 2

Energy converters

Man is different from all other animals. Only man builds machines to work for him. He builds machines to convert and control energy.
At each station write down the energy changes.

Model machines

Take the sun-powered motor into bright sunshine (or shine a very bright light on its photocell).

Turn on the tap and run water through the turbine. The turbine drives the generator which is connected to the electric motor.

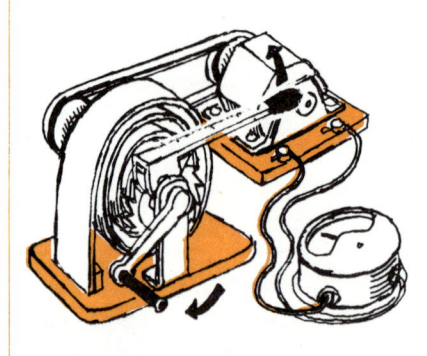

Wind up the spring. Release the ratchet. This lets the spring turn the generator.

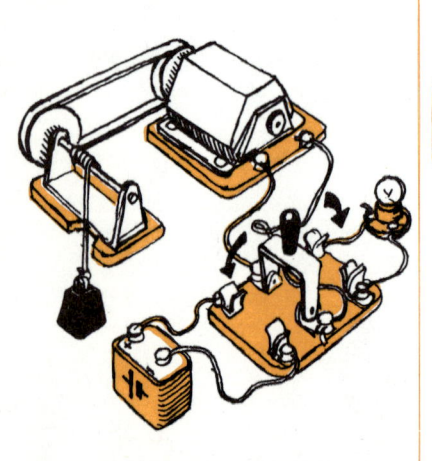

Switch on the electric motor to wind up the weight. When the weight reaches the axle, reverse the two-way switch to connect in the light bulb.

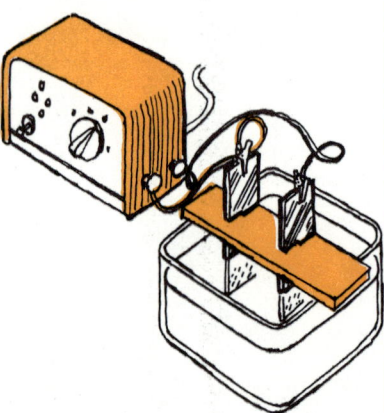

Set the lab pack to 8 volts. Connect the lab pack to the two lead plates in the beaker of acid. Switch on the lab pack for one minute and then switch off.

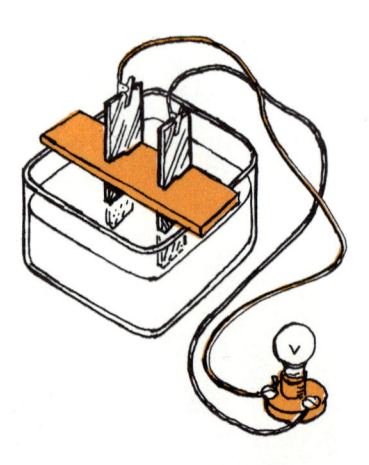

Now connect the lead plates to the bulb.

Switch on the electric motor to wind up the weight. When the weight reaches the axle, switch off and watch your pile driver in action.

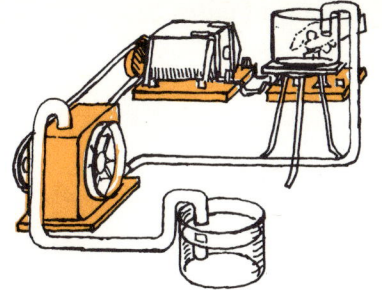

Switch on the electric motor to drive the water pump.

Put on the headphones. Switch on the tape recorder and listen.

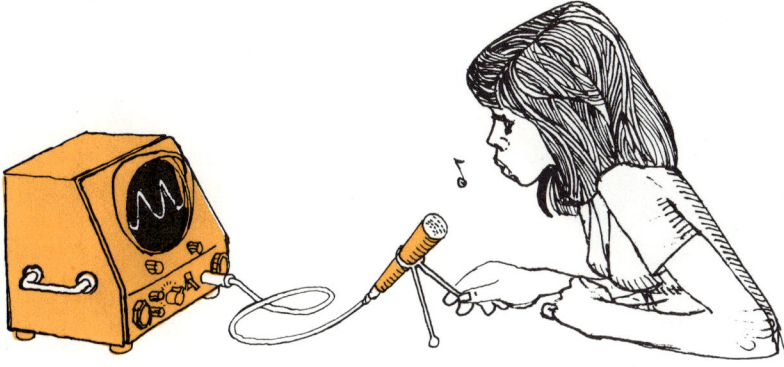

Whistle a note into the microphone. Watch the picture on the screen. Try high and low notes.

Plant puzzle
Plants are the most important energy converters in the world. What energy do they use? What do they make for us that we need?

Old-fashioned machines   Write down the energy changes these machines make.

Water-wheel   Windmill    Horse and cart    Making fire

43

Exploring energy 2

Do it yourself

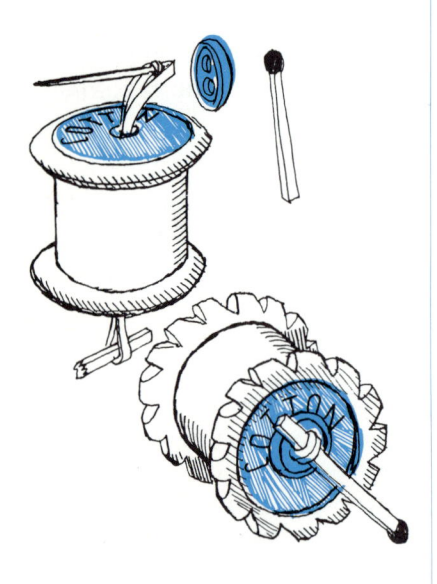

Make this model tank.

Wedge a small piece of camphor at the back of the boat.

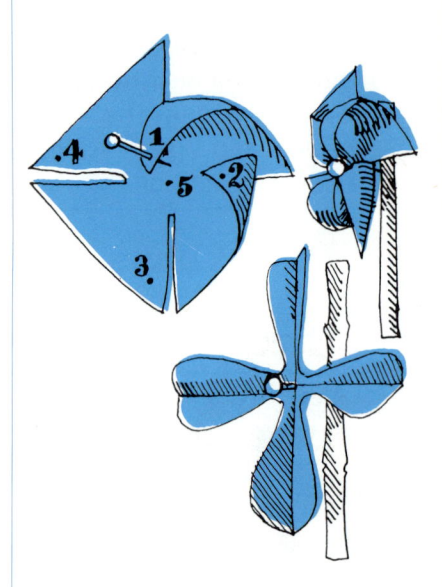

Design and make propellers which spin well.

Make an elastic-powered car or boat.

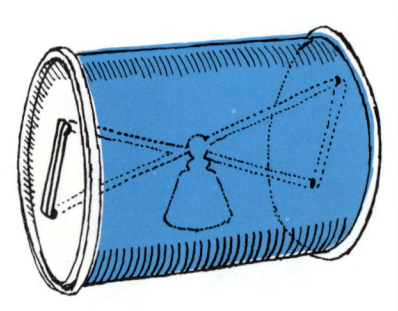

Explain how the comeback can works.

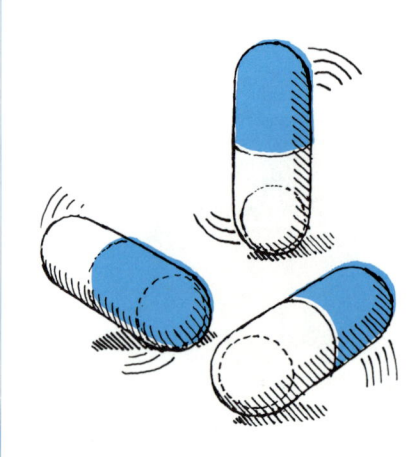

How do the jumping beans work?

Energy controllers

Energy changes can be controlled or uncontrolled. When the change is controlled, useful work is done.

All machines are energy controllers

All machines are energy converters. They are also energy controllers. Machines control how, where, and when energy is changed. Machines may be simple like a bicycle or complicated like a motor car. These two machines seem different but they operate in the same way. Both use stored energy. The bicycle uses energy stored in leg muscles. The car uses energy stored in petrol. The stored energy is converted into working energy. This change is controlled by the machine. And the machine is controlled by a person.

All organisms are energy controllers

All living things are energy converters and energy controllers. Organisms convert and control energy so that they can breathe, and grow, and store more energy. This useful work keeps the organisms alive. Plants control the change of light energy from the sun into stored energy in food. Animals control the change of stored energy in food into moving energy.

At every change some energy does work and some is wasted

Energy controllers never turn all the energy they change into useful work. Some of the energy is always wasted. Wasted energy is work which is of no use. Like the noise you make puffing and panting up a hill on your bicycle. That sound energy does not make the wheels go round any faster. A good energy controller does much work and wastes little energy. A poor energy controller wastes much energy and does little useful work.

Exploring energy 2

Our resources: energy

The big five

We get energy from petroleum, coal, natural gas, hydro-electricity, and nuclear power stations. Our energy needs double every 15 years.

How much is left?

Oil (petroleum)
76 000 000 000 tonnes

Coal
6 641 200 000 000 tonnes

Natural gas
49 900 000 000 000 cubic metres

Hydro-electricity
Many rivers are not as yet used. But the number of places suitable for hydro-electric schemes is limited.

Nuclear energy
761 400 tonnes

How long will it last?

25 to 30 years unless we start to use less of it.

100 to 500 years depending on how fast we can mine it.

27 to 45 years

For as long as we still get rain.

10 years. But different forms of nuclear reactions may extend this time.

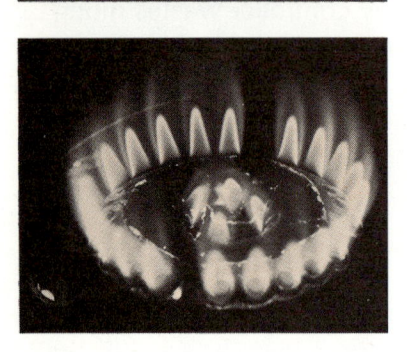

The future Our energy needs double every 15 years. Can we afford this? What will happen if we do not start saving energy?

Exploring energy 2

This can happen: too little energy

Hungry people are caught in a vicious circle. It starts when they have too little energy. They cannot do enough work to get money to buy food. So they have too little energy—to do enough work—to get money—to buy food.

The farmer knows he is hungry. He has eaten too little food. He knows he is tired. He has used up the energy in that food. He knows why he is tired and hungry. He knows he is in the hunger trap.
The farmer realizes that cows turn grass into milk. That cows have calves, that a dead cow will give meat, and that the calves will replace the dead cow. When there is too little food for people, there is less for animals. A hungry cow gives no milk. A starved cow has no calves and gives little meat.

The farmer's wife can see her older child is ill. His stomach and ankles are swollen. She can see the baby is well. His eyes are bright and his hair is shining. The baby is fed with her own milk. The boy was well when he got milk. The cow's milk would make the boy well. The cow is not making milk and the farmer's wife knows why. She knows they are in the hunger trap.

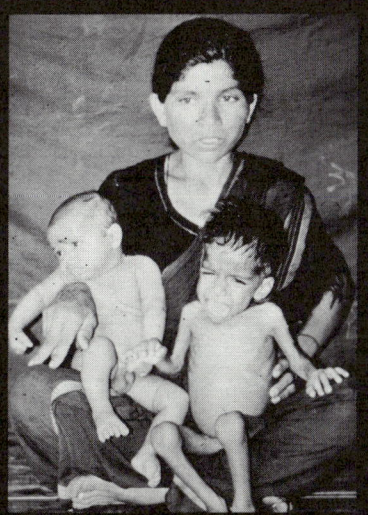

Explaining matter 1

Matter is

Energy and matter are always together like the two sides of a coin. Now that you have looked at the energy side, it is time to have a look at matter.

Solid or liquid or gas or . . .

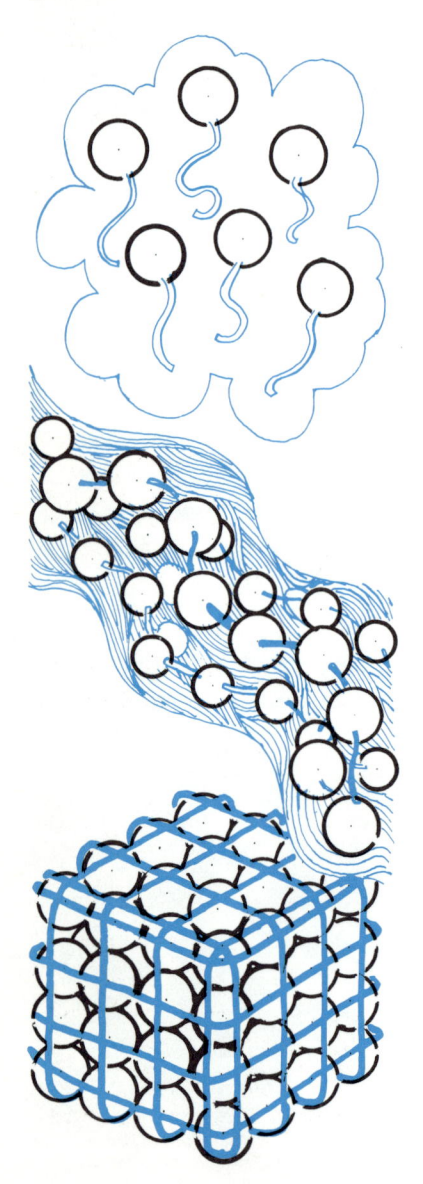

Take a pencil. Tap some ice. Stir some water. Hold it in steam. What is left on the pencil each time? Make sets for the ice, water, and steam. Which of these sets can you put the pencil into? Does the flame heating the water belong with the ice, the water, or the steam?

Put a few drops of methylated spirits on to cotton wool and dab this on your hand. Look and smell. Do not taste. Which set does the cotton wool go into? What about the methylated spirits and the smell of the methylated spirits?

The sand came from a sandstone block. The pumice came from a volcano. Put the sandstone into a set. Does the sand go into that set? When the pumice was in the volcano, which set would it go into? Where does it go now?

There are three sealed containers. Put the contents in each container into a set. Put the materials of each container into a set. Put the materials used to seal the containers into a set.

Put these into your sets:
hair   blood   skin   muscle   leaves   wood   breath   milk.

Into which sets do these substances go:
snow   hail   wind   rain?

Which set does lemonade belong to? What about the bubbles in the lemonade? And the sugar? Do you have a set for ice cream? Or jelly?

Explaining matter 1

The case of the mysterious permanganate

Potassium permanganate colours water purple. You will dilute a mixture of these two substances and watch what happens to the colour. Work accurately. Watch closely. Put 8 test-tubes in a rack and number them 1 to 8. Add 10 ml permanganate and water mixture to tube 1. Add 9 ml water to each of the other tubes.

Use a syringe to remove 1 ml of mixture from tube 1. Add this to tube 2. Stopper the tube and shake to mix well. Wash the syringe and remove 1 ml diluted mixture from tube 2. Add this to tube 3. Stopper, shake, mix. Repeat all these actions until you reach tube 8.

Look at the row of tubes. What changes as you go along the row? What does this tell you about the permanganate in the tubes? Is there any permanganate in tube 8? If you continued with more tubes, would there be a tube which contained no permanganate?

You started with a mixture containing much permanganate. You continually diluted this mixture and the colour became fainter until the mixture became colourless. This shows that there is less and less permanganate in each mixture.

Eventually there will be a tube with no permanganate. That makes the permanganate mysterious. You started with much permanganate and you can finish with none. How?

Now that you can see the problem, the solution is fairly easy. Permanganate is made up of small pieces which separate in water. Some pieces from tube 1 were added to tube 2. Some from the mixture in tube 2 were added to tube 3. As you go along, each tube has fewer and fewer particles of permanganate. Finally there can be a tube with no particles of permanganate.

49

Explaining matter 1

Puzzles with particles

Try to use the particle idea to say what might be happening here:

Last day balloons were filled with air, carbon dioxide, and hydrogen. What has happened to each balloon? How might this have happened? Make your explanation in words, or in pictures, or both.

You put a crystal of copper sulphate in water and another in a jelly last day. Describe what has happened and try to give an explanation.

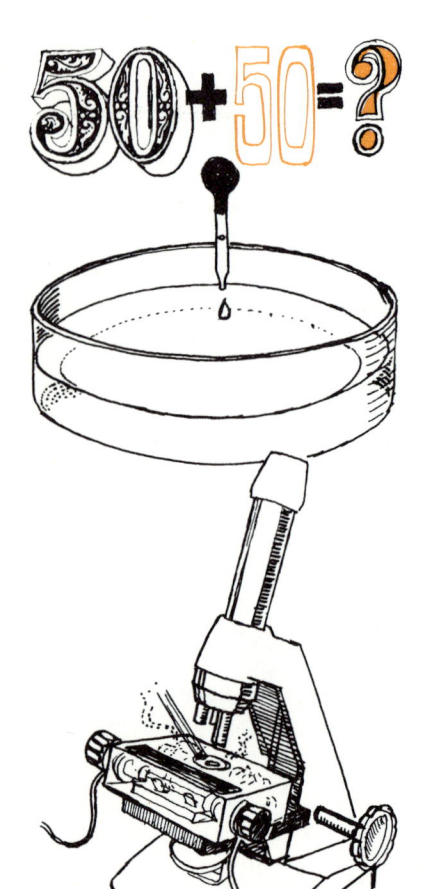

Put exactly 50 ml water in a measuring jar. Measure exactly 50 ml alcohol into another jar. If you add the alcohol to the water what will the total volume be? Now add the alcohol to the water and read the total volume. Were you correct? Use the particle idea to start explaining the difference.

Half fill a large glass dish with water. Sprinkle a fine powder over the surface of the water. Add one drop of oil. What does the oil do to the powder? What happens to the particles in the oil drop when the oil touches the water? In the layer of oil, how many particles of the oil do you think are piled on top of each other?

Look into the microscope at the smoke and air. Watch one of the moving pieces of smoke. Draw the path it makes. What makes it move? What makes it change direction?

Collect your ideas on particles together. Write a sentence on their size, on their shape, on the way they move, on the way they might be arranged.

50

Explaining matter 1

How is all matter built?

How can the same material be a solid, a liquid, or a gas? To answer that we must look to see how all matter is built.

Matter is made of tiny particles

To see how matter is built you looked at the mystery of the missing permanganate. You started with much permanganate and passed some of it from tube to tube. If you had continued long enough you would have ended with no permanganate. How? The permanganate is made of small pieces which can separate and scatter. Perhaps all matter is made up of tiny pieces—the tiny pieces we call particles.

**The particles can move
They have different sizes**

Can that idea explain anything else? Copper sulphate spreads through water; it spreads through jelly. How? The copper sulphate particles move between the water particles or the jelly particles. The smoke particles move in every direction. How? The smaller air particles push the smoke particles about. So the air particles must be moving in all directions. The balloons shrink. How? The gas particles escape between the balloon particles. But how do you explain the balloons shrinking at different rates?

Use the particle idea

Of course the particle idea might be wrong. Right or wrong, it is a very useful idea and we will continue to use it to explain other things. That is how we test an idea. We use it to see how well it can explain things. We will go ahead and use the particle idea to explain the differences between solids, liquids, and gases.

One million

How big is a particle? It is very small. This dot • contains millions of ink particles. Well, how big is a million?

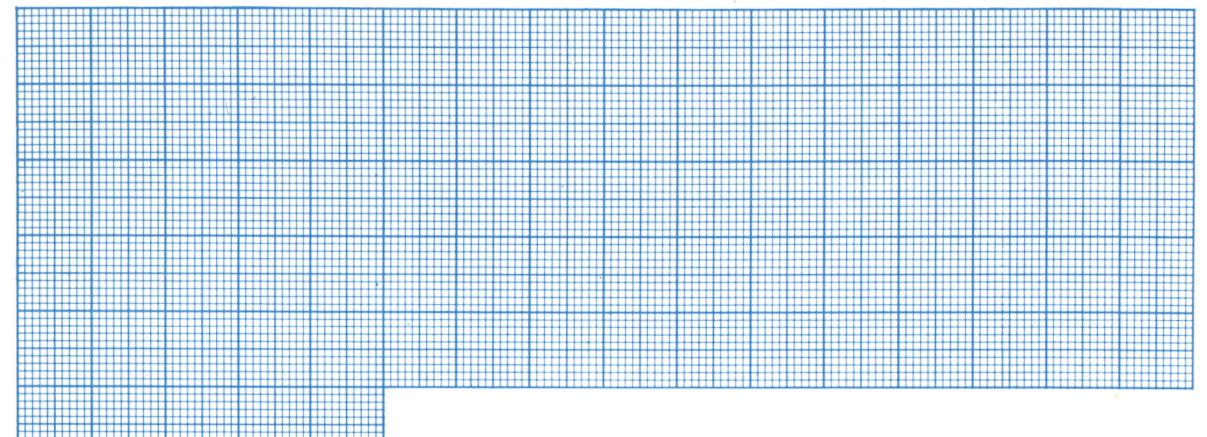

How many things make a million? This piece of graph paper has 10 000 squares. 100 of these pieces will give you a million small squares. How do you know there will be one million square millimetres? Count them and see. If you count at the rate of one square millimetre per second, it will take you 11.5 days. Without stopping to eat or sleep.

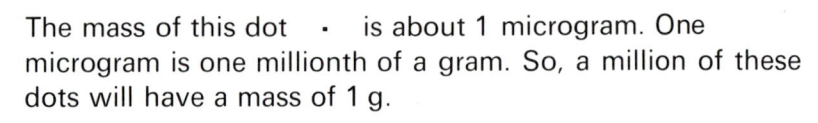

The mass of this dot • is about 1 microgram. One microgram is one millionth of a gram. So, a million of these dots will have a mass of 1 g.

This dot • is about 1 mm across. One million of these dots, joined together, will be 1 km in length.

If one million of these dots were placed end to end then it would take you about 5 minutes to run past them.

$$1\,000\,000 = 10^6$$
$$10 \times 100\,000$$
$$100 \times 10\,000$$
$$1000 \times 1000$$
$$10\,000 \times 100$$
$$100\,000 \times 10$$

Explaining matter 1

Take 20 pupils in your class, each with a mass of 50 kg. Put them together and they have a mass of 1 000 000 g. These 20 pupils have a mass of 1 tonne. You have a mass of about 50 kg. A large postage stamp has a mass of about 50 milligrams. One million stamps will have a total mass the same as yours. On the other hand one million pupils have the same mass as a large passenger ship.

A pupil has a height of 1.5 metres. A bacterium has a length of 1.5 micrometres. A bacterium increased 1 000 000 times would be as tall as the pupil. And if that pupil were magnified 1 000 000 times in length then he or she would be longer than the British Isles.

This sheet of paper is about 0.1 mm thick. A million sheets would be 100 metres thick. In a packet of paper there are 500 sheets. So 2000 packets would contain 1 000 000 sheets.

1 000 000 seconds	=	11.5 days
1 000 000 minutes	=	690 days
1 000 000 hours	=	115 years
1 000 000 days	=	2740 years

If you are now beginning to feel that 1 000 000 is too small a number then you can look at:

1 billion
   1 000 000 000   = 10^9
1 trillion
   1 000 000 000 000   = 10^{12}
1 googol
   10 000 000 000 000 000 000,
      000 000 000 000 000 000,
      000 000 000 000 000 000,
      000 000 000 000 000 000,
      000 000 000 000 000 000,
      000 000 000   = 10^{100}

Explaining matter 2

Examinations and explanations

Matter is made up of very small particles. They are always moving. There are spaces between the particles. Now you will use these ideas.

Squeezing gases, liquids, and solids

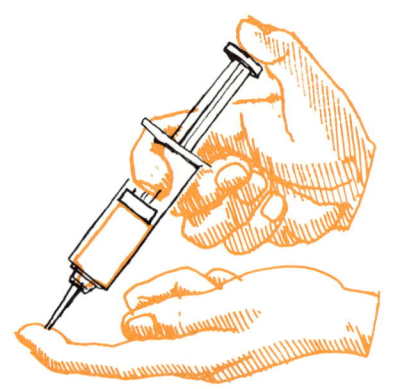

Empty the syringe. Pull the plunger out to the 10 ml mark. What is the volume of air in the syringe? Put your finger tightly over the hole. Squeeze the plunger in as far as you can. What is the volume of air now? Release the plunger. What happens?

Put 10 ml water into the syringe. When you squeeze in, do not let any water escape. Does the volume of water change? Release the plunger. What happens?

Take any of the solids on the bench. Squeeze them. What happens?

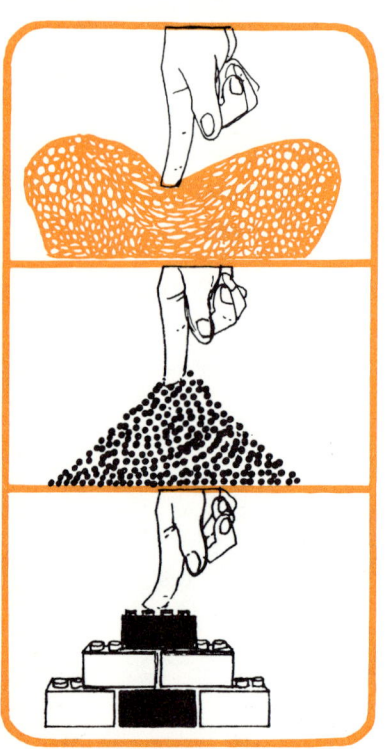

The way solids, liquids, and gases behave depends on how their particles are put together. The way the next solids are arranged will give you clues about how solid, liquid, and gas particles are arranged.

Squeeze a piece of bread. In what way does it behave like a gas? Bread is a solid. How is it put together?

Squeeze some sand. Does it behave like a solid, a liquid, or a gas? Sand is a solid. How is it put together?

Squeeze the Lego. What happens? What does the way the pieces of Lego are arranged tell you about the way particles in a solid are arranged?

Now go back to the first three activities. Finish your explanations of what happens to the particles when solids, liquids, and gases are squeezed.

Explaining matter 2

Squeezers and pushers

Now there is more squeezing to be done. Not by you, nor by your teacher. You have another job to do. Your job is to work out what is doing the squeezing.

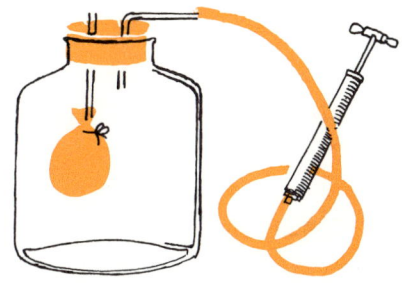

Blow up the balloon in the jar. Bring it down again.

Blow up the balloon. Bring it down and make it flat.

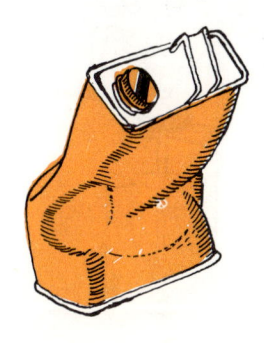

Keep the water in but do not touch the card.

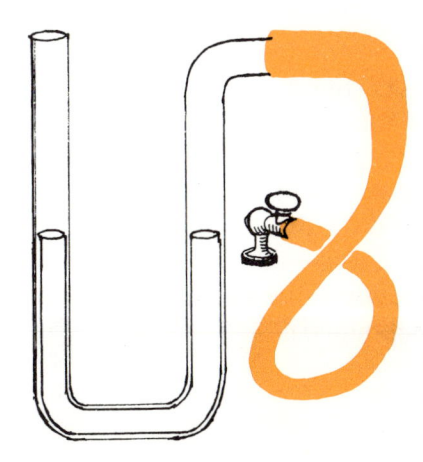

Watch the can being crushed.

Push the water column up.

Use the apparatus to see how the particles are arranged. Adjust the control to make the beads move slightly. The particles in a solid are arranged like this. What is the arrangement like? Make the beads move more rapidly. The particles in a liquid move in this way. How is a liquid put together? Make the beads jump about. The particles in a gas are well spaced out and move very fast. They can push against each other and against the walls of their containers.

55

Explaining matter 2

**Energy for particles;
energy from particles**

What will happen to a solid, a liquid, and a gas when energy is given to their particles? Or when energy is taken from their particles?

Dip the tube from the flask just under the water. Warm the flask with your hands. What happens to the air?
Use the particle idea to explain what happens.

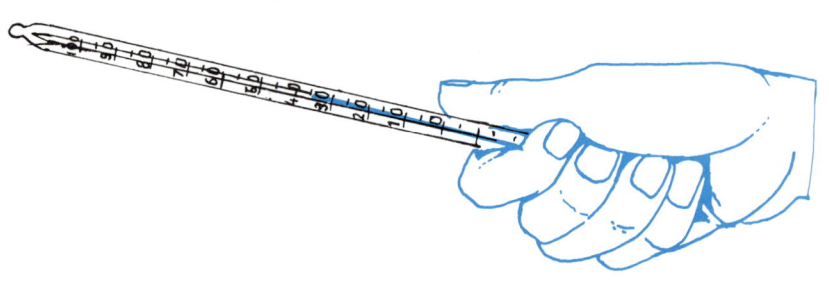

Hold the thermometer bulb carefully in your hand. Watch the mercury. What happens to the column of liquid? What happens to the particles of the liquid?

What do you expect will happen when you heat a length of metal? Use the special apparatus. Heat the metal rod strongly. Watch the pointer. When it has moved, switch off the flame. Did the rod expand? Did you expect this to happen? How did it happen?

Repeat the activity with the flask. Then let the flask cool. What happens? How does this happen?

Put the thermometer bulb into cold water. What happens to the column of mercury? How does this happen?

The metal rod will be cooling down. What has happened to the pointer? How has this happened?

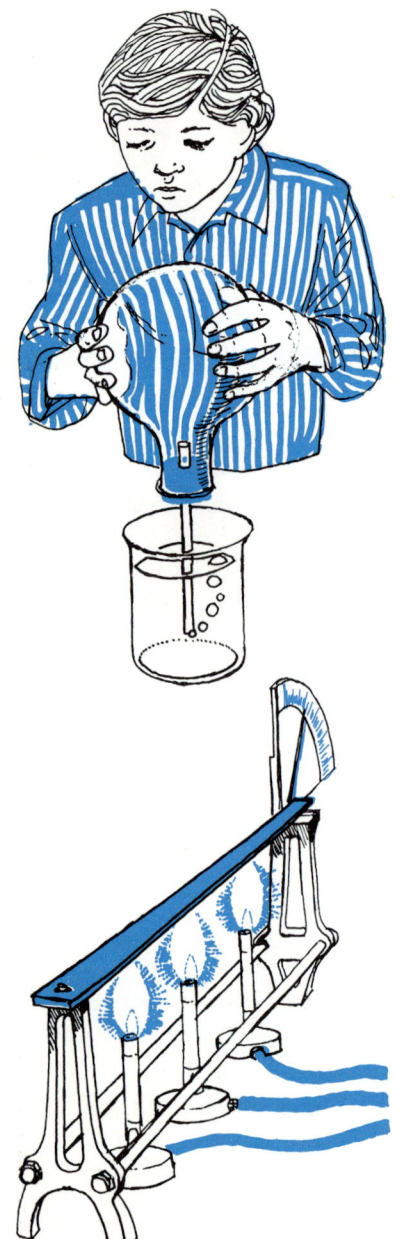

Explaining matter 2

How are particles arranged?

At different temperatures the same substance can be a solid, a liquid, or a gas. The particles in the substance remain the same but they are arranged differently.

Particles in gases are widely separated

In a gas every particle is on its own. They do come together, but bounce away again and keep themselves spread out with much space between them. So gases are light, and can be pushed into a smaller volume. When the pushing stops the particles spread out again. This means gases are springy.

Particles in solids hold each other in place

The particles in a solid cannot be pushed closer together. They are already tightly packed. Nor do they move apart. Instead they hold each other in place and shake. So solids are heavier than gases and solids have a shape which is their own.

Particles in liquids are separate and tightly packed

In a liquid the particles are tightly packed. So liquids cannot be pushed into a smaller volume. With tightly packed particles liquids, like solids, can have a shape. Since the particles do not hold each other together, the shape is not their own, but the shape of the container. Like gases, liquids can flow, because every particle can go its own way.

Turning solids into liquids and gases

When matter is heated, the particles get more energy, so they move more. In a solid the particles shake more, push further apart, and the solid expands. If more heat is added, the particles shake apart, and the solid melts. More heat, more energy, more pushing; the liquid expands. Even more energy and the particles in the liquid separate completely. The liquid boils. It is now a gas.

Explaining matter 2

Describing materials

It can be difficult finding the right word to describe something. Here are some words to help you to say what you mean about materials.

Does it break easily?	Yes:	**Weak** biscuit glass	No:	**Strong** steel nylon
Does it bend easily?	Yes:	**Flexible** leather nylon polythene	No:	**Stiff** steel biscuit bricks
Does it snap in two?	Yes:	**Brittle** diamond iron	No:	**Tough** steel rubber wood
Does it stretch and go back?	Yes:	**Elastic** rubber steel	No:	**Non-elastic** plasticine putty
Does it keep a new shape?	Yes:	**Plastic** plasticine metals polythene	No:	**Non-plastic** rubber
Does it scratch?	Yes:	**Scratchable** most plastics	No:	**Hard** diamond
Is there much stuff in the space?	Yes:	**Dense** gold lead	No:	**Light** air steam
Does it pour easily?	Yes:	**Fluid** water ethanol	No:	**Viscous** syrup treacle

The melting shop

Much of modern civilization depends on steel. To make steel, iron must first be melted. That is not quite the same as melting ice.

On cold, dark, winter mornings the melting shop was a glittering place. It stood out like a lighthouse, warm and inviting as we hurried along to start the day with our usual drink of hot tea. Each furnace in the shop was manned by four melters, with a first hand in charge of the furnace and what was in it.

What makes a good melter is his eyes, not his hands. The melter's eyes were almost his only guide to controlling the heat of the furnace. Today there is help from accurate instruments. That takes a great deal of strain and worry from the melter. It does not make him unimportant. It is as necessary as ever for a melter to know what is happening inside his furnace and what to do about it.

Because we did not know the exact temperature of the furnace, steel making was often a hit or miss affair. Sometimes we could make a ladle full of beautiful steel within four hours of filling the furnace. Then at other times the same type of steel took seven or eight hours to make. We could not use the furnace again right away. Before the next charge could go in it needed hours of maintenance.

At other times the results of high temperatures were calamitous. The first hand would aim for quick steel. He would take a gamble that nothing would go wrong. Then all the mishaps of melting shop life would pile up. Cranes would break down. Supplies of lime or even pig iron would be held up. Then the furnace and its team would be in trouble. The roof and linings would drip into the furnace. The silica in the bricks and the lime in the furnace do not mix well. The furnace would give way.

Then a huge shout would echo over the other noises in the shop: 'A breakaway!' Everyone would hurry to the damaged furnace. There they would tap out the metal into the ladle which usually waited below the furnace. All the time, molten metal would pour through the broken furnace like the flames of hell.

Such an event was a poor finish to high hopes. Even though much of the steel would be saved, there was still the breakaway to disturb the unhappy first hand, who would feel like jumping into the fiery mass in his deep shame. It didn't help when his team suggested he do just that. They had the exhausting job of clearing it all away. Meanwhile, the spectators hoped for an encore.

Explaining matter 3

The periodic table

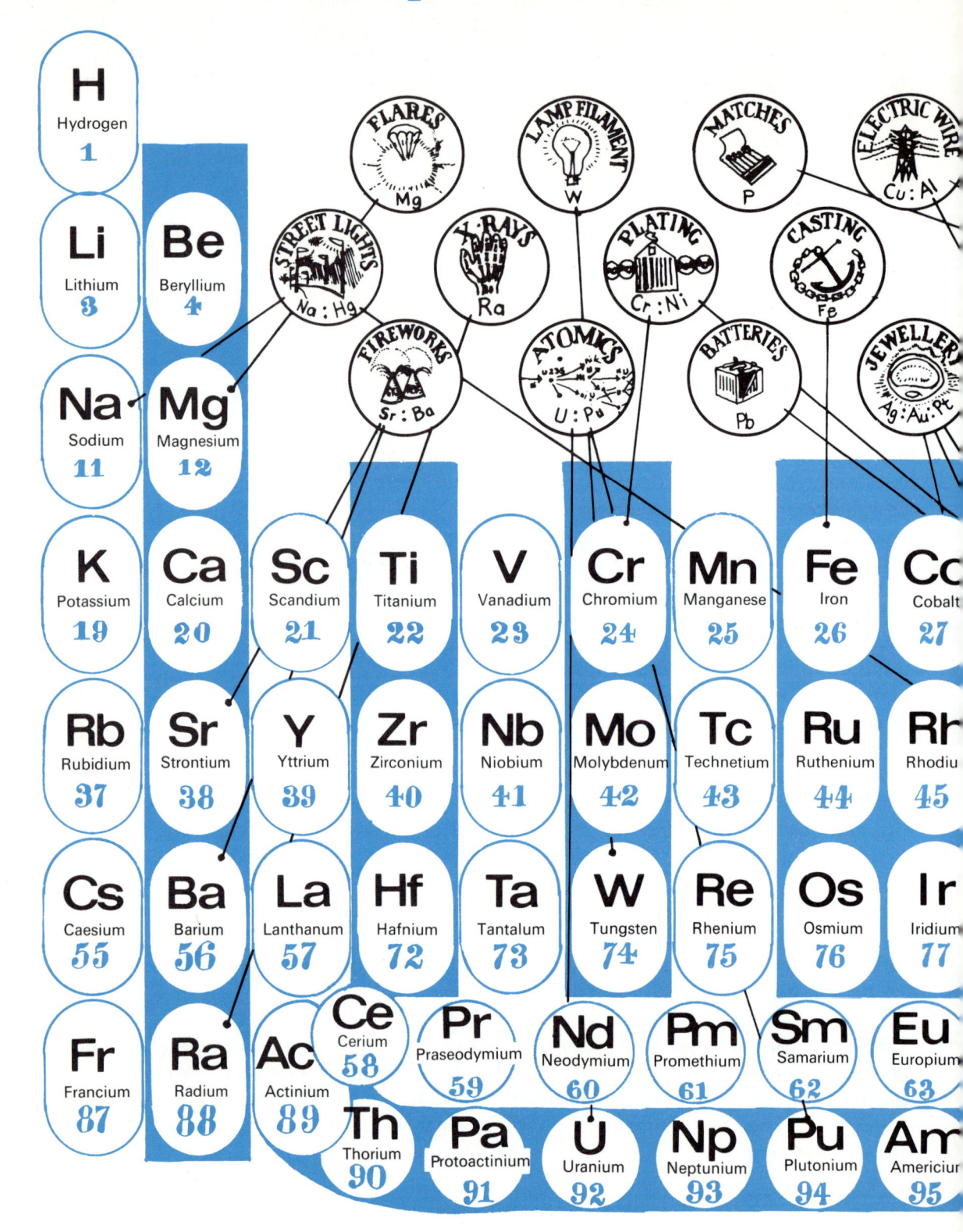

H Hydrogen 1									
Li Lithium 3	**Be** Beryllium 4								
Na Sodium 11	**Mg** Magnesium 12								
K Potassium 19	**Ca** Calcium 20	**Sc** Scandium 21	**Ti** Titanium 22	**V** Vanadium 23	**Cr** Chromium 24	**Mn** Manganese 25	**Fe** Iron 26	**Co** Cobalt 27	
Rb Rubidium 37	**Sr** Strontium 38	**Y** Yttrium 39	**Zr** Zirconium 40	**Nb** Niobium 41	**Mo** Molybdenum 42	**Tc** Technetium 43	**Ru** Ruthenium 44	**Rh** Rhodium 45	
Cs Caesium 55	**Ba** Barium 56	**La** Lanthanum 57	**Hf** Hafnium 72	**Ta** Tantalum 73	**W** Tungsten 74	**Re** Rhenium 75	**Os** Osmium 76	**Ir** Iridium 77	
Fr Francium 87	**Ra** Radium 88	**Ac** Actinium 89							

Ce Cerium 58	**Pr** Praseodymium 59	**Nd** Neodymium 60	**Pm** Promethium 61	**Sm** Samarium 62	**Eu** Europium 63
Th Thorium 90	**Pa** Protactinium 91	**U** Uranium 92	**Np** Neptunium 93	**Pu** Plutonium 94	**Am** Americium 95

Illustrated uses:
- FLARES — Mg
- LAMP FILAMENT — W
- MATCHES — P
- ELECTRIC WIRE — Cu : Al
- STREET LIGHTS — Na : Hg
- X-RAYS — Ra
- PLATING — Cr : Ni
- CASTING — Fe
- FIREWORKS — Sr : Ba
- ATOMICS — U : Pu
- BATTERIES — Pb
- JEWELLERY — Ag : Au : Pt

60

Explaining matter 3

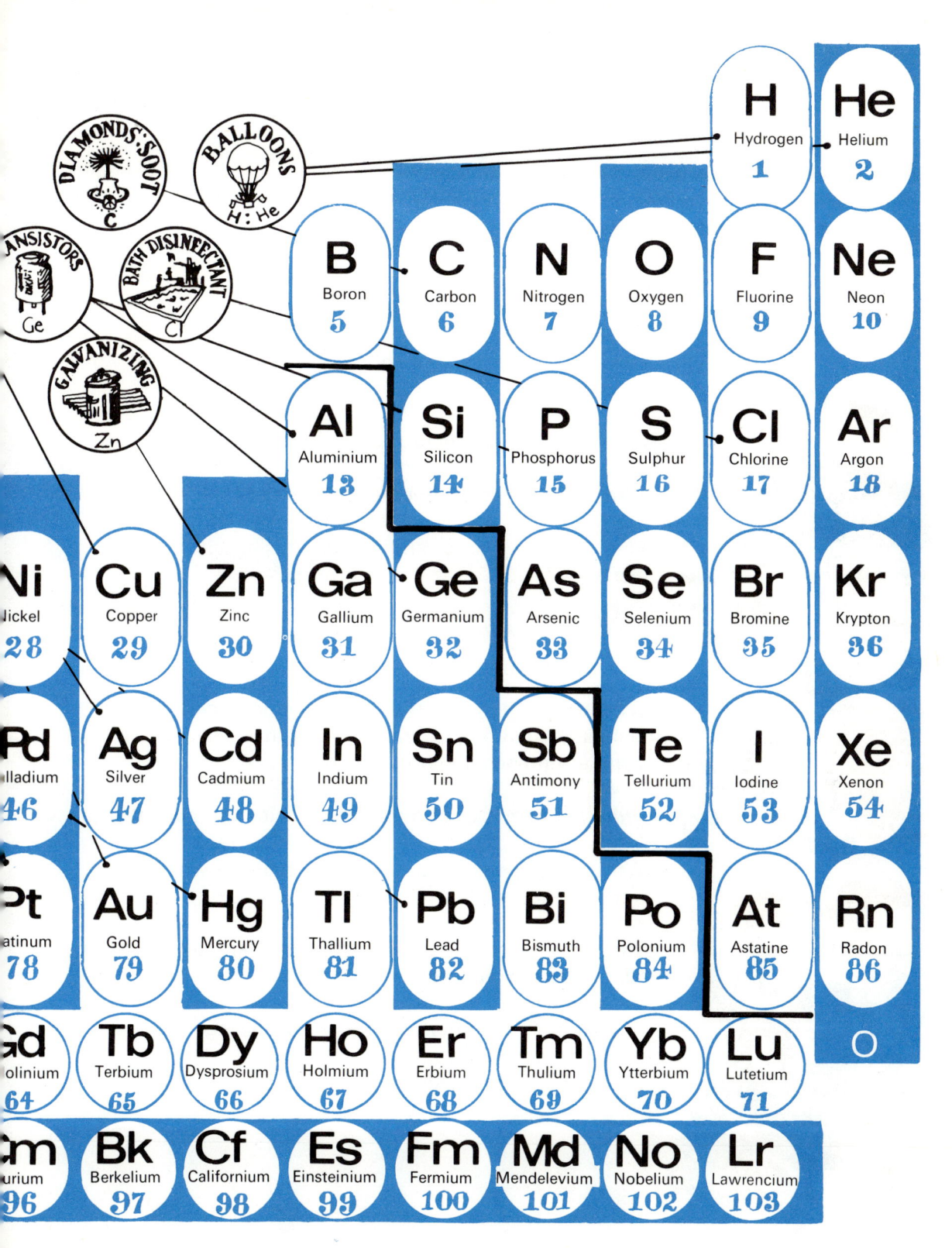

								H Hydrogen 1	He Helium 2
			B Boron 5	C Carbon 6	N Nitrogen 7	O Oxygen 8	F Fluorine 9	Ne Neon 10
			Al Aluminium 13	Si Silicon 14	P Phosphorus 15	S Sulphur 16	Cl Chlorine 17	Ar Argon 18
Ni Nickel 28	Cu Copper 29	Zn Zinc 30	Ga Gallium 31	Ge Germanium 32	As Arsenic 33	Se Selenium 34	Br Bromine 35	Kr Krypton 36
Pd Palladium 46	Ag Silver 47	Cd Cadmium 48	In Indium 49	Sn Tin 50	Sb Antimony 51	Te Tellurium 52	I Iodine 53	Xe Xenon 54
Pt Platinum 78	Au Gold 79	Hg Mercury 80	Tl Thallium 81	Pb Lead 82	Bi Bismuth 83	Po Polonium 84	At Astatine 85	Rn Radon 86

Gd Gadolinium 64	Tb Terbium 65	Dy Dysprosium 66	Ho Holmium 67	Er Erbium 68	Tm Thulium 69	Yb Ytterbium 70	Lu Lutetium 71
Cm Curium 96	Bk Berkelium 97	Cf Californium 98	Es Einsteinium 99	Fm Fermium 100	Md Mendelevium 101	No Nobelium 102	Lr Lawrencium 103

DIAMONDS·SOOT C

BALLOONS H:He

TRANSISTORS Ge

BATH DISINFECTANT Cl

GALVANIZING Zn

Explaining matter 3

A particle catalogue

Matter is made of small particles. Some of these particles are called atoms. The substances which atoms make are called elements. There are about 100 different elements and these are collected together in the periodic table.

Looking at the periodic table

How many elements are in the table?

Write the names of elements whose symbols begin with the letter B.

Find two elements named after countries.

Find two elements named after scientists.

Find the elements Au and Ag. What is special about these elements?

Here are ten symbols:

    He Sn O Fe Al I U Ca N Cl

Write which elements they represent and tick those elements you know. Choose one of these elements and write a sentence about it.

Write the names of two elements which are normally gases.

Write the symbols of another two elements which are normally gases.

The shiny substance used in thermometers is an element. What is the symbol for that liquid element?

Look at the substances to the left of the zig-zag line. These substances belong together in one set.
Give a name to this set of elements.

Explaining matter 3

Looking at elements

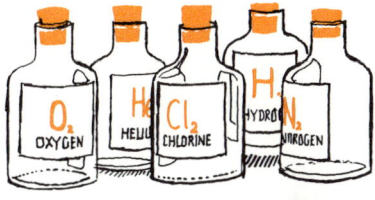

Examine the samples of elements. Write the names of those which are shiny. What are shiny materials like these called? Where do these elements belong in the periodic table?

The sample bottles are not empty. What kind of matter do they contain? In which part of the table are these elements found?

Look at the jar of chlorine gas. What is its colour? This is a poisonous gas, but you have probably met the gas before. Where have you smelled this gas? What does it do to your eyes and nose? Does chlorine belong to the metal set or the non-metal set?

Examine the sample of sulphur. Describe its appearance. Heat a small amount of sulphur gently. What happens? What happens to the sulphur when it cools? On which side of the periodic table will you find this element? Check to see if you are right.

Examine the copper foil. Describe how it looks. Give a reason for this element belonging to the left side of the table. Twist the foil. What happens? Heat the copper for 2 min. Does anything happen to the foil?

Copper is a shiny red metal. Sulphur is a yellow non-metal. What kind of substance do you think you will get when atoms of copper are joined with atoms of sulphur?
Put a small amount of powdered sulphur in a test-tube. Add a thin strip of copper foil. Does anything happen? Heat only the foil. The heat will pass to the sulphur. What happens to the copper when the sulphur heats up? Let the tube cool. Tip the contents on to a mat. Twist the substance. Do you have a new substance? Copper atoms have joined with sulphur atoms. Did you think the new substance would look like this? Invent a name for it.

Explaining matter 3

Looking at compounds

When atoms of one element are joined with atoms of other elements, new substances are made. The new substances are called compounds.

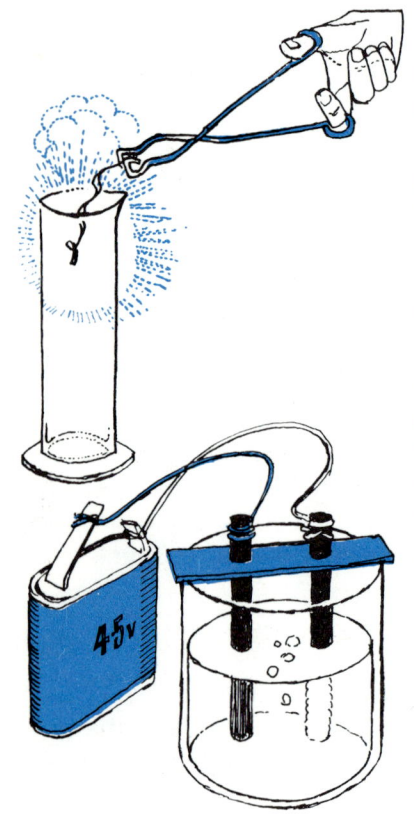

Copper atoms will be combined with chlorine atoms. Since chlorine gas is poisonous, you will not make this compound yourself. Very thin copper foil will be gently heated and placed in a jar of chlorine. What happens to the copper? What do you see forming in the jar? Describe the new substance and give it a name.

Now use electrical energy to break the copper chloride apart. Dip the carbon rods into the solution of copper chloride. Switch on the current for 5 min. Watch the two rods carefully.
What can you see forming on one of these rods?
What can you smell from the other rod?
You started with copper chloride. What has the electrical energy broken the compound into?

Look at the compounds on display. On the labels you will see the symbols for these compounds. These symbols tell you what kinds of atoms make up the compound. Use the periodic table to say what elements make up these substances.

Write the names of these elements:

Fe   Mn   Ca   Na   Si

Now write which compounds in the display contain atoms of these elements.

You have many chemical compounds at home. One example is sugar. Write the names of five others you can find at home.

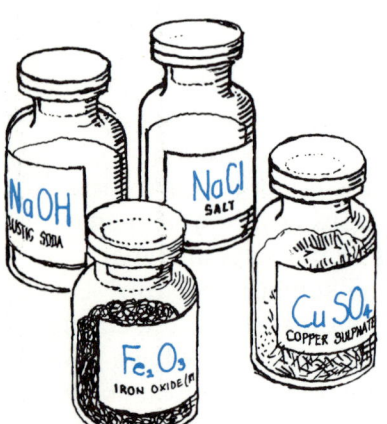

Explaining matter 3

Atoms

You quickly worked out that matter is made of particles. It would have taken you a long time to work out that there are two main kinds of particles.

Atoms are the building blocks of matter

The first kind are called atoms. The second kind are made of atoms joined together. That means atoms are the building blocks of all matter. There are about 100 different kinds of atoms. Atoms of the same kind belong to the same set. This set is called an element. Atoms of the same element behave in the same way, but they behave differently from atoms of other elements.

Atoms can be joined together

Atoms of one element can be joined with atoms of other elements to form new substances called compounds. The compound particles are no longer atoms, although they are atoms joined together. The joined atoms are the second main kind of particle. Compounds can have very unexpected properties. You saw this when red copper was joined with yellow sulphur. This made the black compound copper sulphide, whose particles are copper sulphide particles. Perhaps the most surprising compound is made from the gaseous elements hydrogen and oxygen. This is the compound water.

Energy is needed to join atoms or to pull atoms apart

Energy is needed to make atoms join together to make compounds. When compounds are broken the same atoms come apart and energy is needed again. In this way the work of a chemist goes in a circle. Chemists work with atoms and energy to get new compounds. Chemists work with compounds, breaking them up to find out what elements are present. They then recombine these elements in different ways or combine them with other elements. From this they make new compounds. Look around at these compounds and their surprising properties.

Explaining matter 3

Scientists working with materials

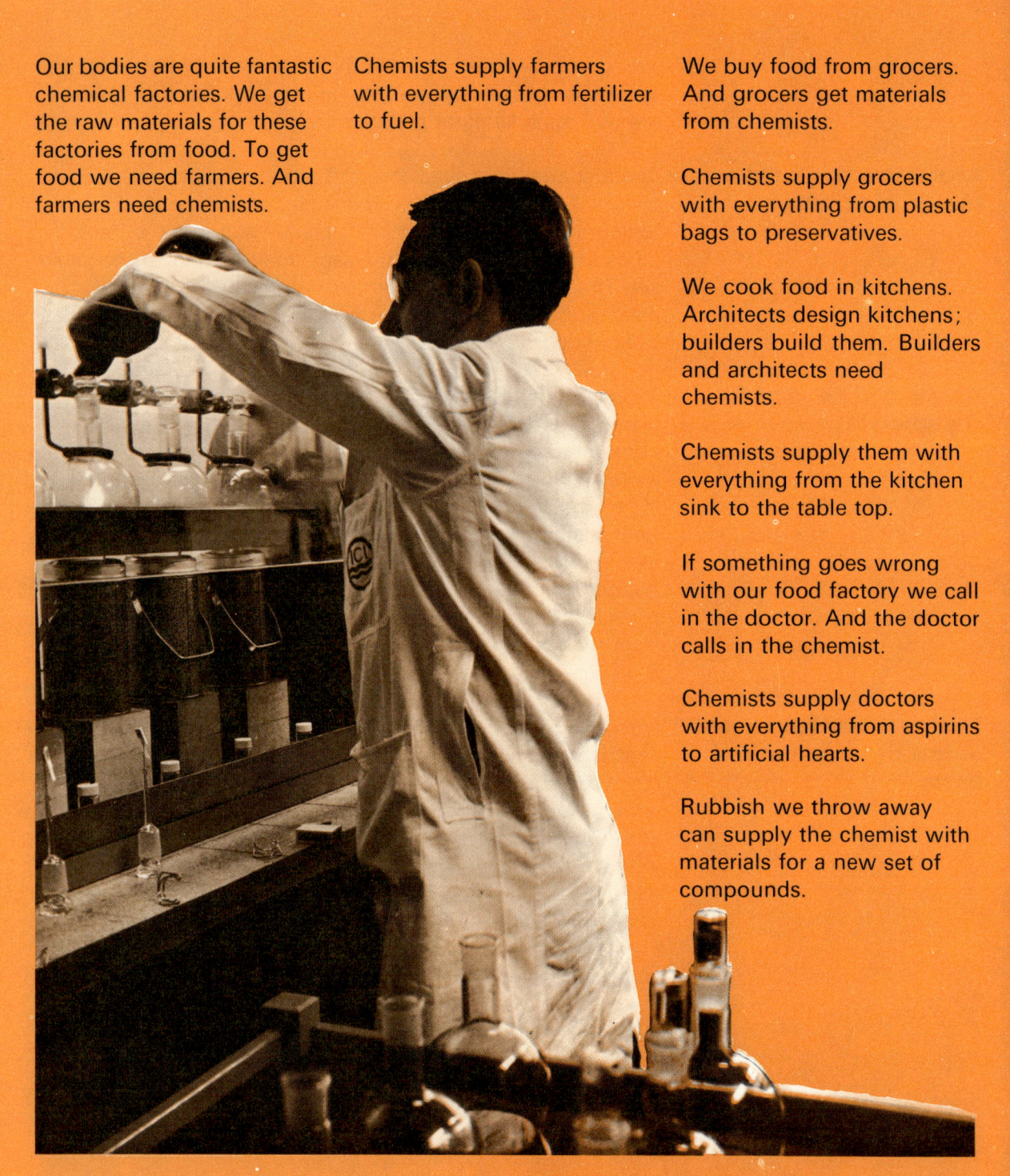

Our bodies are quite fantastic chemical factories. We get the raw materials for these factories from food. To get food we need farmers. And farmers need chemists.

Chemists supply farmers with everything from fertilizer to fuel.

We buy food from grocers. And grocers get materials from chemists.

Chemists supply grocers with everything from plastic bags to preservatives.

We cook food in kitchens. Architects design kitchens; builders build them. Builders and architects need chemists.

Chemists supply them with everything from the kitchen sink to the table top.

If something goes wrong with our food factory we call in the doctor. And the doctor calls in the chemist.

Chemists supply doctors with everything from aspirins to artificial hearts.

Rubbish we throw away can supply the chemist with materials for a new set of compounds.

Explaining matter 3

Mr. Tanimoto's story

Atoms are not simple particles. They are made up of even smaller pieces arranged together in a complicated way. These pieces are held together by large amounts of energy. If an atom is split this energy is released. This energy can be released destructively in an atom bomb. This is the story of a family who survived the explosion of the first atom bomb.

Mr. Tanimoto was afraid for his family and his church. He ran towards them by the shortest road. He was the only person making his way into the city. He met hundreds and hundreds of people who were fleeing. They all seemed to be injured in some way. Many were naked or in shreds of clothing. On some of the undressed bodies, patterns could be seen. On the skin of some of the women the patterns were in the shape of flowers—the flower patterns of their kimonos. The dark material of the flowers had passed the heat flash through to their skin. Many, although injured themselves, helped relatives who were worse off. Almost all had their heads bowed. They were silent; their faces bore no expression.

Mr. Tanimoto ran all the way and as he approached the city centre he saw that all the houses were crushed and that many were on fire. The trees were bare, their trunks charred. Under many houses people cried for help. But no one helped. That day survivors could assist only their friends. They could not stand any more misery. They could not bear to see more suffering. Mr. Tanimoto also ran past. He was a good and kindly man and as he ran, he prayed: 'God help them and take them out of the fire.' He thought he would avoid the fire but he could not. Every street he tried was blocked. He was staggered by the extent of the damage. He ran out to the suburbs. All the way he overtook burned and wounded people. In his guilt he turned to them as he hurried and said, 'Excuse me for having no wound like yours', for he was the only one.

He came to the bank of the river but there was fire all around. There was no fire on the other bank, so he threw off his shirt and shoes and jumped in. In midstream the current was strong. Fear and exhaustion caught up with him. He went limp and drifted with the current. He prayed, 'Please God, help me to cross. It would be nonsense for me to be drowned when I am the only one uninjured.' He managed a few more strokes and landed on the other bank.

He climbed up the bank and ran along it till he came to a shrine where there was a fire. He turned left to go round it and by a piece of unbelievable luck he met his wife. She was carrying their baby son. Mr. Tanimoto was worn out in every way by now. Nothing could surprise him any more. He simply said, 'Oh, you are safe.'

Water 1　　　　　　A very common substance

You have been exploring two very important ideas: energy and matter. You can now use these ideas to explore a very common and a very important substance: water.

How is water, water?

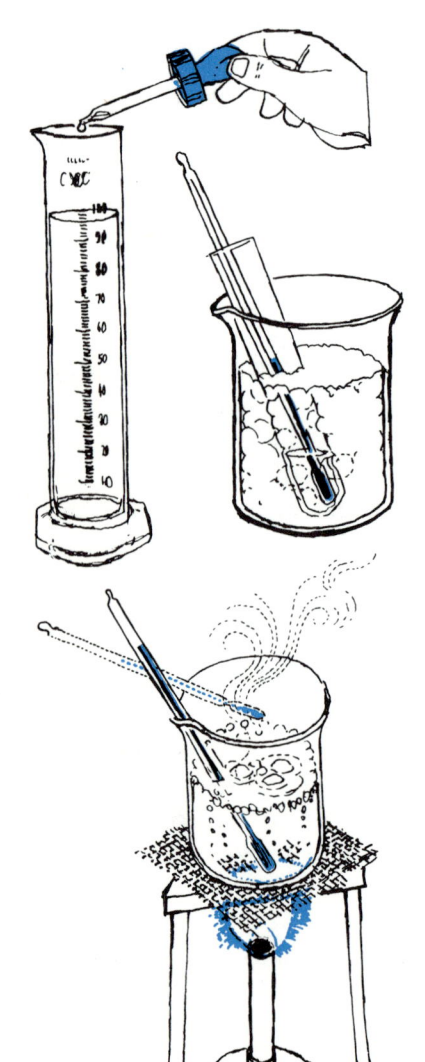

Put almost 100 ml water in a measuring jar. Add more water from a dropper to get exactly 100 ml.
Write five things you notice about the water.

Half fill a test-tube with crushed ice. When the ice begins to melt, put a thermometer in the melting ice.
At what temperature does ice melt?

Add salt to some crushed ice in a 250 ml beaker. This makes a freezing mixture. Put 3 ml water into a test-tube and put the tube into the freezing mixture.
Where does ice begin to form?
At what temperature does water freeze?

You will now find the temperature of boiling water. Take great care. Boiling water causes very painful burns.
Put 50 ml water into a 100 ml beaker. Heat the water until it boils. Put a thermometer gently into the water. What is the highest temperature reached by the boiling water?
At what temperature does water boil?

Remove the thermometer from the boiling water. Be very careful. Steam can be more dangerous than boiling water. Hold the thermometer at an angle and hold it so that the bulb is just above the boiling water. Read the temperature on the thermometer.
At what temperature does steam condense?

Now turn out the burner. Carefully place a clean watch glass on top of the beaker of hot water. What collects under this glass? Write two sentences saying how you think that substance got there.

68

Water 1

When is water, water?

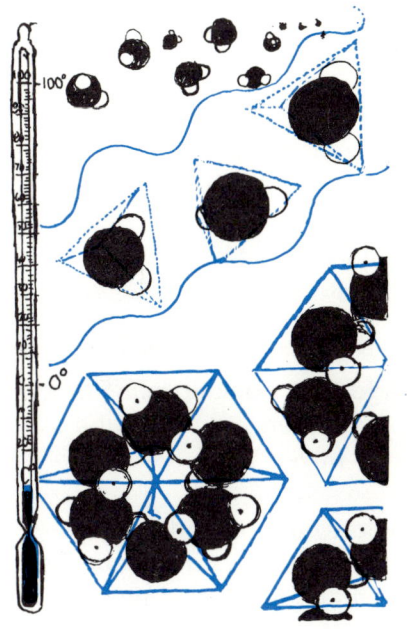

You know these sentences:

Water changes into ice. Ice changes into water.
Water changes into steam or water vapour.
Steam and water vapour change into water.

Match the sentences with these words:

condensation   freezing   melting   evaporation

Complete these sentences:
Water will freeze when enough energy is taken from it. It freezes at ___°C. Ice melts at ___°C. Ice melts when energy is _____ to ice. Water boils at ___°C. Steam _____ at 100°C. Water boils when enough _____ is added to water.

Water puzzle   To keep water boiling heat must be added all the time, but the temperature of boiling water does not change. The temperature stays at 100°C. If the heat does not make the water hotter, what does it do?

Solutions and problems

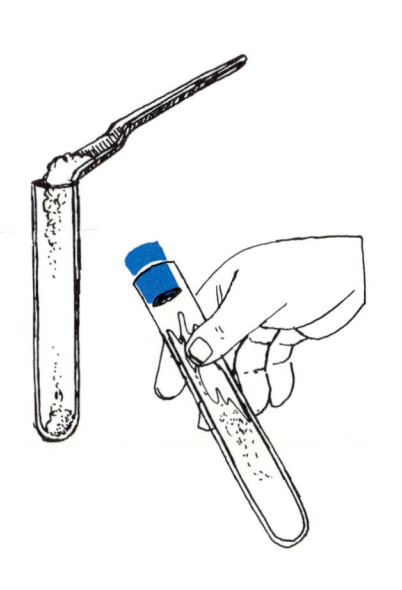

You will now mix everyday substances with water. One substance you will use is salt. The salt you will use is called sodium chloride.

Put one spatula heap of sand in a test-tube. Half fill the tube with water. Put a stopper in the tube. Shake the tube to mix the pieces of sand with the water. Do the pieces of sand stay mixed? How do you know?

Put one spatula heap of sodium chloride in a test-tube. Half fill this tube with water. Stopper and shake for one or two minutes. Do the sodium chloride particles settle out? Where are these particles?

You cannot see the sodium chloride particles. If you tasted the mixture, you would know that the sodium chloride particles are still present. Work out another way of showing that these particles are present.

Water 1

Solutions and problems

Put one drop of the sodium chloride and water mixture on a clean slide. Gently heat the slide. What happens to the water? What is left on the slide? How could you be sure of this?

When a substance mixed with water disappears and stays mixed, like sodium chloride, we say the substance has dissolved. Mixtures which stay mixed are called solutions.

It looks as though pieces of sand do not stay mixed with water. You cannot be sure just by looking. How can you check there are no sand pieces in the clear water?

Put 1 ml water in a test-tube. Add 5 ml cooking oil. Stopper and shake for two or three minutes, then hold the tube still. Do the two kinds of particles stay mixed?

Add 5 drops of washing-up liquid to the oil and water. Stopper and shake for two or three minutes, then hold the tube still. What happens to the oil and water this time?

Put 50 ml water in a 100 ml beaker. Add a small quantity of powdered starch to this water. Stir the starch and water. Does the starch dissolve in the water?

Place the beaker carefully on a tripod. Heat the mixture, stirring all the time, until it boils. Has a solution been made?

Half fill a test-tube with cooled starch and water mixture. Half fill another tube with sodium chloride solution. Hold both tubes in a beam of light. What can you see? Use your ideas on particles to explain the difference.

Water 1

A very interesting substance

Water is a very important substance. Water is a very common substance. It is often mixed with other substances. All this makes water an interesting material.

What is water like?

Water is a liquid. The particles in water hold on to each other, so pieces of water shape into drops. The particles hold together very lightly. They can still slide past and around each other. So water can flow and can fit into any container and take the shape of the container. Water has no shape, no colour, no smell, no taste. It has a feel. Water feels wet.

When is water, water?

Water can store heat well, but there is a limit to how much heat it can hold. That limit is reached at 100 °C. At that temperature more heat can be added to the water, but it does not make the water hotter. The water boils away, changing from liquid to gas. Instead of water there is now steam. There is also a limit to how much heat can be taken from water. That limit is reached at 0 °C. Then water freezes. It changes from liquid to solid, and instead of water there is ice. So water is water between 0 °C and 100 °C.

What is in water?

When substances are mixed with water, some, like sand, do not stay mixed. Others, like sodium chloride or starch, stay mixed and spread all through the water. Mixtures of this kind are called solutions. Sodium chloride and starch make different kinds of solutions. They are spread through the water in different ways. In a sodium chloride solution, the sodium chloride particles are completely separate from each other. This kind of solution is called a complete solution. In a starch solution, small numbers of starch particles are collected together. These collections are spread through the water. This is called a colloidal solution.

Water 1

Scientists working with water

The water cycle affects us all. It affects us in many ways. What happens can be good (enough rain falls). It can be bad (rain falls too quickly, or it falls too early, or it falls too late). We want to know more about the water cycle. We need to know more about it. One person can find out a little. Many can find out a lot. Here are some of the people who explore the water cycle.

Physicist Interested in matter and energy. Concerned with freezing, melting, evaporation, condensation in water cycle. Always fascinated when these happen when they should not. Always excited when these do not happen when they should. Must know why.

Meteorologist Studies weather. Often very friendly with physicist. Work together to explain rainfall, hail, and snow. Forecasts improving all the time. Trying to control rainfall in some parts of world.

Hydrologist Tries to put numbers to different parts of the cycle. How much rain falls? Where does every drop go? How great an effect does this cause? Does it all add up? Is any wasted? How much?

Water 1

Engineer Works very closely with hydrologist. Concerned with controlling flow of rivers and streams. Builds dams to store water. Builds dykes to prevent flooding.

Geologist Scientist curious about Earth and how it is built. Water cycle responsible for shaping much of land. How does it do this? Is it still going on? Are glaciers becoming larger or smaller? Why? What will this mean?

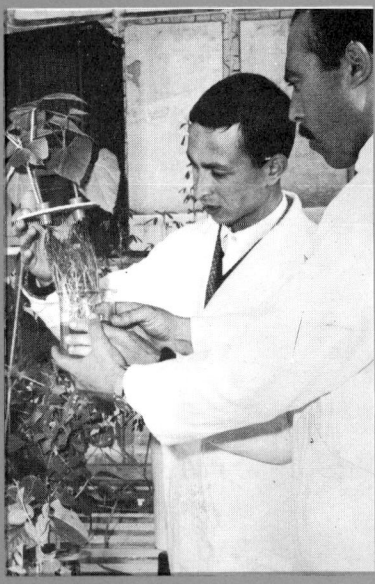

Botanist Plant biologist. Plants get water from soil. How much water does each plant need? Can it do with less? Will it still grow as well? Will it give as much food? Can it grow where there is little rainfall? Trying hard to breed these kinds of plants.

Geographer Looks at water cycle in different way from others. Concerned with many aspects. Works with all these people. Ties everything together and connects this with how human beings live.

Water 2 # Stopper and shake

Water is the best solvent there is. Many substances dissolve in it to make complete solutions. It is worth exploring what water can and cannot do.

How many particles can be packed into water?

That is a sensible question to start with. But it does not ask how much water will be used, nor how much substance will be added. You will always use the same amount of water: 10 ml. You will measure out the substance to be dissolved in spatula heaps.

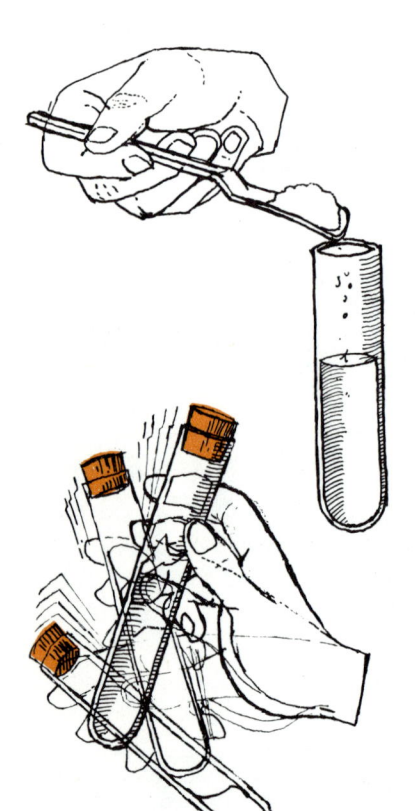

Put 10 ml water into a test-tube. Add one spatula heap of sodium chloride to the water. Stopper the tube. Shake until the sodium chloride has dissolved. Add a second spatula heap of sodium chloride to the solution. Stopper and shake until the solute has completely dissolved. Add more sodium chloride in this way until no more will dissolve.

Is there a limit to how much sodium chloride 10 ml of water can hold? How many spatula heaps of sodium chloride can 10 ml water hold?

Will 10 ml water dissolve the same amount of other solutes? To find out, work the same way as in the last activity. Put 10 ml water in a test-tube. Add one spatula heap of a new solute to the water. Stopper and shake until it has completely dissolved. Continue this way with the new solute until no more will dissolve. Do the substances dissolve in water? Is there a limit to how much can be dissolved in 10 ml water? How many spatula heaps of each solute can be dissolved in 10 ml water?

Water 2

Can more particles be squeezed in?

Shaking moves the solute particles among the solvent particles. What will heating do?

Put 250 ml water into a 500 ml beaker. Carefully heat the water to 55 °C. Do not turn out the burner. Use a low flame to keep the water at about this temperature. Put 10 ml water in a test-tube. Place this tube in the heated water bath. Let the water in the tube heat to 50 °C. Take the tube from the bath and add one spatula heap of sodium chloride to the water. Stopper and shake until all the solute dissolves.
Replace the tube in the bath. Let the solution heat to 50 °C, then remove the tube. Add one more spatula heap of solute. Stopper, shake, dissolve, replace. Repeat this until no more solute will dissolve.

Does more sodium chloride dissolve at the higher temperature? How many spatula heaps of sodium chloride will dissolve in 10 ml water at 50 °C?

Will 10 ml water at 50 °C dissolve the same amount of other solutes? Find out by working with other solutes in exactly the same way as the last activity. Can more of other solutes be dissolved at the higher temperature? How many spatula heaps of each solute can be dissolved in 10 ml water at 50 °C? Record your results in a table.

You have made solutions which can hold no more solute particles. These solutions are saturated with solute. Use a dropper to remove some of the clear, warm, saturated solution. Put one drop on a microscope slide. Look at the solution through a hand lens. What happens to the solute when the warm saturated solution cools?

solute	spatula heaps
sodium chloride	....
copper sulphate	....
potassium permanganate	....
alum	....

Solution puzzle What would happen if you let the solution cool slowly?

Crystals

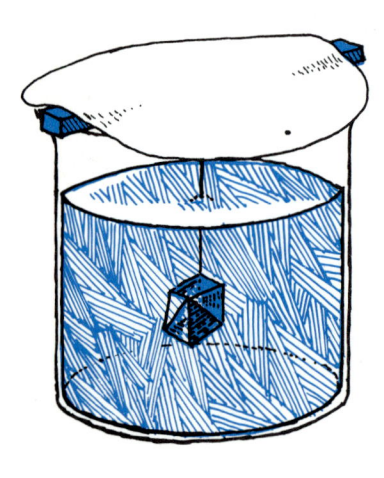

Take a clean test-tube. Carefully pour some warm saturated solution into this tube. Take care that the undissolved solute is left at the bottom of the first tube. There should be no undissolved solute in the second clean tube. Leave this saturated solution to cool slowly. What happens to the solute?

Take a clean 250 ml beaker. Pour all the saturated solution of copper sulphate into this beaker. Take care that no undissolved copper sulphate is added to this beaker. Choose a small crystal of copper sulphate. Tie a nylon thread round this crystal. Hang the crystal in the cool saturated solution. Cover the beaker with a filter paper to keep out dust.
Watch and wait for several weeks. What happens to the small crystal as the solvent evaporates?

Potassium alum was also used as a solute. Do the same with potassium alum as you have just done for copper sulphate. Watch the potassium alum crystal. Do different solutes form the same kind of crystal?

The instructions and questions have guided you this far. To solve the next problems you must guide yourself. You will have to provide your own instructions and questions. Here are the problems:

Which dissolves faster:

Large copper sulphate crystals or small copper sulphate crystals? Stirred crystals or unstirred crystals? Crystals in cold water or crystals in hot water?

Plan your work carefully. Then carry it out.

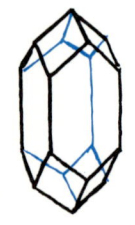

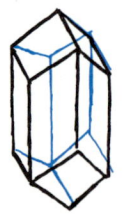

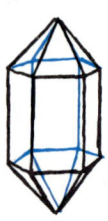

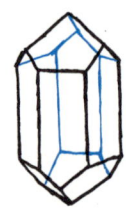

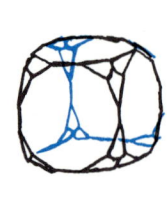

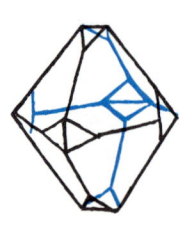

Solutions

Water is the commonest liquid of all. Pure water is very uncommon. There are usually many other substances mixed with water. Here are some of these mixtures.

Solvents and solutes

There are always two parts to a solution. One part is the solute, the other is the solvent. The solute is the substance which is mixed through the solvent. Sodium chloride, copper sulphate, and potassium alum are solutes. These are solids, but solutes can also be liquids or gases.
Usually the solvent is a liquid, and usually that liquid is water. Other liquids can dissolve solutes and some solids can be solvents.

Dissolving

When a solute dissolves in a solvent two things happen. First, the solute particles separate from each other. Somehow the particles no longer hold on to each other. Second, the particles spread out. The particles are all moving. They bump into each other and move apart. When the solution is heated, the particles move faster, so they spread out faster.

Saturation

The solute particles spread out and move among the solvent particles. When no more solute particles can squeeze among the solvent particles, the solution is saturated. When a solution is heated, all the particles jostle each other. More solute particles fit in. So a hot solution holds more solute particles than a cool solution.

Crystals and crystallization

But warm solutions cool. Then fewer solute particles can squeeze in among the solvent particles. The solute particles cannot stay dissolved. Solvent particles evaporate from solutions. Now there are fewer solvent particles to hold the solute particles. Again the solute particles cannot stay dissolved. Some solute particles collect together again. They collect in a pattern. We can see the pattern when the particles collect slowly. They collect into crystals.

Water 2

Our resources: the sea

The ocean is the biggest and most complicated solution there is. The materials in it are ours to use, but they are not free. Energy must be used to extract them. Equipment must be built to arrange for this. Energy is money. Equipment is money.

Sodium chloride This has been cheaply removed from the sea for thousands of years. The energy source is free: sunlight. The equipment is cheap: huge shallow pits on the seashore. Sodium chloride is the most common solute in sea water.

Gold There is a fantastic amount of gold in the oceans. There is an even more fantastic amount of water around it. One very good chemist spent ten years on the problem of removing gold from sea water. His conclusion: you can never get enough gold out to pay the price of getting that gold out.

Uranium At the moment it is cheaper to get uranium from expensive uranium ores than from the sea. In future we may run out of uranium ore. Then uranium from the sea will appear to be cheap, no matter how expensive it is.

Water The biggest supply of this priceless substance is found in the oceans. It takes much energy and equipment to remove enough solutes so that the water is fresh. Scientists and engineers are working very hard to make this cheaper.

As you can see it is expensive to take materials from the sea, even though the sea does not belong to anyone. So is it cheap to dump substances into the sea? The answer to that question is no. There are many links between ourselves and the sea, and we have no idea how much we might damage these links by using the sea as a dump.

Jacques Cousteau: the manfish

Jacques Cousteau spends much of his time working under the sea. He works as an explorer, observer, and experimenter. He is also an inventor. He and Emil Gagnan invented the aqualung in 1943. Here is the story of his first dive.

My friends fitted on the last piece of equipment. It was very heavy, so I staggered as I walked into the sea. In the sea I felt like a trespasser and I have felt like that ever since. The sand sloped into the distance. A small valley opened below, full of dark green weeds, black sea urchins, and small white seaweeds.

I put my arms to my side and kicked the fins lightly. I travelled down, gaining speed, watching the beach rush past. I stopped kicking and still moved on in a fabulous glide. When I stopped, I slowly emptied my lungs and held my breath. My body became a little smaller. There was less body for the water to push against so I sank down, and reached the bottom in a state of great excitement.

A school of silvery fish, round and flat as saucers, swam amongst the rocks. I looked up and saw the surface of the water like a trick mirror. I saw my wife Simone. She was the size of a doll. I waved. The doll waved back.

I became fascinated with the way I breathed out air. The bubbles swelled as they rose to the surface. They were flattened like mushroom caps as they pushed against the water. I realized how important bubbles would be in all future dives. As long as air bubbled on the surface, all was well below. If the bubbles disappeared there would be anxiety and emergency measures.

I thought of the helmet diver with his big clumsy boots, struggling to walk a few metres, thinking always of his life-line to the surface. On skin-dives I had seen them leaning dangerously forward to make one step. The diver in his copper helmet and his lead boots was a cripple in an exciting land. But from this day on, men would swim free as fish. They would swim across country no man had known.

I experimented with all possible ways of moving with the aqualung. I looped, I did somersaults, I did barrel rolls, I stood upside down on one finger. Whatever I did, nothing stopped the flow of air. Free from gravity, I flew around in space. I soared up and passed my own bubbles. I kicked and could reach a speed of 4 kilometres per hour. I pushed down to 20 metres. I was testing myself and the aqualung. I wondered about our invention. I wondered how far it would take us. I knew one thing. Our new key to the hidden world promised wonders.

Water 3

What's in the mixture?

How do you make something invisible? By painting it with invisible ink, of course. You cannot see the particles in a solution. So how do you make them visible?

Tests and testing

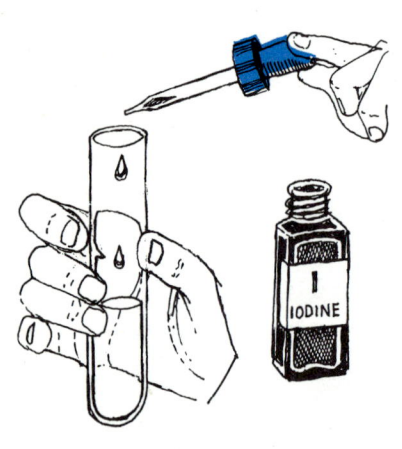

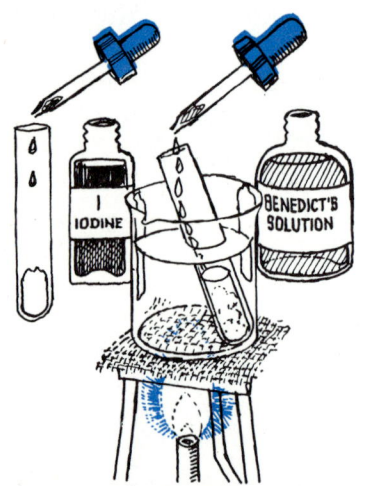

Put 2 ml starch solution in a test-tube. What is the colour of the starch solution? What is the colour of iodine solution? Add 2 drops iodine solution to the starch solution. What is the colour of the new mixture?

Put 5 ml glucose solution in a test-tube. What is the colour of glucose solution? What is the colour of Benedict's solution? Add 10 drops Benedict's solution to the glucose solution. Set up a water bath with a 250 ml beaker. Heat the mixture of glucose solution and Benedict's solution in the water bath. What colour is the warm mixture?

Try the iodine test with glucose solution. Is there a colour change with this mixture? Warm starch solution with Benedict's solution. Is there a colour change with this mixture?
Is iodine solution a special test for starch?
Is warming with Benedict's solution a special test for glucose?

You will test food samples to see if the foods contain starch or glucose.
To test for starch, add 2 drops iodine solution to a small sample of the food.
To test for glucose, the food must first be mixed with water. Put 5 ml water in a test-tube. Add 0.5 cm food to the tube. Heat this mixture in a water bath for a few minutes. Add 10 drops Benedict's solution and continue to heat the mixture in the water bath.
Make 4 lists. These will be foods containing: starch only, glucose only, starch and glucose, and no starch or glucose.

FOODSTUFFS CONTAINING—			
Starch only	Glucose only	Starch and Glucose	No Starch or Glucose

Water 3

Separating substances

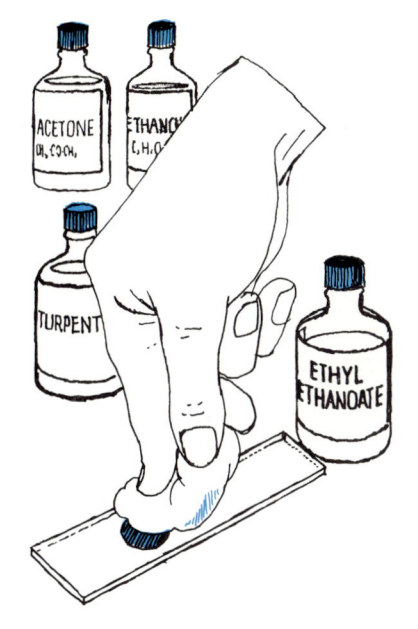

Tests can tell us what is in a mixture. We need to know this to separate the substances from each other. Each substance is separated in a special way. Here are some of these ways. There are many, many more.

Paint a small circle with nail varnish in the centre of 5 microscope slides. Let the varnish dry. Wet a small piece of cotton wool with water. Rub the varnish on one slide with the damp cotton wool. Does anything happen to the varnish?
Repeat this with these liquids:
acetone, alcohol, ethyl ethanoate, turpentine.
Use a new piece of cotton wool for each liquid.
Which liquids remove the varnish from the slide?
How do these liquids do this?

Rock salt is a mixture of sodium chloride and dirt.
The substance we want is sodium chloride.
Put 2 spatula heaps of rock salt in a test-tube. Add 10 ml water to the tube. Stopper and shake.

Fold a piece of filter paper into a cone. Place this in a filter funnel. Support the funnel in a tripod stand. Place a 100 ml beaker under the funnel. Pour the rock salt and water mixture into the filter paper cone. Rinse the filter paper with water when the mixture has passed through.
What has collected on the filter paper?
What has collected in the beaker?
Have the sodium chloride and dirt been separated?

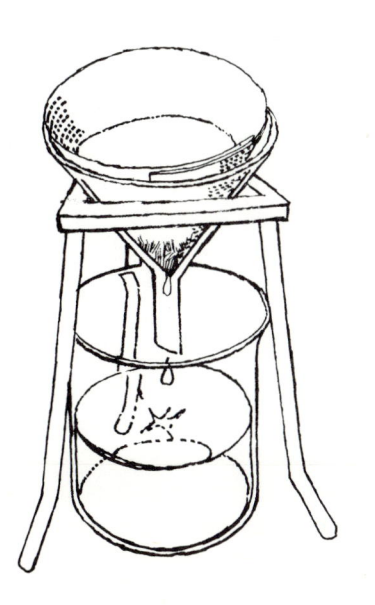

Separation puzzle How can you separate the sodium chloride from the water?

Water 3

More separating

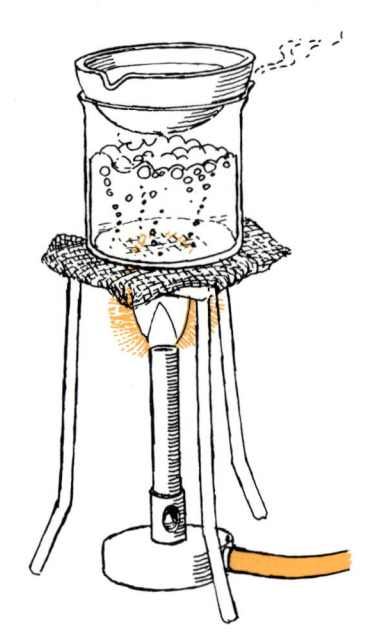

Now you will separate the sodium chloride from the water. Put the sodium chloride solution in an evaporating basin. Half fill a 250 ml beaker with water. Put the beaker on a tripod stand. Place the evaporating basin on the beaker. Boil the water in the beaker. How does this separate the sodium chloride from the water?

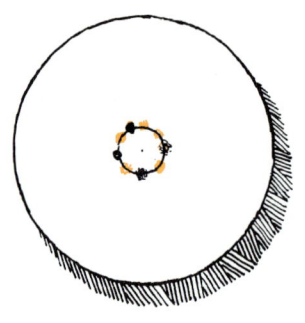

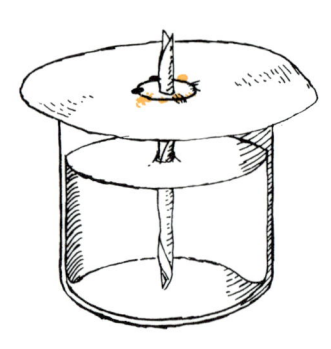

Use a pencil to draw a circle at the centre of a sheet of filter paper.
Put a spot of ink from a felt-tip pen on the edge of this circle. Put spots from other coloured pens round the circle. Take a small piece of filter paper. Roll it up tightly. Poke it through the centre of the spotted circle. Keep it there and let one end dip into water in a beaker. The spotted paper will be supported on the rim of the beaker. Leave for a short time.
What is the job of the rolled paper?
What happens to the ink spots?

Chromatography puzzle Chromatography is a neat and colourful way of separating substances. It can also be used to identify the substances in a mixture.
Here is the puzzle. You have one drop of black ink. It contains 5 different colours. You have 10 bottles of black ink. How can you find out which bottle contains exactly the same ink as the drop?

Water 3

Identify and separate

We use tests to find out what substances are in a mixture. Then we can decide how to separate the substances.

Making the pieces visible

Often we cannot see what is in a mixture. We have to find ways of making the substances visible. We can do this by colouring particles. We can colour in special ways, using many different colours to show up the different substances in a mixture. If starch is in a mixture, we get a blue/black colour when we add iodine solution. If glucose is present, we get an orange colour on warming the mixture with Benedict's solution. We can measure the brightness of the colour. That will tell us how much of a substance is present. With this knowledge we can separate the substances in a mixture.

Separating the insolubles

The easiest substances to separate from a mixture are the insolubles. Light substances can be floated off or shaken out of mixtures. Heavy substances settle by themselves. Insolubles can be trapped in many ways. Some can be collected by magnets or electricity. Some will hold on to other materials. Others can be trapped because they are too big to pass through small holes.

Separating the solubles

At first this is simple. The solvent is evaporated. This leaves the solute. It is trickier when both solute and solvent are liquids. The solvent is evaporated. This might not leave the solute; it might evaporate with the solvent. That can be a problem. A solution can hold many solutes. How can one and only one of these solutes be separated from the others? That is the same problem as separating the many substances in sea water. How do you get rid of the solute and keep the solvent? You will solve that problem in the next part of your work.

Water 3

Gold

It is always hard to separate substances. It becomes harder when there is very little of the substance you want. It becomes very hard when you want to collect a lot of that substance. Gold is a substance many people want. Gold can be mixed in many ways with different substances. There is never much gold present in these mixtures but people want as much as they can get. And when they do get it they usually just bury it again.

Fine gold dust in fast-flowing streams
Method   Trap pieces of gold in tangled hairs.

A sheep's fleece is placed on the bed of the stream. The gold dust is caught among the wool fibres. Jason and the Argonauts went looking for these fleeces.

Coarse gold dust in sand and gravel
Method   Shake out lighter material (sand).

Water and dirt are put into a big shallow pan. The mixture is swirled around. This makes the water spill out. The water carries the sand with it. Gold specks and tiny nuggets are left in the bottom of the pan.

Very fine gold dust in rock
Method   Dissolve. Make insoluble. Filter.

The pieces of gold are so fine a microscope is needed to see them. A really cheap method is needed to make separation worthwhile. The ore from the mine is crushed. It is added to a cyanide solution. The gold dissolves. The rock dust settles out. The cyanide and gold solution is removed. Zinc is added to this solution. The zinc particles push the gold particles out of solution. The gold is filtered off.

Pike's Peak or bust   The Colorado Gold Rush of 1859

The story of the American West is the story of the gold discoveries in California, in Colorado, in Nevada. Each new discovery brought a new stampede of men seeking riches beyond dreams. For a few that dream came true. For a very, very few.

One white, bitterly cold morning in the dead of winter, George Jackson, Indian trader and miner, cousin of Kit Carson, set out up Clear Creek. He was warm in his heavy windbreaker, fur cap, leather boots, and buckskin gloves. His pack was heavy with food, blankets, gold pans, and cooking pots. His rifle was on his shoulder.

He searched in all the likely places, sometimes digging into deep drifts to try his luck, but time and again he failed to find the colour that meant gold. With his food running low, Jackson realized he had to get home. He made his way south on Clear Creek, and came across a long low sand bar. It looked promising so he built a huge fire on the sand and kept it blazing all night to thaw the sand out.

His diary, January 7, 1859, reads, 'Clear day. Removed fire embers. Dug down to rock. Panned out 80 loads of dirt. Found nothing but fine yellow. Got one nugget. Dug and panned till big knife wore out. Will have to quit or use sharp skinning knife. Have about 13 grams gold so will quit. Will return later. Feel good tonight.'

Having marked his strike, he returned down the creek. He told one friend only. 'Tom Golden is the only man who knows I found gold at the head of the creek. I am not uneasy. His mouth is as tight as a number 4 beaver trap.' But there is no way to keep gold a secret. At the beginning of May he went to Denver for supplies. He paid for them in gold dust. Hundreds of gold-hungry prospectors followed him to his camp. The news spread fast.

The canyon was soon solid with miners. Thousands poured into the tiny valley. Overnight Denver was deserted. Merchants locked up their stores. Saloon keepers packed up their bottles. Gamblers pocketed their cards. Carpenters building cabins left their tools where they were. One and all—the county judge, the sheriff, lawyers, doctors—everyone joined the rush to the new El Dorado.

In the next few months 50 000 men entered the region. It was a human stampede with a continuous stream of wagons, of men on horseback, of men on foot. They had one thought, 'Gold'. They had one motto, 'Pike's Peak or bust'.

Water 4   A matter of life or death

Here is a piece of bad news. You and the laboratory are stranded on a desert island. There is no fresh water. There is sea water and that is good news. It is also a problem.

The problem
Put 100 ml tap water into a clean beaker. Dissolve 3 spatula heaps of sodium chloride in the water.
Taste what you have made.
The problem: make this water drinkable.

The problem started
Where do you start? You start by deciding what the problem really is.
Which two substances are in the solution?
Which substance do you want?
Which substance do you not want?
You have now made the problem simpler.

The solution started
How do you start to solve the problem? You start with what you know. You know how to separate sodium chloride and water. How did you separate these substances before?
To make the water drinkable, you must separate sodium chloride and water again. But your earlier separation was the wrong way round. You kept the sodium chloride. You let the water go. You must now turn the separation the right way round. You must ignore the sodium chloride and discover how you can keep the water.

You always start with what you know. Then look at it in many different ways.

Water 4

The solution working

You can now see how to get drinking water from salt water. You separate the two substances in the solution, ignore one of the substances, and collect the other. Here you will collect water vapour.
Now you must decide how you will arrange apparatus to do this.

To separate solvent from solute particles, heat is needed. What equipment is necessary for this?

The solution must be held in a container. The solvent particles evaporating from the solution must not escape. They must be kept together. What container will you use for this?

When the solution boils, the solvent particles evaporate. You could not drink these particles. They are too hot and too scattered. How can they be cooled? How can they be kept together while cooling? What will the cooled water be collected in?

When you have discussed your arrangements, the equipment will be collected. It must be safely connected and built. It must be safely operated.

When you have distilled some water, take a drink. You will need it. You deserve it.

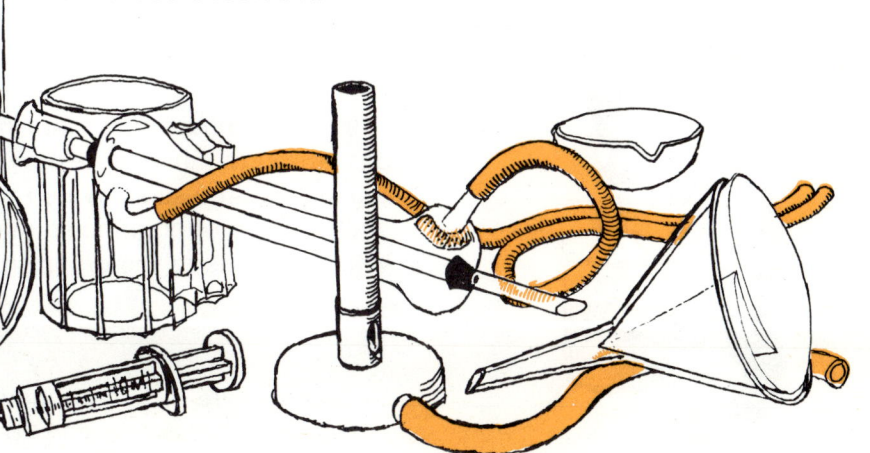

Drinking water

Look at a sample of pond water. Stir it up. What kind of materials are in this sample? What size are they? How could they be removed? Do they need to be removed?

Put a drop of the stirred-up mixture on a microscope slide. Look at this mixture under a microscope. What do you see now? What size are the objects? How could they be removed? Do they need to be removed?

Let the mixture settle. Put a drop of the clear mixture on a slide and evaporate it carefully. What is left? How is this mixed through the water? How could it be removed? Do we need to remove this?

Look at tap water exactly as you looked at pond water. Are there any large materials visible in tap water? Are there any small animals present in tap water? Are there any substances dissolved in tap water? What must be removed from pond water to make it like tap water?

In waterworks, the filters used to clean the water are made out of sand and gravel. You can use the same materials to make a filter in a glass tube. Slide a few stones into the tube. Add some gravel. Pour sand over this to a depth of about 5 cm. Support the tube carefully. Place a 250 ml beaker under the tube. Pour the muddy pond water into the filter column. What is held back by the column? Does the water come out clear? Keep passing the water through until it is clear.

Filtration removes most, but not all, microbes. Those which pass through must be destroyed. Put a drop of water full of organisms on a slide. Watch this through a microscope while a drop of chlorine solution is added to this water. What happens to the organisms in the water?

Water puzzle If you added chlorine solution to your clear, filtered water, would you get water fit to drink?

Water 4

Fit to drink

It is always surprising to find that the water we drink is not absolutely pure. In fact you might not like water free from all dissolved substances. We like to drink water free from unpleasant smells and tastes. We must drink water free from germs.

What must be taken out?

Rain, melting ice, and snow keep streams and lakes filled. From these rivers and lakes we get our drinking water, but it is not yet ready to drink. Many materials are carried into the water, and human beings add more. Many of these materials must be removed. Some substances, like pieces of dead plants, are harmless but unpleasant. These should be removed. Other substances, like the germs causing typhoid or cholera, are harmful. They must be removed.

How are they taken out?

Water can be separated from all these substances by distillation. This process is expensive because it uses so much energy. It is unnecessary because we do not need to take out all substances. The substances which must be removed are the dangerous and unpleasant ones. They are usually large and are not in solution, so they are removed by filtration. In waterworks, filters made of large beds of sand and gravel remove the substances we do not want.

What is left?

Some solutes will be present in the filtered water. They do not matter. A few germs will not be trapped by the filter. These germs will be present in the filtered water. They do matter. To destroy these germs another solute is added, chlorine gas. Chlorine kills most of the germs that are left. A few may survive. They are so very few that they do us no harm. The water is now fit to drink.

Water 4

How the Bushmen get their water

Laurens van der Post is an explorer. Here he describes a meeting with one of the last groups of Bushmen in the Kalahari desert of South-West Africa.

We were convinced that the Bushmen could continue to exist only if they were able to get a supply of water from the deep sands of the central desert. The site of these sip-wells was a secret and I had never found one on all my journeys. But an old friend had told me how he had been saved by a Bushwoman. She had found him dying of thirst. He had been dragged to a place he did not know. There she sucked water out of a hollow stick pushed into the hot sands. This water she squirted straight from her mouth into his. It seemed fantastic. Was it true?

We took great care to be polite, helpful, and friendly to the first group of true Bushmen we met. In the evening, I mentioned the problem of water. Immediately four Bushmen, Stone Axe, Powerful Wildebeest, Wooden Bowl, and Lips of Finest Fat, offered to show us. They led us some miles away to the deepest part of an old dry river bed. There was no water to be seen. The supply was hidden. Hidden safe from evaporation by sun and wind, safe beneath the sand.

Stone Axe knelt down and dug into the sand to arm's length. Some moist sand but no water eventually appeared. He took a tube, about two metres long, from the stem of a bush with a soft core. He wrapped some grass round one end of the tube, and put that end into the hole. When everything was in place he packed the sand back into the hole and stamped it down with his feet.

He then took some empty ostrich eggs from Lips of Finest Fat and wedged them into the sand beside the tube. A piece of wood was placed in the hole of the egg. The other end of the little stick he put in the corner of his mouth. Now he put his lips to the long tube. For about two minutes he sucked mightily with no result. His broad shoulders heaved with the immense effort and sweat ran like water down his back. But at last the miracle happened. A bubble of clean, bright water ran out the corner of Stone Axe's mouth. The drop clung to the little stick. It ran straight down the side into the ostrich egg without spilling.

So it continued, faster and faster, until shell after shell was filled. Stone Axe's whole being and strength joined in the single task of drawing water up out of the sand. Why he did not fall down with exhaustion I do not know. I tried to do it. My shoulders and lungs are good but I could not bring up a single drop.

Water 5

Food and water

When we drink water it goes down into our gut. The water passes through the gut wall and into the blood. How does food pass into the blood?

In your mouth

Count the number of teeth you have. How many teeth are in your upper jaw? Your lower jaw?

Make two half circles to show your upper and lower jaws. Mark your teeth on these.

Divide the diagrams of your teeth into right and left halves. How many teeth are in your right jaw? Your left jaw?

There are three different kinds of teeth in your mouth. How many of each kind do you have? Where in your mouth do you find each type?

Eat a potato crisp. What do your teeth do to this crisp? What does your tongue do to the crisp? What happens to the amount of saliva in your mouth while you are eating?

Take a bite from an apple. Which teeth do you use to take the bite? Which teeth chew the apple afterwards?

Use your teeth to bite a piece off a hunk of toffee. Which teeth are used to tear off this piece of toffee?

Here are some instruments used for breaking materials into smaller pieces: pliers, mortar and pestle, scissors.
Match these instruments with these teeth: front, side, back.
How do teeth help to make food soluble?
What is food mixed with in the mouth?

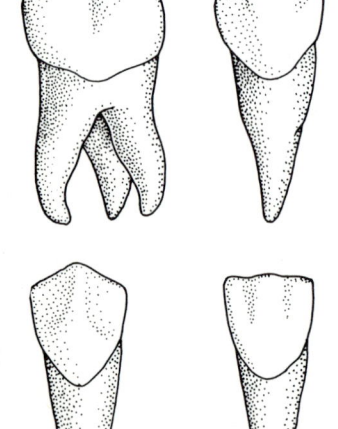

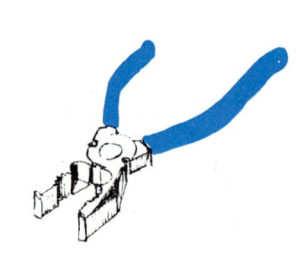

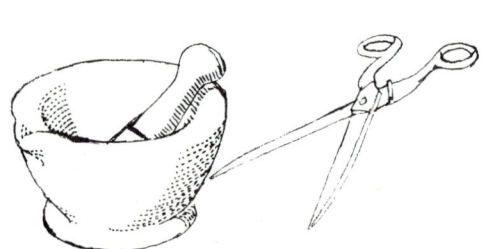

Making a gut

Now we must look further into the gut. But this is impossible for us. What we can do is make a working model of the gut and look at it.

Soak a 10 cm piece of cellulose tubing in water for one minute. Rub one end between your fingers to open it up. Blow down the tube to open it completely. Tie one end with string. This is your model gut.

Add 5 ml starch solution and 5 ml glucose solution to this gut. Tie the open end tightly with string. Check for leaks. Wash this whole gut in running water to clean any starch or glucose from the outside.
Put the gut into a 100 ml beaker and cover with water.

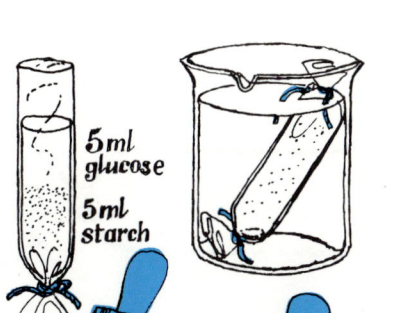

Use Benedict's solution to check that the glucose solution you put in the gut really is glucose. Use iodine solution to check that it was starch you added.

Then take samples of the water around the gut. Test one sample for glucose. Test the other for starch.
Has starch passed through the wall? Has glucose passed through?

Make a neat drawing of the model gut. Show what you put into the gut. Show what passed through the gut wall. What did this pass into? What does this represent?

Try to explain how this happened, using the particle idea. Draw the particles on either side of the gut wall. Make your drawings explain what happens.

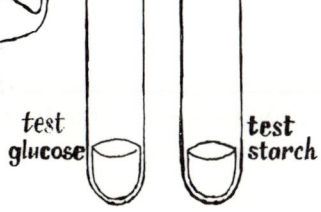

Starch and saliva

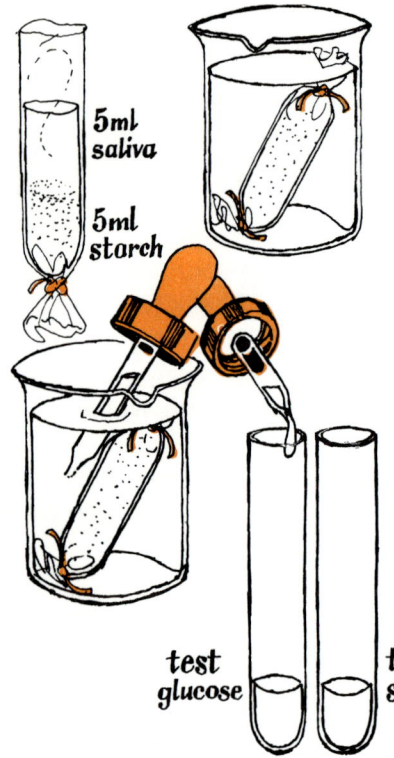

A lot of the food we eat is starch. The starch must pass somehow into our blood. Even in solution starch particles are too big to do this. They must be made smaller.

Make a new model gut. Tie one end of it with string.

Add 5 ml starch solution and 5 ml saliva to this gut. Tie the open end tightly with string. Check that there are no leaks. Wash any starch or saliva off the outside with water.
Put the gut into a 100 ml beaker and cover with water. Leave this for 10 minutes.

You know that the starch is starch. Check that there is no glucose in the starch. Then check that there is no glucose in the saliva.

Take samples of the water around the gut. Test one for glucose and the other for starch.
What do you find? Where did it come from?

Make another neat drawing of the model gut. Show clearly what is inside the gut and what is outside the gut.

What did you put into the gut? What did you not put into the gut?
What did you find outside the gut? What did you not find outside the gut?
Where did the substance outside the gut come from?
What substance did it come from?
What substance made this happen?

Write a short story about how a piece of starch in a piece of cake passes into the blood. You can start: 'I bit the cake. It tasted delicious...'

Water 5

Through the gut

Many foods are insoluble. It is the job of the gut to make these foods soluble. It does this by making the food particles small and separate.

Biting, tearing, and crushing

Much of our food comes to us in large pieces. The teeth break up these pieces. The sharp front teeth bite off smaller chunks. The pointed side teeth tear off strips from tough foods. The jagged back teeth crush these pieces down into even smaller pieces. While the chewing is going on, the tongue mixes the food with saliva and any other liquid in the mouth. This makes a coarse watery paste.

Separating food particles

The tongue pushes the paste to the back of the mouth. The throat muscles grip the paste and squeeze it down into the stomach. All the way down the gut, muscles squeeze in and out, mixing the food and water more and more. Gradually the paste becomes a finer mixture. The food particles are well spread through the water, but they are not yet soluble and they will not pass through the gut wall.

Breaking the particles

The food particles are too big to pass through the gut wall. The big particles must be changed into smaller particles. To make this change chemicals made by the body are used. These special chemicals are called enzymes. It was enzymes which changed each big starch particle into many smaller glucose particles. For each kind of big food particle there is a special enzyme.

Passing into the blood

When the particles are soluble they can pass with water through the gut wall. They pass into the blood and are carried by the blood to every cell in the body where they are needed. Enzymes in the cells can rebuild the small particles into bigger ones.

Water 5

Water in your body

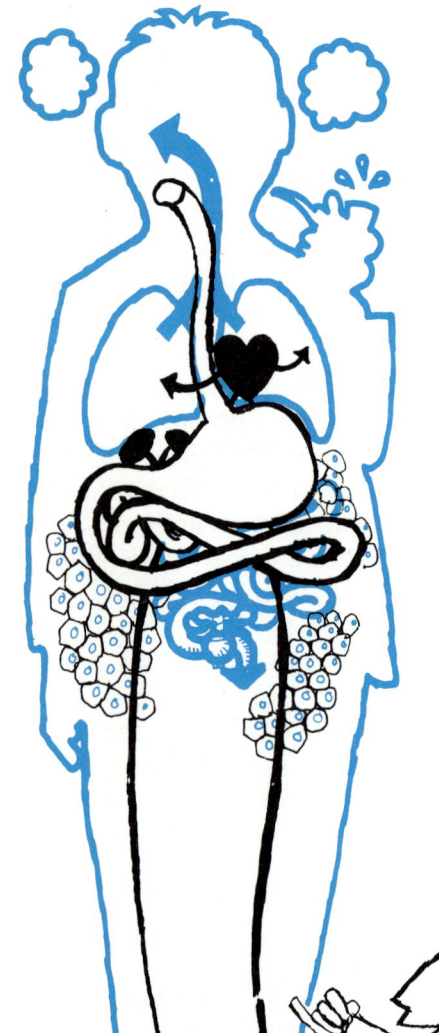

Water circulates round and round our bodies. We usually call it blood; 85% of blood is water. The cells of our bodies are mostly water too and the spaces round cells are also filled with a watery substance.

An average teacher will be about 70% water (and you too). This will be made up of about:

  5000 ml in the blood;
11 000 ml between cells;
30 000 ml in the cells.

Much of the food we eat is water:

Potatoes are 90% water.
Meat is 70% water.
Tomatoes are 95% water.

Each day:

you drink about 1000 ml water;
you get about 1200 ml water from food;
you get about 400 ml water from the chemical reactions in your body;
you lose about 500 ml water from your lungs;
you lose about 1500 ml water as urine;
you lose about 150 ml water with your faeces;
you lose about 450 ml water as sweat.

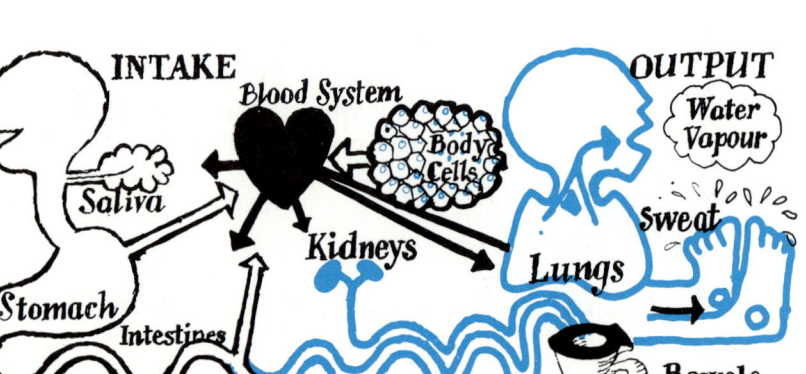

Looking into the gut   A living gut

It is impossible for us to look into a living gut and see it working. But every once in a while the impossible happens. It happened to Alexis St. Martin. He was accidentally shot in the stomach. The wound did not heal properly and left a hole to the outside. His doctor, Dr. Beaumont, treated him and used the opportunity to study the workings of the stomach. It is not a pleasant story that Dr. Beaumont tells. It is an interesting one.

'On June 6, 1822, I was called to attend Alexis St. Martin. He was 18 years old and very healthy.'

'I saw him about 30 minutes after the accident. A piece of lung was sticking out through the wound. Below this I found a piece of his stomach. The coats of the stomach were torn right through and the food was pouring out. The hole in the stomach was large enough to admit a finger.'

Alexis St. Martin was tough. Very tough. He survived. His wounds healed but not perfectly. There was still an opening from the stomach to the outside. The wound had healed but the hole had not closed. Dr. Beaumont understood how important this was. He could be the first, perhaps the only, person to look into a living gut. St. Martin, after much persuasion, gave him permission to try some experiments.

'August 1, 1825. At 12 noon I took some foods and passed them through the hole into St. Martin's stomach. The foods included: a piece of very spicy boiled beef, a piece of raw fat pork, a piece of raw lean beef, a piece of stale bread, and some raw sliced cabbage. Each piece weighed about 3 g. These were tied on to a piece of silk string and carefully pushed into the stomach.'

'At 13.00, I withdrew the silk string and examined each piece of food. The cabbage and bread were half digested. The pieces of meat were unchanged. I returned them to the stomach.'

'At 14.00, I removed them all once more. I found the cabbage, bread, pork, and boiled beef all cleanly gone. The other pieces were unchanged. I returned them to the stomach.'

St. Martin shortly after this complained of being unwell. The undigested food was taken out so the experiment was stopped.

Alexis St. Martin did not write his story. He did show his feelings about being a human laboratory. Although Beaumont paid him for the experiments he kept running away. No matter how far he went Dr. Beaumont always managed to find him.

Growing and developing

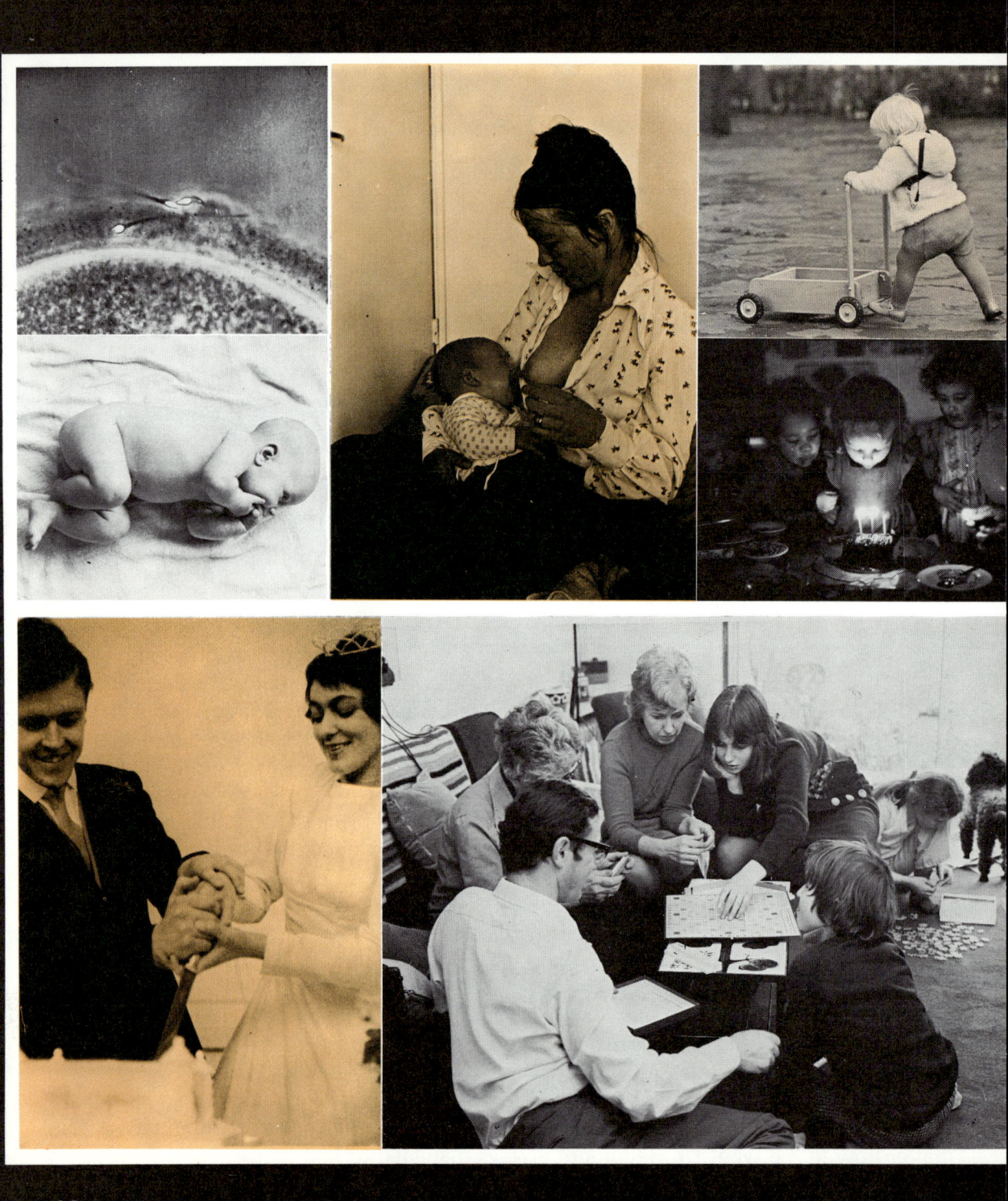

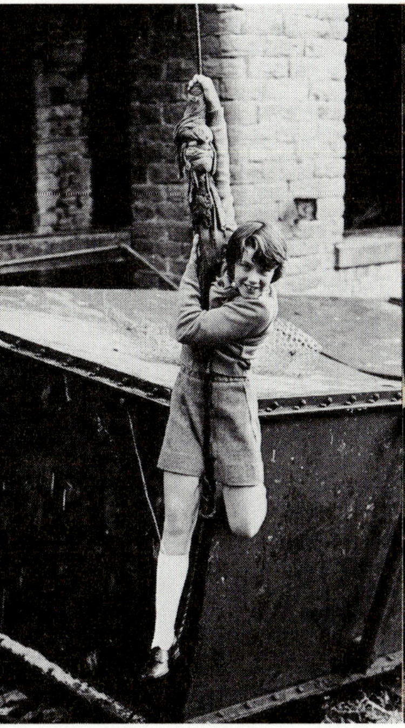

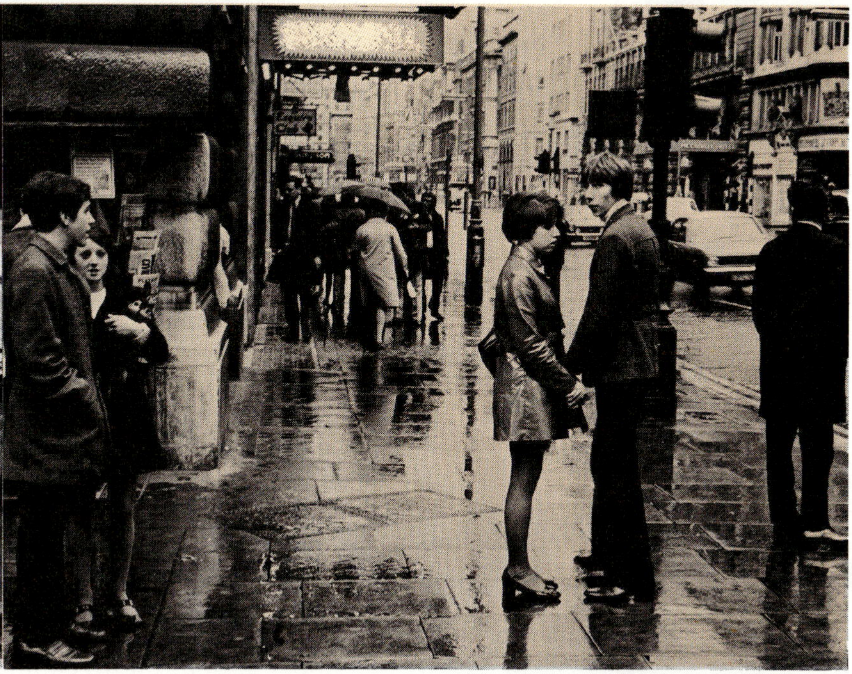

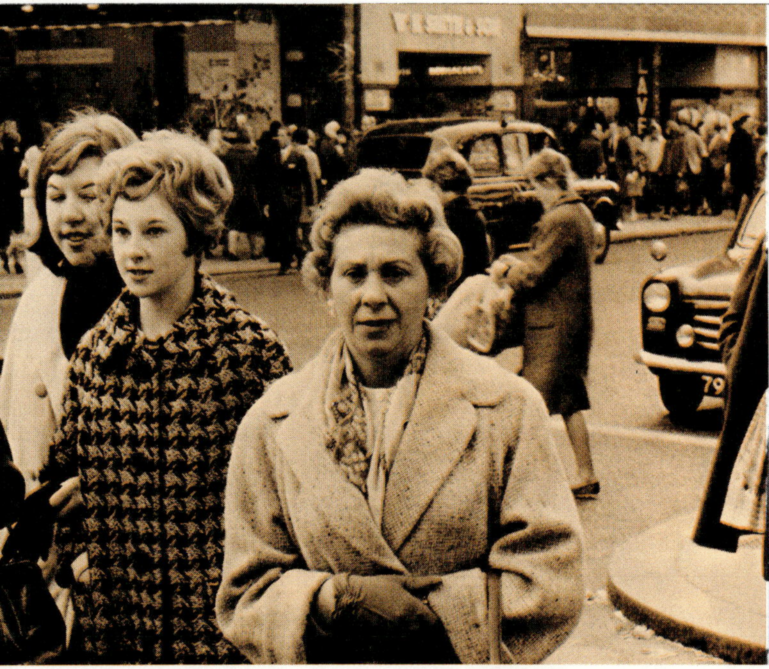

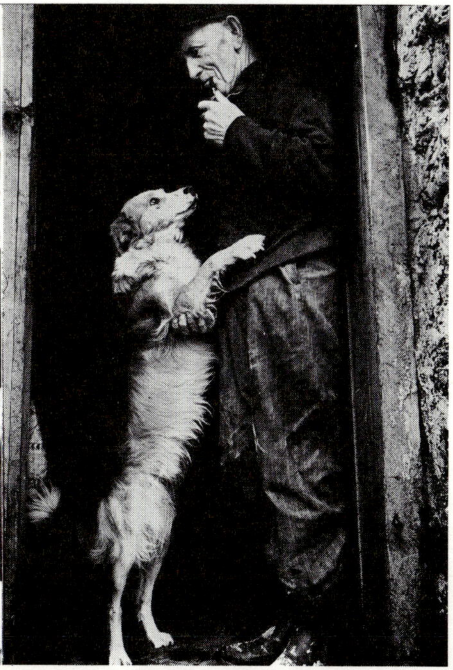

Growing and developing 1

From cells

Your body is made up of millions of cells. All the cells of your body can be traced back to one cell. So our work begins with cells, especially that first cell.

Using a microscope

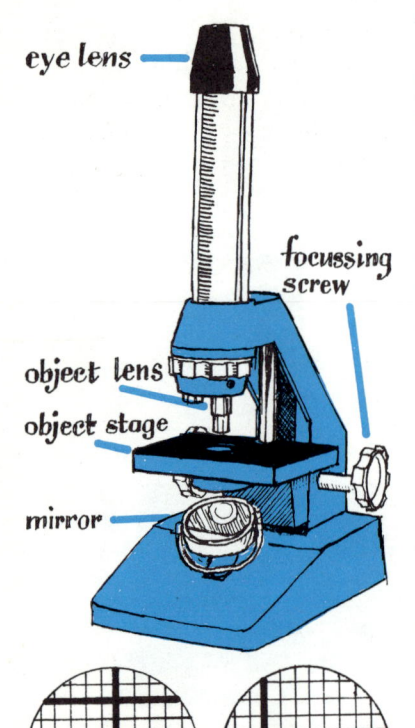

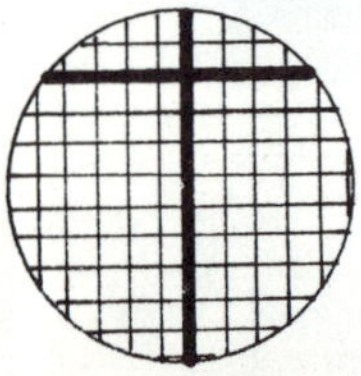

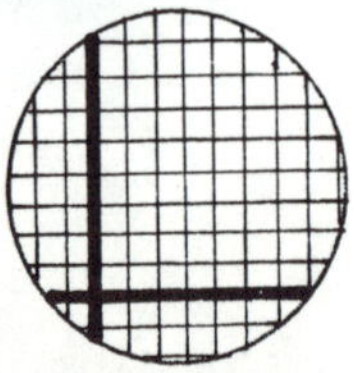

Microscopes make objects appear bigger. This is done by special pieces of glass called lenses. Find the eye lens and the object lens. The object to be looked at is placed on the stage under the object lens. Look down through the eye lens. Make sure that a bright light is shining up at you. The magnified picture of the object may not be clear. To make the picture clear you must use the focussing screw.

Lenses make big clear pictures possible but they are easily damaged. What is wrong with touching the eye lens? You will look at objects on a piece of glass called a slide. To focus this lens use only the fine focus screw. Why?

Look at the edge of a piece of blotting paper.
Look at a piece of millimetre square graph paper.
Move the paper so that the thick lines form a cross, a T, and an L. Look at a little square. What size is it?
Carefully change to the high power object lens. What size is the square now?

On the graph paper draw a letter H so that it just fits the field of view under the low power object lens.
Make a letter A of the same size and look at it. Then make a letter F and look at it. In what ways do things look different under the microscope?

Make a cross with two short pieces of hair. Look at the crossing point under the microscope. Can you keep both hairs in focus at the same time? Which hair is above the other?

Look at as many different things as you can.
Look at hair, dust, a photograph.

100

Growing and developing 1

Looking at living cells

You would not call yourself a master of the microscope. That takes much practice. But you can use the microscope to see many objects. You will now use it to see living cells.

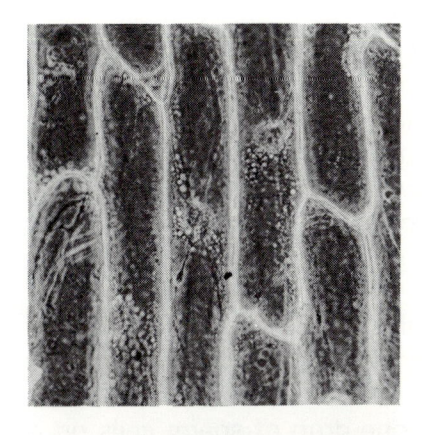

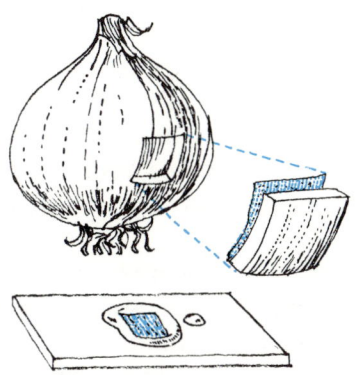

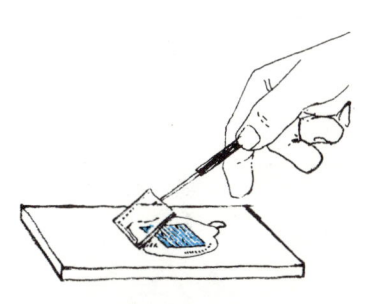

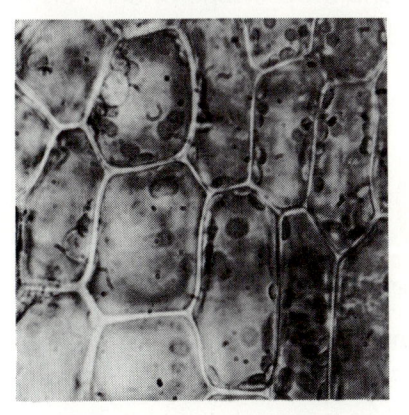

To prevent cells drying out they must be covered with water. Place a drop of water in the centre of a slide. Take a leaf from an onion bulb. From the hollow side of the leaf tear off a piece of the thin silvery skin. It will curl up, so flatten it as you place it in the water on the slide. Use a pin to lower a cover glass on to the skin. Look at your slide under the microscope. Find the round nucleus in the cells. The nucleus controls what happens in a cell.

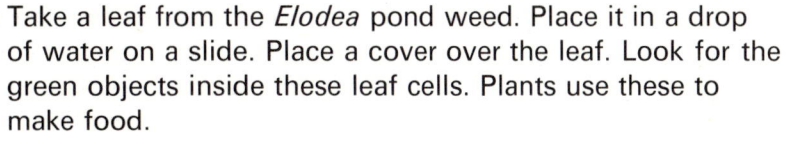

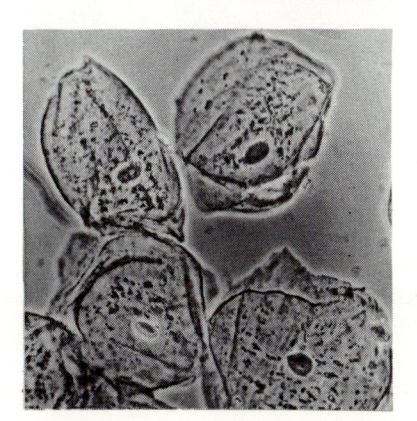

Take a leaf from the *Elodea* pond weed. Place it in a drop of water on a slide. Place a cover over the leaf. Look for the green objects inside these leaf cells. Plants use these to make food.

Gently scrape the inside of your cheek. Smear this on to a slide. Add a drop of water and a cover. Look at your cheek cells. The cells will not be very clear. Make up a new slide with cheek cells. Add a drop of iodine solution to the cells, then cover. Look for the nucleus in these cells.

Put a drop full of organisms from the tube on a slide. Cover this drop.
Many of the organisms will consist of only one cell.
Describe in words and pictures any three of the organisms.

Growing and developing 1

Cells that start organisms

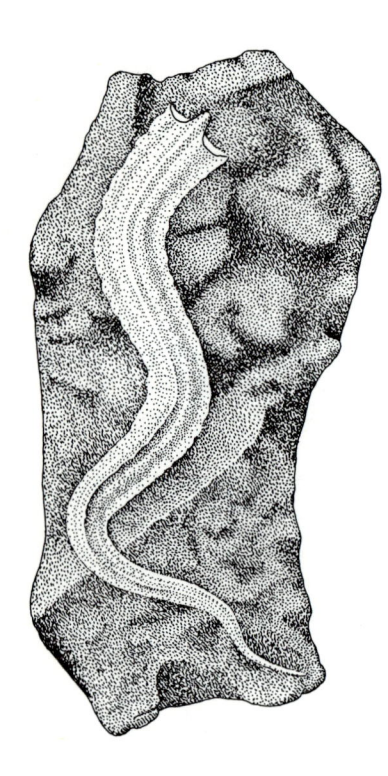

Most organisms start life when a male cell and a female cell join together. These cells are called gametes. Egg cells are female gametes. Sperm cells are male gametes.

Pomatoceros is a small worm found on the sea-shore.
It is easy to get the gametes from these worms.
Make a slide with the pink female cells.
What is the shape of these gametes? Do they move?
Make a slide with the cloudy white male cells.
How big are these compared to the egg cells?
How else could you tell sperm cells from egg cells?

When the nucleus of a male cell joins up with the nucleus of a female cell a new organism starts. This getting together is called fertilization.
Mix one drop of egg cells and one drop of sperm cells on a slide. Look at the mixture with a microscope.
Where are the sperm cells?

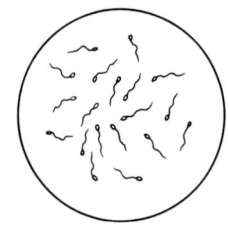

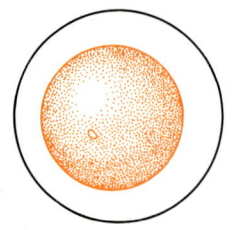

Put a mixture of egg and sperm cells in the refrigerator.
Look at them on your next laboratory day.
What do the eggs look like now?
Is each egg just one cell?
What is happening to the fertilized eggs?

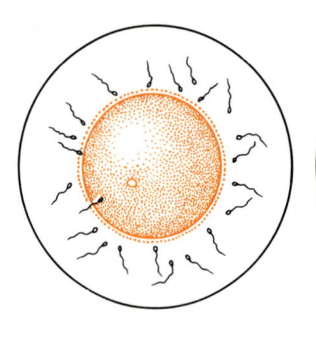

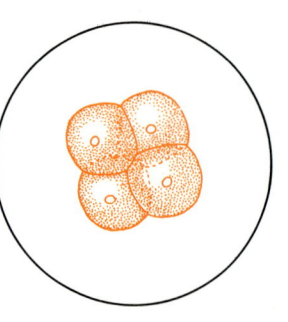

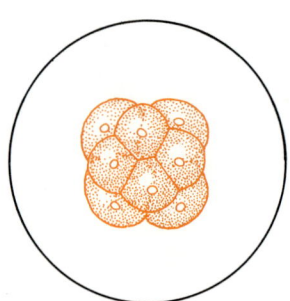

Growing and developing 1

Life cells

All things are made of particles. Living things are made up of many different kinds of particles, organized into working units. These working units are called cells.

Our body cells work together

We are made of millions of tiny cells. All these cells have a nucleus which controls the work of the cell. Each cell works with others. Not all cells are of the same kind. There are many different kinds of cell, each kind doing a special job. All the cells of our body fit together and work together. They work together to make us what we are.

Sex cells start new lives

There is one group of cells all of us must have. These cells do nothing to keep us alive. Their job is to start new lives. These are the sex cells made by women and men. Women make an egg cell once a month. Two weeks later this egg cell passes out of their bodies with a little blood. Doctors call this the menstrual cycle. Women call it their period. Men make sperm cells. These are much smaller than eggs and can swim by lashing their tails. Sperms swim towards eggs.

A sperm enters an egg to start a new life

When sperm cells meet an egg they swim beside the egg. Soon one sperm enters the egg. The nucleus of the sperm joins with the nucleus of the egg. There were two cells each with a nucleus. Now there is one cell with one nucleus. The mixing of the sperm nucleus with the egg nucleus to form one nucleus is called fertilization. Fertilization is the beginning of a new life.

Growing and developing 1

Starting a family

In humans a new individual starts when a male sex cell fertilizes a female sex cell. In this way we are the same as many other organisms. We are also like other organisms in that there are many steps which lead up to fertilization. There are also many important differences. The most important difference is that we can decide to start a family.

A man and woman meet.

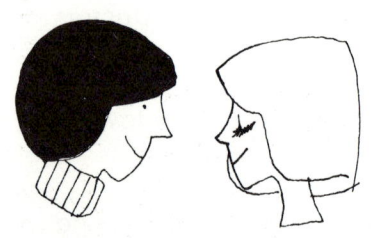

They like one another.

They meet again and again, getting to know each other better.

They decide to be together all the time.

They look for a house together.

They make this house into a home.

Sooner or later they decide to have children.

To fertilize an egg the man's penis is slipped into the woman's vagina.
Sperm cells are passed into the vagina.
The sperm cells swim to the egg cell.
One sperm fertilizes one egg cell.

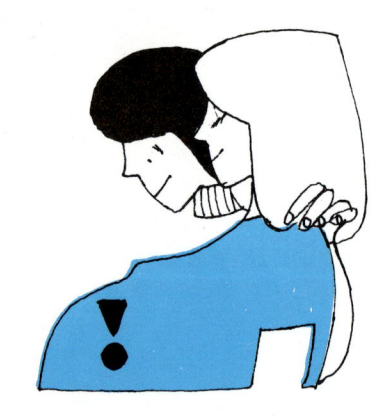

A new person has been started.

280 days later a baby is born.

Growing and developing 1

Other ways of starting a family

Fertilization is much the same in most organisms. The steps leading to fertilization can be very different.

Finding a mate

Scent Many male moths find mates by following female scent.

Sight Male fire-flies flash in the dark. Females twinkle back.

Sound The death-watch beetle knocks against his tunnel to attract females.

Keeping the mate

Fighting Bull elk use their antlers to fight off rivals.

Forewarning Bears rub their smell on trees to warn off other males.

Frightening Gorillas call out to frighten off other males.

Mating

Outside The male salmon sheds sperm over the eggs laid by the female.

Inside The sex organs of birds are pressed together so that the gametes can join.

105

Growing and developing 2

Into a baby

Fertilization does not look a spectacular event. Yet it leads to spectacular events. It leads to the growth and development of a complete organism.
From a family tree we can work out part of what happens at fertilization. We can look at different families and work backwards. Working backwards always takes us to fertilization. That is where we all begin.

Exploring a family

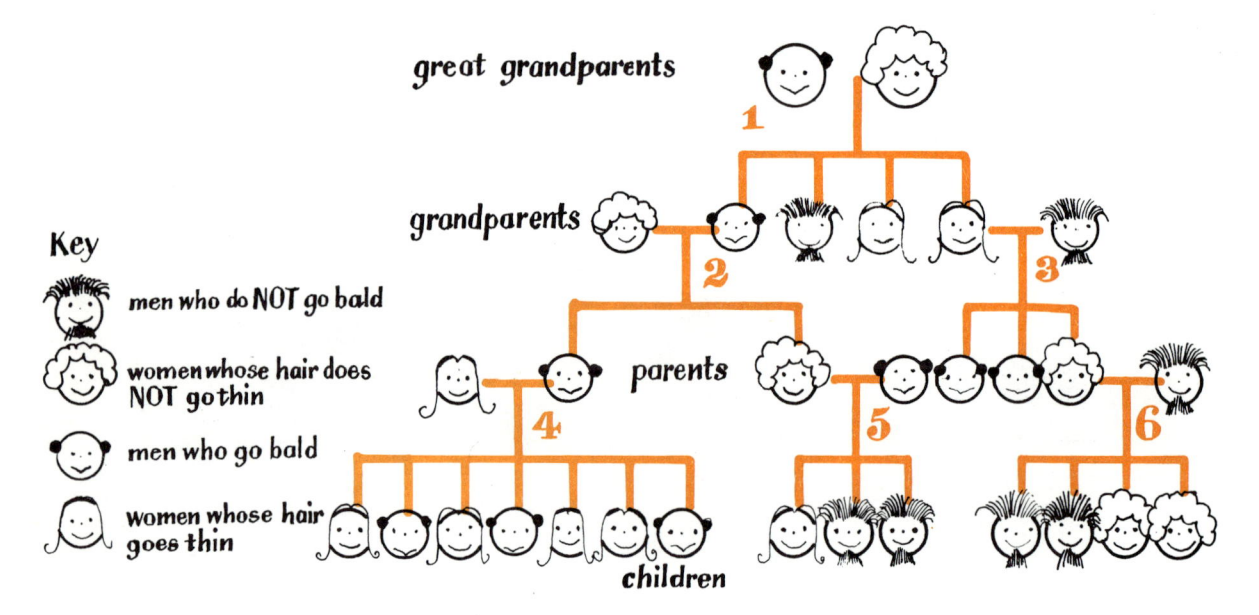

Key
- men who do NOT go bald
- women whose hair does NOT go thin
- men who go bald
- women whose hair goes thin

Which family is the largest? How many children are in it? Which family has the smallest number of children? How many sons are there in family 3? In which family is no one bald or thin-haired? Which family has a bald father and a thin-haired mother? Which families have bald sons and thin-haired daughters? In which family is the daughter thin-haired while the sons have full hair?

What do the parents and children of family 6 look like? What do the parents and children of family 4 look like? From whom did the daughter in family 5 get her plans for thin hair? Does baldness just happen in a person or does it depend on what that person's parents are like?

Growing and developing 2

In family 1, the father is bald, and his daughters have thin hair. One of these daughters has sons who go bald. Do parents pass baldness itself to their children? Or it it likely that only plans for baldness are passed on? To start a person, what does the father give? What does the mother give? What passes the plans on? In which part of the cells are the plans probably found?

Multiplying by dividing

Time	Bacteria
Start	1
30 minutes	2
1 hour	4
1.30	8
2 hours	16

A fertilized egg is one cell. We are made up of millions of cells. How does that one cell form millions?

Bacteria also start as one cell. In some bacteria that cell can grow to full size in 30 minutes. It then divides to give two cells. These cells do not stay together. Each cell becomes a new bacterium. Work out quickly how many cells there will be after a day.

Make a table to show how the bacteria increase. How long before there will be:
1000 bacteria?   10 000 bacteria?   1 000 000 bacteria?
How many bacteria will there be after 12 hours?
Why is the world not filled with bacteria?

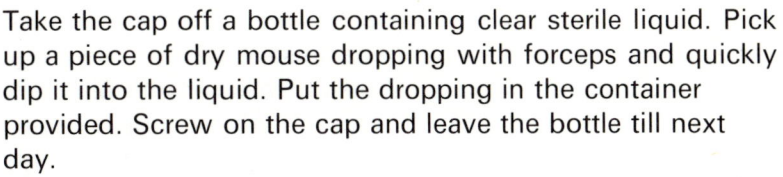

Take the cap off a bottle containing clear sterile liquid. Pick up a piece of dry mouse dropping with forceps and quickly dip it into the liquid. Put the dropping in the container provided. Screw on the cap and leave the bottle till next day.
What change takes place in the appearance of the liquid? How can you explain this change?

Growing and developing 2

Developing

Organisms change in many ways as they grow from one cell. They develop.

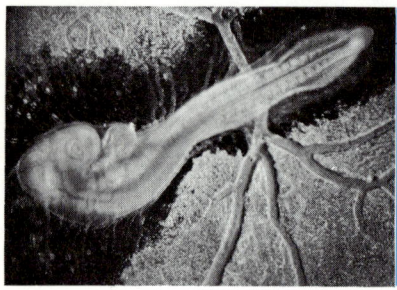

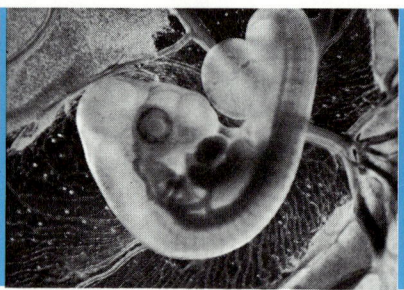

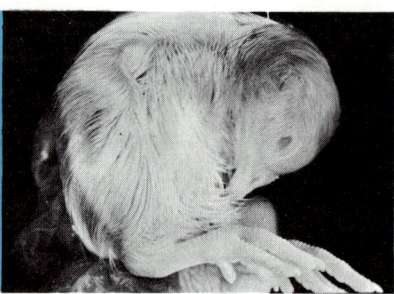

Look at the eggs. They were fertilized at the same time. Open them carefully on different days after you get them. Then you can see what happens as the chick develops. How old is the fertilized egg before you can see anything? How old is the fertilized egg before you can see the heart beating? Eyes? Blood vessels? Limbs? Wings? Head? Feathers? Beak?
Leave at least one egg to develop completely. Let it hatch.

Look at the dissection of a pregnant rat. How many young rats are there? How were they fed inside their mother?

The pond organism *Daphnia* carries its young in its body. Find these *Daphnia* using a microscope and a cavity slide.

Seeds are found inside fruits. Very young plants are found inside seeds. Find the young plants inside pea and bean seeds. These young plants have stopped growing. How can this growth be started again?
The coats protecting young plants in seeds can be built in many ways. Look at many different fruits and say how you think each arrangement suits the young plant.

Take some stick-insect eggs home. Let them hatch in a covered jar. Their food is privet leaves so make sure your jar has some fresh leaves of privet in it. When they have hatched bring them back to the class.

Growing and developing 2

Egg to adult

How does a fertilized human egg develop into a human being? Why is one person different from all other people? The answer is in the plans: one set from the mother, one set from the father.

Sperms start eggs growing

Egg cells do not start growing on their own. Sperm cells are needed to make them grow. One sperm going into the egg starts the egg growing. It grows by dividing. It divides first into 2 cells, then into 4, into 8, into 16, 32, 64—until all the cells are there. Between each division the cells grow in size. In this way one very small cell becomes a very large person.

Plans are handed on

In the nucleus of the sperm cell there is one complete set of plans. There is another complete set of plans in the egg nucleus. So a fertilized cell contains two sets of plans: one set from the father, one set from the mother. Every time a cell divides, each new cell gets a complete copy of the two sets. Bit by bit the plans are put into operation. Some plans come into operation early, like the plans for the number of fingers you have. Others come into operation later. Baldness is one of these.

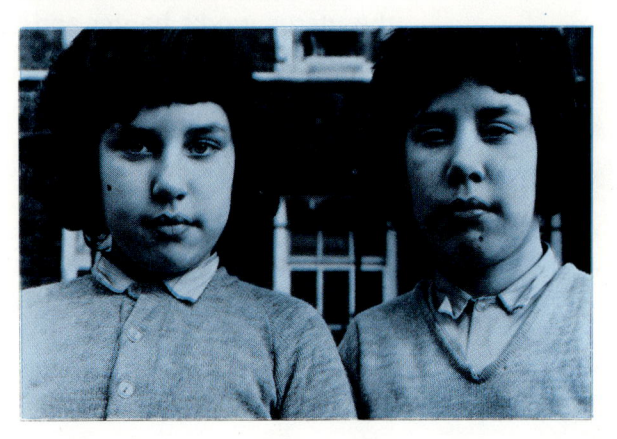

No two people are identical

The plans are complete and a human being develops. The main parts of the plans for each human being are the same. But the details are different for different people. No two people, except identical twins, receive the same plans. And even identical twins grow up to be different.

Growing and developing 2

Our first journey

Birth is our shortest journey. It is our most difficult journey, but the most important one. It is our journey into the world of people.

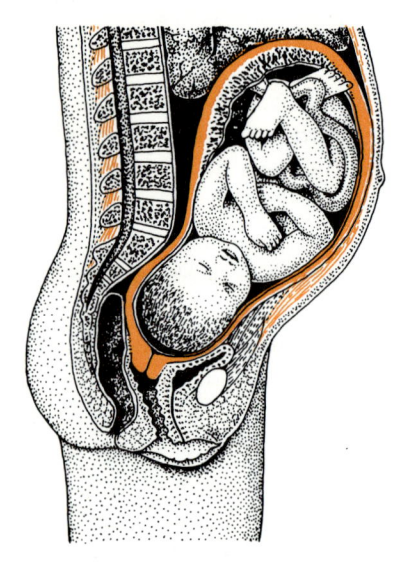

The mother gets plenty of warning that the birth is near. The first sign is that the uterus muscle starts contracting. The uterus has been the baby's home for nine months and now it is preparing to push the baby out into the world.

The uterus muscle practises first, squeezing gently and opening the channel the baby will pass through.

As time goes on, the squeezing gets stronger and more frequent. The muscle of the uterus works harder and harder, pushing the baby down the birth canal.

No wonder the woman is said to be in labour. It is hard work. The mother is sweating with the effort.

A big push and the head appears. A few more pushes and the baby is out.

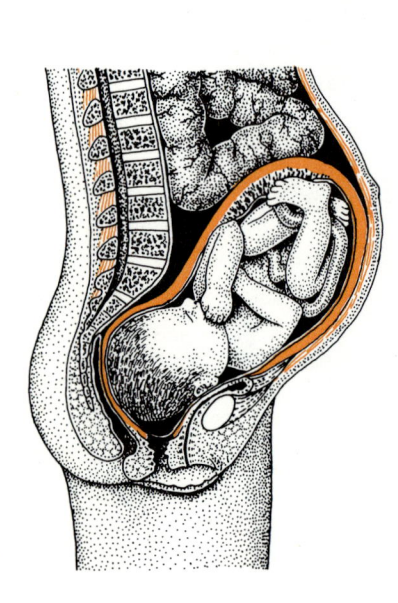

Growing and developing 2

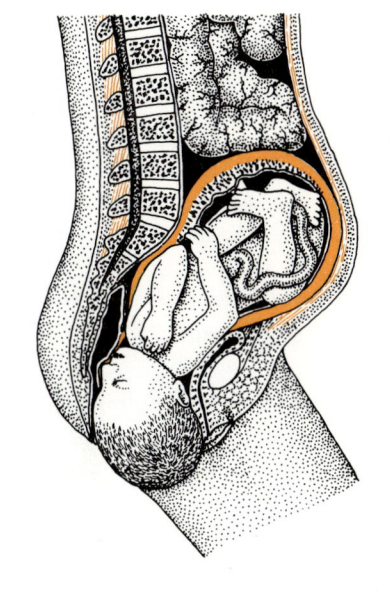

The first thing the mother wants to know is that the baby is all right—fit and healthy. Then she wants to know what sex it is. She gets a quick answer and the baby is no longer an it!

Boy or girl—it's all the same—the baby has to start breathing. If it does not start by itself, the doctor or nurse gets it going, sometimes with a sharp smack on its bottom.

The cord is painlessly cut and tied to prevent any blood loss. A name tag is put round its wrist or ankle. The baby is wrapped in a clean, warm towel and is put in a warm cot for a long rest.

The mother deserves a rest too. She has worked very hard bringing her baby into the world. The nurses make sure she has that good rest.

Father makes sure she has that rest and his baby too. He has an important job. He has to take care of his family.

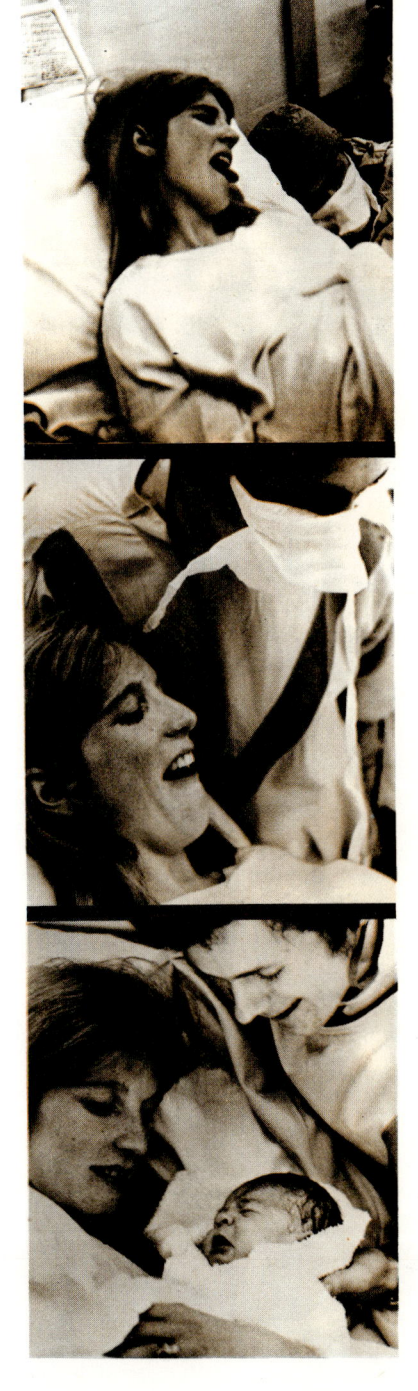

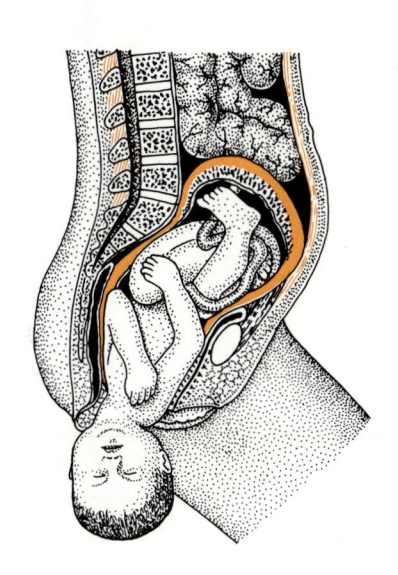

Growing and developing 3

Into boys and girls

Babies are small human beings who will grow to be full sized people. But they have a lot to learn. They learn as they grow and develop.

Growing taller

Years		0	1	2	3	4	5	6	7	8	9	10	11	12	13	14	15	16	17	18
Boys	cm	57	77	89	98	105	112	118	124	129	134	139	144	149	154	159	164	168	174	179
Girls	cm	56	76	87	96	104	111	117	123	128	133	138	145	151	156	161	164	168	169	169

Are you tall or short for your age? Is anyone you know exactly average? What is the average height of the boys in your class? What is the average height of the girls?

Between which years do boys grow fastest? Grow slowest? During which years do girls grow fastest? Grow slowest? At birth boys are usually longer than girls. At what age do girls overtake the boys in height? When do the boys become taller than the girls again?

Growing heavier

Years		0	1	2	3	4	5	6	7	8	9	10	11	12	13	14	15	16	17	18
Boys	kg	3	10	12	14	16	18	21	24	27	29	32	35	38	42	48	54	58	61	63
Girls	kg	3	10	12	14	16	18	21	23	26	28	31	35	39	44	49	51	53	54	54

Are you heavy or light for your age? If you were tall for your age are you heavier or lighter than average? Are the boys and girls in your class an average group for their weight?

Between which years is there the greatest increase in weight? Which other years have the next biggest weight increase? At what age do girls become heavier than boys? How does this compare with the age at which girls become taller than boys?

Growing and developing 3

Measuring development

We learn to crawl, then walk, then run and everyone learns these things at about the same age. On this page and the next are some more stages in a baby's development. Put these stages in order and link them to the ages in the boxes.

Learning to walk

6 months
7 months
9 months
10 months
11 months
12 months

Walks on hands and feet like a bear.
Can crawl, but usually goes backwards.
Walks sideways, holding on to furniture.
Holds chair and repeatedly lifts one leg up and down.
When held bounces up and down with happiness.
When held can support himself for a short time.

By the age of 15 months most babies can walk by themselves. Why does walking take so long to learn?

Learning to use hands

9 months
10 months
15 months
18 months
2 years
$2\frac{1}{2}$ years

Scribbles with a pencil.
Touches objects with her first finger.
Forever throwing toys on to the floor.
Can hold a pencil in her hand, instead of her fist.
Can turn door handle.
Picks up small objects with her thumb and first finger.

Babies at a certain age enjoy playing a game of throwing toys on the floor. Why is this an important game? Why is it important to play this game often?

Growing and developing 3

Learning to speak

1½ months
3 months
4 months
5 months
7 months
8 months
15 months
22 months

Laughs aloud.
Smiles when his mother speaks to him.
Coughs or makes other sounds to get attention.
Blows raspberries.
Talks all the time but no one knows what he is saying.
Can make the sounds 'da-da' and 'ba-ba'.
Always squealing with pleasure.
Can use the words: 'I', 'me', 'you'.

Babies like people talking to them. They need people to talk to them so that they can learn the language. Some people talk to babies in baby talk, others in adult talk. How do you talk to babies? Why?

Learning by playing

4 months
5 months
6 months
7 months
10 months
12 months
18 months

Plays at sweeping the floor, or dusting.
Claps her hands with happiness.
Will stick out her tongue when asked.
Likes to play peek-a-bo.
Blows bubbles.
Gets excited when she sees toys.
If people enjoy what she is doing, she will repeat it.

Babies spend much of their waking time playing. Why is playing a good way of learning? What do you learn when playing? Is it easy to learn when you do not enjoy it?

Shape puzzle
Everyone here has been made the same height, so you can see the shape changes during growth. Find five changes.

Before birth   2 years   5 years   9 years   13 years   18 years

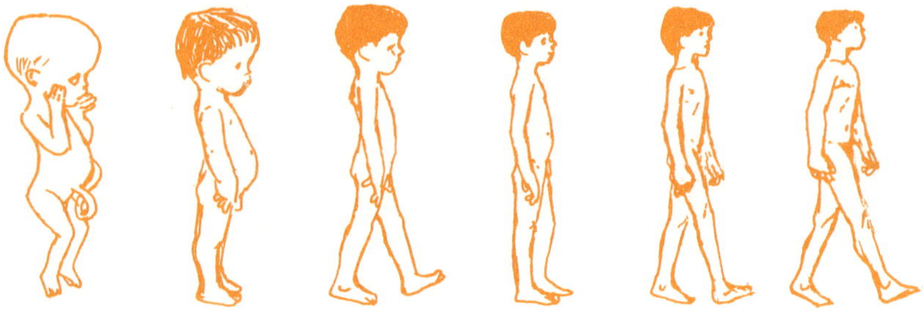

Growing up

'Mam, can I . . . ?' 'No dear, I'm sorry'. 'But why not?' 'Well you are too young. Maybe when you are older'. This is part of growing up. So is getting heavier, learning to walk, learning to talk . . .

Becoming taller and heavier

Babies grow very fast at first, then slow down. For girls there is a spurt of growth in height and weight starting at about eleven years. This means that the girls in your class may be bigger than the boys. Boys catch up again by the age of fifteen and keep growing for a longer time than girls. In the end most men are taller and heavier than most women.

Getting things working

Babies are born with all the parts needed for living. Some, such as the heart, are already working. Others, like the lungs, must begin to work immediately at birth. The eyes and ears are working but babies have to learn how to notice the important things. This learning takes time. Babies start with simple actions and they practise until they are expert. They practise by playing. So then they can go on easily to more complicated actions. Slowly and surely, they fit all the things they have learned together.

·Learning to live

While they are learning to use their bodies, babies learn who they are. They also learn who other people are. None of this is easy. It looks easy because it is learned so happily. It is learned as a game. The game starts when a mother looks at her tiny baby, speaks softly, and the baby looks up and smiles.

Growing and developing 3

Scientists working with people

We are all given plans at fertilization. We all grow and develop before and after birth. Here are some of the scientists who specialize in these matters.

Geneticist Concerned with the plans. What do the plans actually consist of? What happens if part of the plan is missing?

Embryologist Interested in the development and growth of organs from fertilization onwards. Works with the geneticist to see how the plans are put into operation. How do the organs grow in the right place at the right time in the right way?

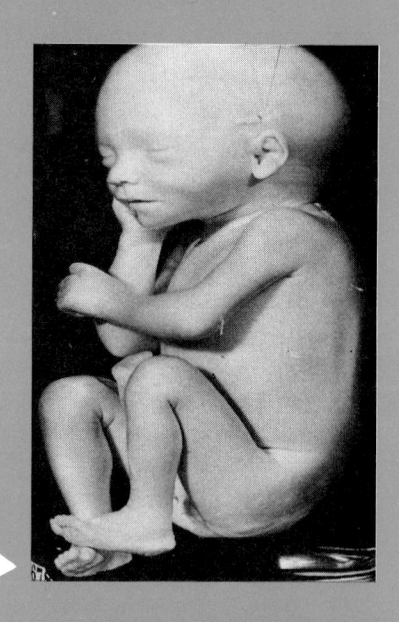

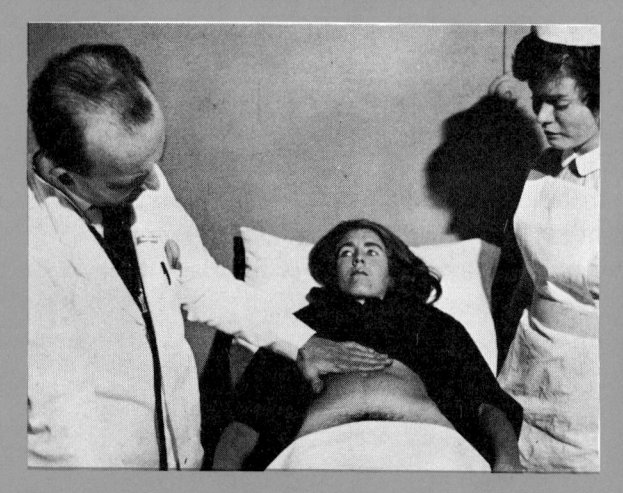

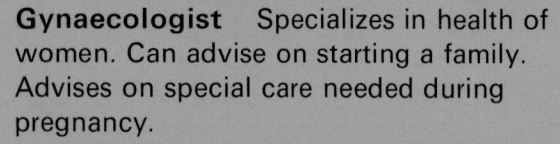

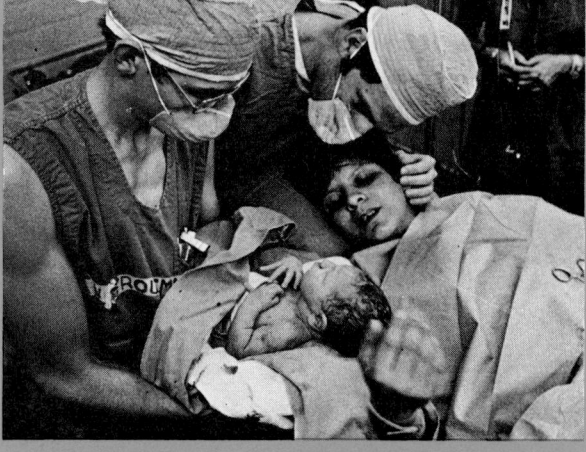

Gynaecologist Specializes in health of women. Can advise on starting a family. Advises on special care needed during pregnancy.

Obstetrician Takes up where the gynaecologist leaves off. Most concerned with mother and baby before, during, and just after birth. How can birth be made easier for mother and baby?

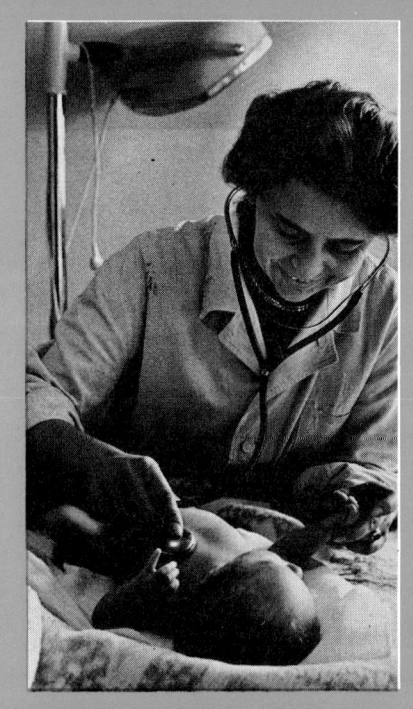

Paediatrician Specialist in health of babies and children. What is the normal pattern of growth? What diseases are most common in children? How do we prevent these?

Psychologist Concerned with the development of learning and behaviour patterns. Works closely with paediatrician. How do we learn? When do we learn different things?

Anthropologist Looks at different behaviour patterns all over the world. What patterns are common to all mankind? What patterns of behaviour are learned and what patterns of behaviour are laid down in the plans at fertilization?

Teacher Works with the psychologist to find easier ways for people to learn. Is sometimes wrong.

Growing and developing 4

Into men and women

There is more to being a woman than wearing ear rings or having babies. And more to being a man than shaving or having male sex organs.

Differences

Men and women are built differently. Make a list of the differences. Make a note of any exceptions.

Men	Women	Comments
taller	shorter	true on average only
bearded	smooth-faced	Boys are smooth also

Boy	Girl

Males and females of most ages behave differently. This is true for chimpanzees too. Sort the behaviour patterns of the young chimps into two lists: boy and girl.

better behaved, sit longer   friendlier
run away when not watched   fight more
fond of bright colours   use their hands well
begin to walk earlier   more destructive

Make your own lists for human boys and girls.

Make a collection of behaviour patterns that you think are true for men and women.

Often men and women dress differently. Make a list of these differences and comment on the exceptions. These exceptions can include men and women from the past and men and women from other countries.

Men	Women	Comments

Growing and developing 4

Men better than women?

Men are usually more muscular than women. How does this body pattern help men do the work they usually do? Take another building pattern for men or women. Show how it might be important for that sex.

Women are often friendlier than men. How might this behaviour pattern help women with the things they do? What other behaviour patterns are important in this way?

Match these patterns to the way they may be caused.

Body patterns   due to way person is brought up.
Behaviour patterns   due to plans given at fertilization.
Patterns of dress   due to both.

Make a collection of the world records for these races.

Race	100m	200m	400m	800m	1500m	3000m	5000m
Men							
Women							

Are all men better runners than all women? Will women ever be as good at sport as men? Explain your answers.

In this country at present most doctors, engineers, lawyers, and managers are men. Does this mean that men are smarter than women? Talk about this in small groups.

There are more men in prison than women. Does this mean that women are smarter than men? Talk about this in small groups.

Growing and developing 4

Women better than men?

The list shows some causes of death in men and women:

Cause of death	Men	Women
Heart disease	275 000	175 000
Pneumonia	40 000	35 000
Ulcers	7000	1000
Car accidents	24 000	7000
Murder	3000	1000
Diabetes	12 000	20 000

Do the items on the list show that women are healthier than men? Which causes of death depend on the way people live? Which depend on the way they are made?

These life expectancy tables start with the same numbers of boy and girl babies. They show how many are expected to be living at different ages. The figures are calculated from questions answered in a census.

Age	Men	Women
0	100 000	100 000
40	90 000	92 000
70	50 000	61 000
85	10 000	15 000
95	500	1000
100	50	140

Make a graph of these figures. Then estimate the age at which 1000 men would still be alive. Estimate the ages at which 90 000, 50 000, 10 000 women would still be alive. Do women live longer than men?

There are many ways of measuring toughness. Here is one way. Get into a sitting position with your back against the wall. Time how long you can stay like this. Are the boys tougher than the girls?

The in-between age

Children are easily recognizable as children. Adults are clearly adults. You are in between. You are moving into the world of adults.

From girl into woman

Female sex organs are inside the body. They are present long before birth but do not begin to work until a girl is about 10 or 11 years old. At about this time her sex organs usually begin making egg cells in fits and starts. Soon they settle down to produce one egg each month. The sex organs called ovaries make more than eggs; they make chemicals called hormones. These hormones cause the breasts to grow, fat to accumulate under the skin, the hips to grow wider, and the body to become rounder. Female hormones make a girl look like a woman.

From boy into man

The male sex organs are held in a little bag just outside the body. They are called testes and begin to make sperm cells about the age of 12. They also make male hormones. Male hormones make hair grow on the face and body and cause the voice to break and deepen. Male hormones make a boy look like a man.

Men and women

Growing up is a very different matter from actually becoming a man or a woman. Having all the parts of the body working like an adult is not the same as being an adult. Becoming an adult happens early with some and later with others. It depends on being responsible. On doing what needs to be done. And on thinking of others.

Being able to start a family

Children become men and women not when their sex organs are mature and functioning, but when their minds mature. Responsible men and women take responsibility for their own actions. They have fun but they act with regard for others. They do not start a family without thinking if they can support the new baby. Becoming a man or a woman means growing up not so much in body but in mind.

Growing and developing 4

Men and women

The painting below shows Adam and Eve in the Garden of Eden. It was painted by the great German artist Albrecht Dürer. To paint a picture as well as this, the artist must study his subjects carefully. That is why this painting has been used instead of a photograph. It shows very clearly the differences between men and women that are due mainly to hormones.

Men

Heavier brow

Squarer jaw

Larger face and head

Taller and heavier

Broader and squarer shoulders

Larger and more muscular limbs

Narrower hips

Facial hair

Stronger body hair

More muscular and angular body

Women

Smaller head

Rounder, broader, and more delicate face

Rounder and more sloping shoulders

Wider and more rounded hips

Smaller body, brain, lungs, etc.

Lighter body hair

Angle greater between upper and lower part of limb

The long history of trousers

Although trousers have a long history, the Romans at first knew nothing of them. The Romans first discovered trousers when they conquered Gaul. They found the natives of that country wearing loose rags round their legs. They called their conquest Trousered Gaul. When they were fighting in Germany they thought these trousers were a good idea and started to wear them themselves.

At first the new fashion was not popular in Rome. Politicians spoke out against following the ways of conquered barbarians. The Roman Senate passed laws: only sick and elderly people were allowed to wear this garment—trousers. So anyone else wearing trousers was really a weakling. It was no use; if people like a new fashion nothing will stop them from following it.

This was true during the Middle Ages as well as Roman times. At that time trousers were two sleeves, one fitting over each leg. That is why we still talk of a pair of trousers, although it is now one garment. Gradually these sleeves got wider and wider and wider. Eventually some men were wearing trousers a metre wide.

The fashion changed. Trousers became tighter and tighter. Eventually they were so tight that walking was impossible. So the legs of the trousers were cut at the knee. That was not all. Just above this slit it was decided to add a little padding. Then a little more, and more and more. Soon it took 6 metres of cloth to make the bag above the knee and 20 metres of silk to pad out the bag. Then one trouser designer decided it would be interesting to extend the bag to the ankle, with all the padding.

That was too much. Sermons were preached, pamphlets were printed, laws were passed against this ridiculous fashion. It was, as in Roman times, no use. Then the King of Brandenburg decided he would stop this fashion. He fought fire with fire. If anyone wished to wear these trousers he would let them. In fact, they could wear even bigger and longer and baggier trousers. And they would wear them in public. They would show them to everyone at special fashion parades. If anyone refused to parade, then the King's police cut the belts holding their trousers up ... The fashion did not last long.

Modern long trousers were first worn by the French revolutionaries. But the fashion was not encouraged. One king tried to stop it. He dressed criminals in top hats and long trousers and sent them out to work on the roads. In that way he hoped to make the fashion ridiculous.
But as a king can break a fashion, a king can make a fashion. One morning King Frederick of Prussia appeared wearing the new long trousers. Men have been wearing them ever since.

Electricity

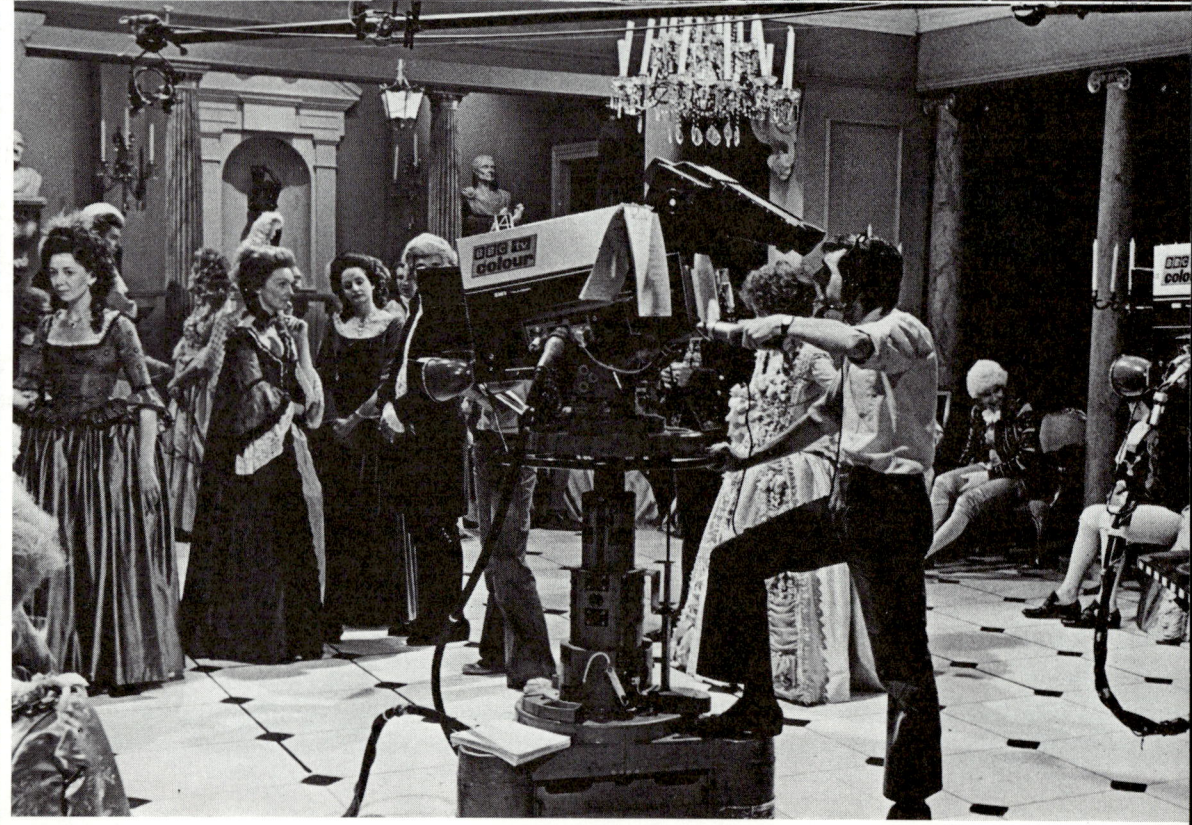

124

125

Electricity 1

Electrons standing still

There is electricity in you. There is electricity on you and around you. You use it and need it. But what is electricity?

What is electricity?

Electricity is one kind of energy. It can be changed into other kinds of energy. Write down the energy changes that take place when you:
Switch on the TV.
Record on a cassette.
Switch on a light.
Use a bicycle dynamo.
Turn on an iron.
Use a vacuum cleaner.

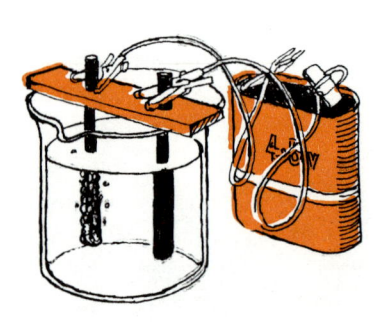

Dip the carbon rod into the copper chloride solution. Switch on the electricity for 5 minutes. Watch the rods and see what happens.

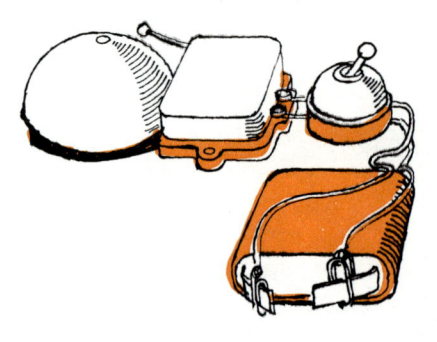

Switch on the circuit with the bell and battery. Listen to what happens.

Switch on the bulb. What do you see? Hold your hand over the bulb. What do you feel? If this were a light bulb in your home what would you feel when you touched the glass?
In each case some changes took place. What were they?

Electricity 1

Keeping it simple

To see further into the idea of electricity you will use static electricity.

Rub a balloon on your jacket. Stick the balloon on a wall. Can you do this with an unrubbed balloon? Tie a thread on to each of two balloons. Rub each balloon. Bring the balloons together, holding them by the threads. What happens?

Put some tiny pieces of paper on your desk. Comb your hair. Bring the comb to the paper. What happens? Rub a plastic rod with a dry cloth. Bring this rod to the paper. What happens?

Turn on a water tap so that a thin, even trickle comes out. Rub a plastic rod with a cloth. Hold the rod near the water. What happens?

Look back at what you have just done. Where did you find static electricity: on the inside or outside of materials?

You can build up some rules of electricity using simple equipment. You will need a pair of clear rods, a pair of dull rods, a dry cloth, and a watch glass. Rub one of the clear plastic rods with the duster. Balance this rod across the watch glass. Rub another clear rod and bring this near the end of the balanced rod. What happens? Which way does the first rod move? If you do the same for the two dull rods what do you think will happen? Now do that and check your answer. Put a rubbed clear rod on the glass. If you rub a dull rod and bring it to the clear rod what do you think will happen? Now check to see if you are correct. Is a rubbed clear rod the same as a rubbed dull rod? Is the static electricity on the outside of a rubbed clear rod the same as the static electricity on the outside of the dull rod?

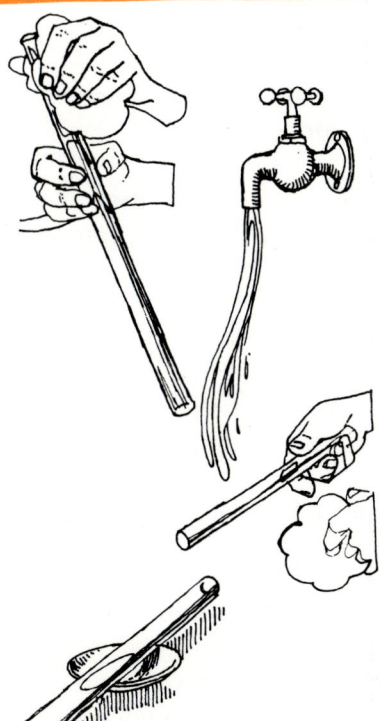

127

Electricity 1

A shocking display

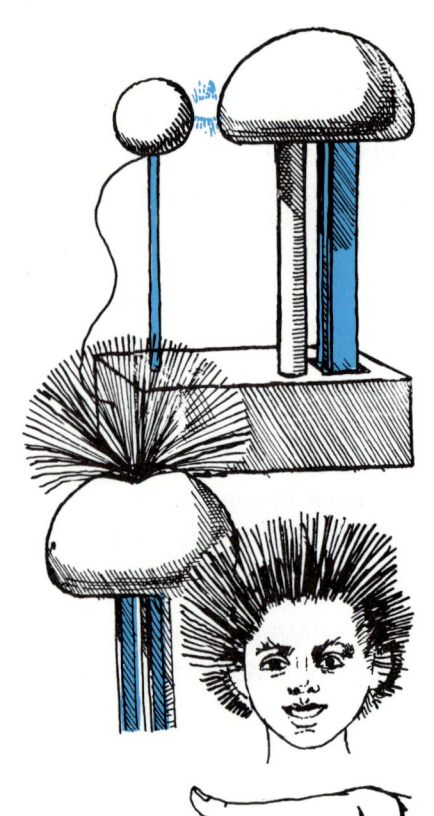

The Van de Graaff generator works in the same way as rubbing the plastic rods. It works better and faster. It collects more electricity in the big ball.

The small ball is connected by a wire to the earth. What happens when you switch the generator on and bring the earthed ball close to the big ball?

What happens if you point your finger at the big ball when the generator is on?

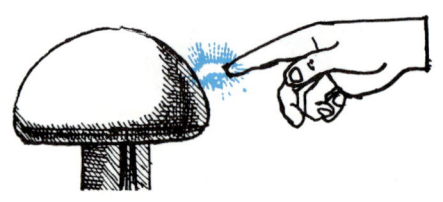

Put a piece of fur on top of the big ball. What happens to the fur when the generator is switched on?

Stand on a plastic basin. Put one hand on top of the generator. The generator will be switched on. What happens to your hair?

Keep standing on the plastic basin with one hand on top of the ball. Try to light a gas burner with your finger. Before you step off the basin touch the bench. You could get a shock if you do not do this.

Point a small neon bulb at the big ball. What happens when the generator is switched on?
If this bulb were in a torch, what would make it light up?
What makes the light bulbs in the classroom light up?

There is electricity in rubbed plastic rods, in the Van de Graaff generator, in batteries, and in the wires in your home. Is all this electricity the same?

Electricity 1

Electrons and electricity

You cannot see electricity. You can see what it does. From your observations you can begin to explain what it is.

Simple materials

To start making sense out of electricity, you worked with very simple materials. You rubbed a pair of clear rods with a dry cloth. You brought these rods together and they pushed each other apart. You rubbed a pair of dull rods and brought them together. They also pushed each other apart. But when you rubbed a dull rod and a clear rod and brought them together, they stayed together.

Simple explanations

With these simple materials and simple events we can make some simple explanations. We can make a guess that the cloth is rubbing something on and off the rods. That something has to do with energy because rubbed rods can move each other. That something has to do with electrical energy. But what is it? And what makes the two kinds of rod behave differently?

Simple particles

These questions can be answered if we look at atoms more closely. Atoms are made up of smaller pieces. Some of these pieces are called electrons. Electrons can be taken away from atoms. Electrons can be added to atoms. When you rubbed the clear rods you rubbed electrons off the atoms on the clear rod. When you rubbed the dull rods you rubbed electrons on to the atoms on the dull rod.

Simple language

We say that rods, or any material which either gives up or gets electrons, is charged. There are two kinds of charge. There is the charge which is due to extra electrons. This is a negative charge. There is the charge due to fewer electrons. This is a positive charge. In most materials the charges cancel each other out.

Electricity 1

The big sparks

Electric charges can build up on clouds. When the electric charges on a cloud become very large the cloud discharges. You see this as lightning; you hear it as thunder.

There are different kinds of lightning. The most common is forked lightning.

Another kind of lightning is sheet lightning. Sheet lightning is the reflection of a hidden flash of forked lightning.

A flash of forked lightning travels to the ground at a speed of up to 1600 km per second. After this another flash of lightning usually travels up to the sky. It moves up very much faster at a speed of 140 000 km per second.

The temperature of a lightning flash can be as high as 45 000 °C.

Lightning can strike twice. In fact, Park Ranger Roy Sullivan of America has been struck 5 times—and he is still alive. In 1942 he lost one of his toe nails. In 1969 he lost his eyebrows. In 1970 his shoulder was burned. In 1972 his hair was set on fire. His hair grew again but was unfortunately burned off again in 1973.

Possibly the record is held by the Empire State Building. In 3 years it was struck 63 times.

Ball lightning

Ball lightning is not common. It is very spectacular, and most people who have seen it write about it. Here are some accounts of ball lightning.

The whole family was sitting at the supper table when a ball of lightning came into the room. It was about 10 cm in diameter and fluttered about the centre of the table. It made a buzzing noise and hung about 25 cm above the dishes. Its colour was a mixture of blue and orange and it may have had some red. It fluttered about for five or six seconds. I could easily have grabbed it if I had dared to do so. Then it exploded like a large firework and gave off a smell of gas. After it exploded, the table was left as before; no dishes had been broken or moved about.

I was outdoors during a very bad thunderstorm in Iowa. I heard a heavy rushing noise like an extra strong wind. I looked around and saw a ball of fire, yellowish white, about the size of a bath tub bouncing down the dirt road. The ball was travelling a little faster than you could run. I couldn't see where it came from but I saw it move to a small shed. There was a horse in that shed when the ball hit the shed. The shed seemed to explode and the horse was killed.

During a thunderstorm I saw a huge, red-hot ball come down from the sky. It struck our house, cut the telephone wire, burned the window frame, and buried itself in a large basin of water which was underneath the window. The water boiled for some minutes afterwards. When the water was cool enough to search I found nothing.

I was standing in the kitchen of my home in Omaha while a terrible thunderstorm was going on. A sharp cracking noise made me look to a window screen on my left. I saw a round, shining object about the size of a tennis ball come towards me. It curved over my head and went through the glass door of the oven. It hit the back of the oven, spattering into brilliant streamers. There was no sound and no effect on me except a tingle as it passed over my hair. When I looked at the screen there was a tiny hole with scorch marks, and the back of the oven was marked with small holes.

Electricity 2   # Electrons moving

We do not use static electricity with electrical equipment. Instead we use a cell or the mains. What is special about electricity from these sources?

Round in a circle

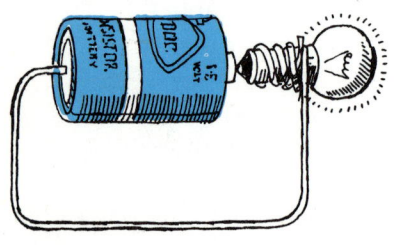

To answer that question you will need a small, simple, and safe supply of electrons. You will get that from an electric cell.

Connect the bulb and cell so that the bulb lights. What supplies the electrons here? What uses the electrons? What are the wires for? What are the electrons doing in the wire?
All electrons are built in the same way. What is the difference between the electrons in the wire and those on the surface of the plastic rods?

The wires were arranged in a special way to light the bulb. This arrangement is called a circuit. Now make a drawing to show this arrangement.

When electricians draw circuits they use special symbols. Here are the symbols for a bulb, a cell, and a wire.
Join these symbols to show your circuit.

Which of these diagrams will let electrons move round?
Which of these instructions will get the bulb to light?

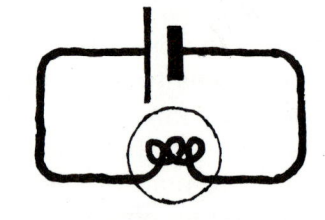

Join two wires to a cell and a bulb.

Join two wires to the bulb.

Join two wires to a bulb and cell so that a complete circuit is made.

Why will the other instructions and diagrams not get the bulb to light?

Electricity 2

Follow my leader

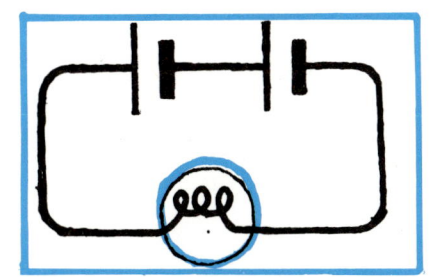

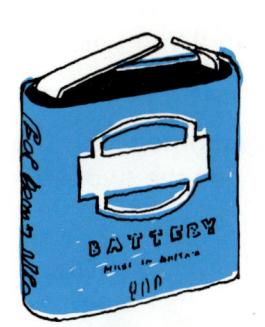

Look at this circuit diagram. How many cells are there? How many bulbs are there? Is it a complete circuit? Will the bulb light? How brightly will that bulb light compared to a circuit with one cell only?

You will build this circuit. First you will check that each cell is working. How can you do this?

Cells in a line must be joined correctly. On each cell a positive point is marked. There is also a negative point. These points are called terminals. Find the positive and negative terminals on each cell.

Electrons flow from the negative terminal to the positive terminal. That means the negative terminal of one cell will be joined to the positive terminal of the next cell. Join two cells together in this way.

The bulb can then be put in to complete the circuit. Do two cells in a line light a bulb more brightly than one cell? What does this tell you about two cells joined in a line?

What do you think will happen when a circuit is made with three cells in a line to light a bulb? Your teacher will show you how to check your guess.

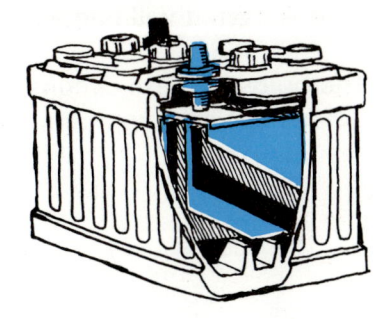

Examine the transistor battery. It is made up of a number of cells. How are these cells connected? Examine the car battery which has been cut open. How many cells are there in this battery? Trace the connections from one cell to the next. Is the negative terminal of one cell connected to the positive terminal of the next cell?

In one or two sentences say what an electric battery is.

Electricity 2

Different paths

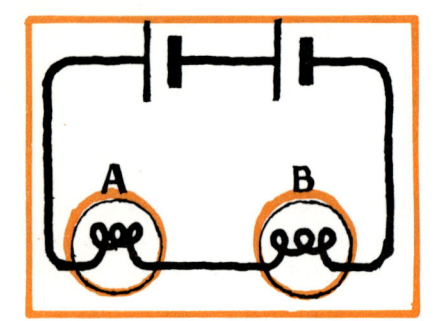

Look at this circuit diagram. How many cells are there? How many bulbs? Will the bulbs light if you build this circuit? How brightly will they light?
Make the circuit. How brightly do the bulbs light? Explain what will happen to the flow of electrons if you unscrew bulb A. What will happen to bulb B?

Look at this circuit. How many cells are there? How many bulbs are there? Will the bulbs light if you build this circuit? How brightly will they light compared to each other? How brightly will they light compared to the bulbs in the first circuit you built?
Make the circuit. Were your answers correct? In both circuits 2 cells were used and 2 bulbs. Why do the bulbs in one of these circuits light more brightly than in the other circuit?
In this second circuit what will happen if you unscrew bulb A? What will happen to bulb B?

The bulbs in these circuits are arranged **differently**. The differences are important. Try to **describe** the two different set-ups.

Electricity puzzle
If a bulb in your home burns out, do all other lights go out? What kind of circuit is there for the lights in your home?

Electricity 2

Electrons in circuits

Electrons do not just happen to move. They must be pushed. They do not move just anywhere. They move in special paths.

Electrons are pushed

The electrons you use in your home have been pumped out from a power station. For work in the laboratory you must use a simpler and a safer supply of electricity. You use electric cells. To get a little push of electrons you use one cell. For stronger pushes you can use two or three cells joined together.

They move from negative to positive terminals

These cells must be joined in a special way. They are joined so that electrons will pass from one cell to the next. The rule for this is that the negative terminal of one cell is joined to the positive terminal of the next cell. The electrons pushing out from the first cell join the electrons pushing from the next cell. So the push of electrons from a battery of cells is stronger than the push from one cell.

They move in circuits

But no matter how strong the electron pump is, no electrons will move unless there is an electron pathway. The pathway is made of wires and these wires always end back at the electron pump. That means the electrons are pumped from the cell back to the cell. They move in a circle which must be complete. Without a complete circuit there can be no current of electrons.

Comparisons

It is difficult to understand what is happening in an electric circuit. The electrons are so small you cannot see them. Electricians have many ways of thinking about electrons moving. One way is to compare electricity to water moving through pipes. Another way is to imagine that electrons are like pupils moving through corridors. But be careful. Water particles are not electrons. A class of pupils is not electricity.

Electricity 2

Electricity in your body

When you read these words messages pass from your eyes to your brain.
When you understand these words messages pass round your brain.
When you move your eyes along this line messages pass from your brain to your eye muscles.

The messages pass along nerve cells. They are electrical messages.
There is very little electricity passing in any part of your body but it can be measured. We know a little about nerves and their messages. We know a little about electricity. Put this together and we can make machines to help people.

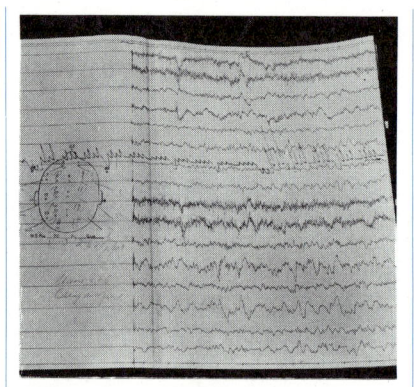

This electroencephalograph measures the electrical activity of brains.

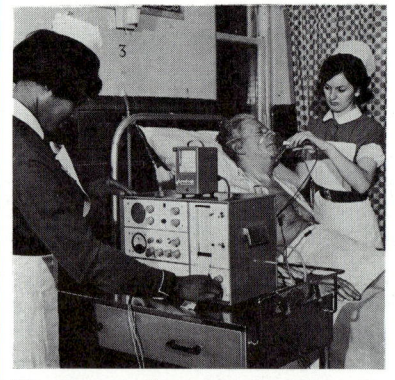

Electrocardiographs measure the electrical activities of hearts.

This device produces electrical messages to keep a heart pumping properly.

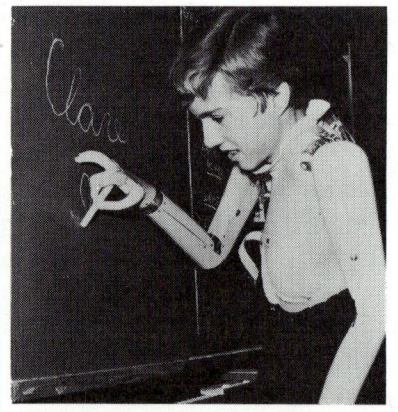

Messages are always being passed to muscles. The messages which would go to the real arm are passed to the artificial arm.

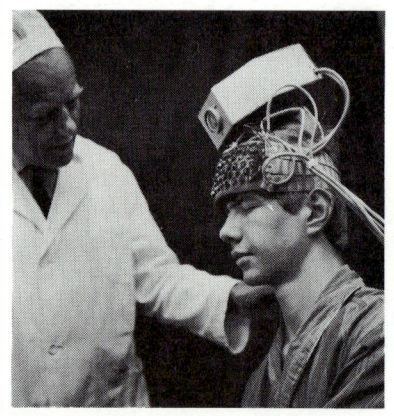

This man is blind. He can pick out objects using the electric device connected to nerve cells in his skin.

136

Electric messages are always passing from senses to the brain, around the brain, and from the brain to muscles. Very little electricity is needed for all the messages passing every second. Add a little more electricity and the messages become confused. Our muscles stop working properly and that means we stop working properly.

How much electricity will damage us? That depends on how strongly electrons are being pushed through us. And that depends on the path they take. And that depends on how long the electricity takes to pass through us. But it takes a very small electric current to damage us.

Electricity can damage you when you are in contact with a current. That means bare wires of any sort. A current is all the more dangerous if you are a good path for the electrons. You are a good path if you are touching another good path, like water or metals. You are not a good path if you are touching a poor path, like rubber or wood. Do not depend on that, however.

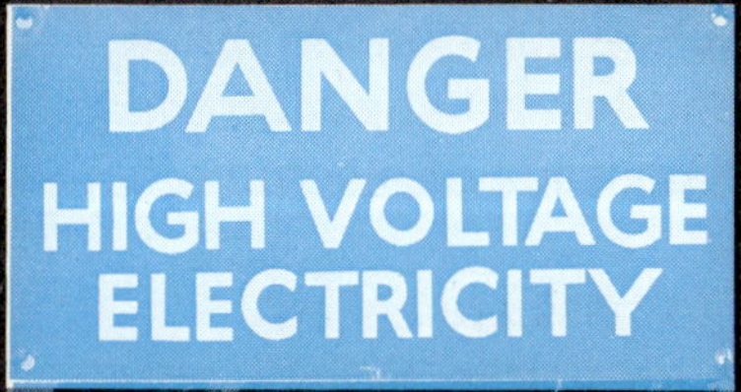

The least that happens is great pain. Too many senses are passing too many strong messages to the brain. The electricity starts muscles working when they should not. Your hand will keep a tight hold of the source of electric current when your brain is saying 'Let go'. Some muscles stop working properly. Like your breathing muscles, or heart muscle. You know what will happen then.

Electricity 3   # Electrons pushing

Electrons can move along pathways. That gives an electric current. To use that current well we need to know more about the electrons in the pathway.

Conductors and insulators

Make a working circuit with a bulb, cell, and wires. When the bulb lights, what does that tell you about the circuit? What does that tell you about the cell? What does that tell you about the wires?

When you have checked that everything is working, take out one of the wires. In its place put an iron nail. What happens to the bulb? Is this circuit complete? Can electrons pass from the cell through the nail to the bulb?

Take out the nail. Put a rubber band in the place of the nail. Is the circuit completed by the rubber band? Does the bulb light? Can electrons move along the rubber from the cell to the bulb?

Take other materials and place them in the gap. Make a list of the materials which allow the electrons to move from the cell to the bulb. Make another list showing the materials which do not allow the passage of electrons.

Conductors	Insulators

The materials allowing electrons to pass are called conductors. The others are called insulators. What kind of materials are the conductors?

Cut a wire and look at the cut end. What is in the centre of this wire? What is on the outside? Why is the wire made this way?

Look at a light bulb, an electric plug, an electric switch. They are built with different materials. Why are these materials used where they are?

Electricity 3

Looking along the wire

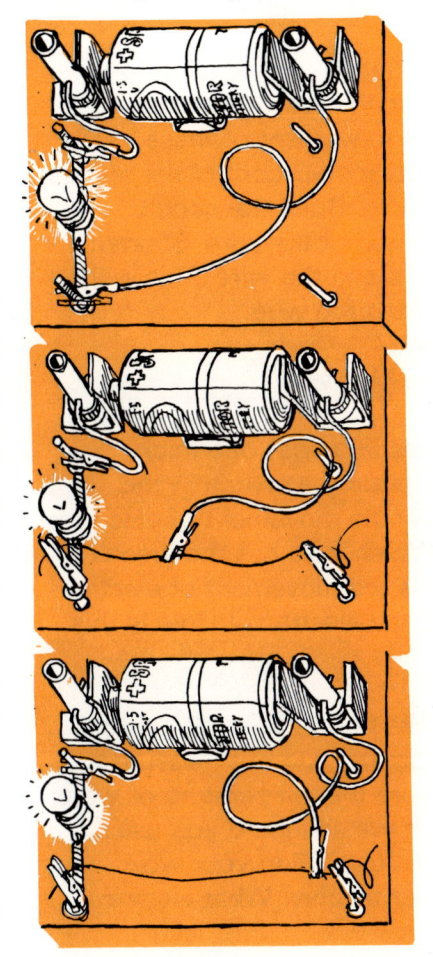

What happens when electrons move in a wire? To answer that you will use one kind of wire but in different lengths and thicknesses. This wire is nichrome wire. You may have met it before. Where?

Set up a working circuit with a cell, a bulb, and two wires. Look at the bulb. Does it shine with the same brightness all the time? What does that tell you about the number of electrons reaching the bulb? What does that tell you about the number of electrons pushed out by the cell? What does that tell you about the number of electrons moving along the wires?

Add the nichrome wire into this circuit so that there is still a complete circuit. Around the wire there is a clip. What can this clip do to the length of nichrome wire in the circuit?

Set the clip to give a short length of wire in the circuit. Then move it so there is a much longer length in the circuit. What happens to the brightness of the bulb? What does that tell you about the number of electrons reaching the bulb? What is causing the change? Can the electrons move easily through the wire?

Electron puzzle The nichrome resists electrons passing through. Does a thin wire hinder the electrons more than a thick wire? You do not need to guess the answer to that. You can set up a circuit with thin and thick wires. How will you tell which is the more resistant wire?

You can now compare the resistance of copper wire and nichrome wire to the passage of electrons. You will have to use wires of the same length and thickness. Why? How will you know which kind of wire allows more electrons to pass through? Now set up your circuits.

Electricity 3

Looking into the wire

What happens to the energy of the electrons moving in a wire? You will look into these wires to find out.

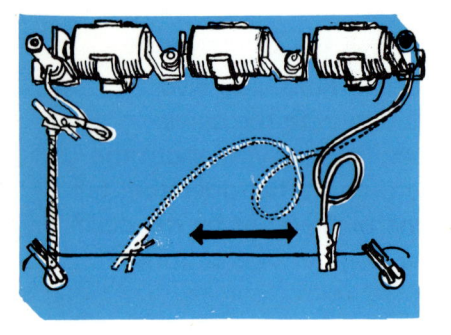

This line of cells will give the circuit many electrons. The very thin wire will resist the movement of these electrons. Moving the sliding contact will control the number of electrons passing along the wire. Build the circuit. Connect the contact at the free end of the wire. Shorten the wire by moving the contact along the wire. This will allow more electrons to pass along the wire.
What happens to the wire? How?
Where is this idea used at home? Why?

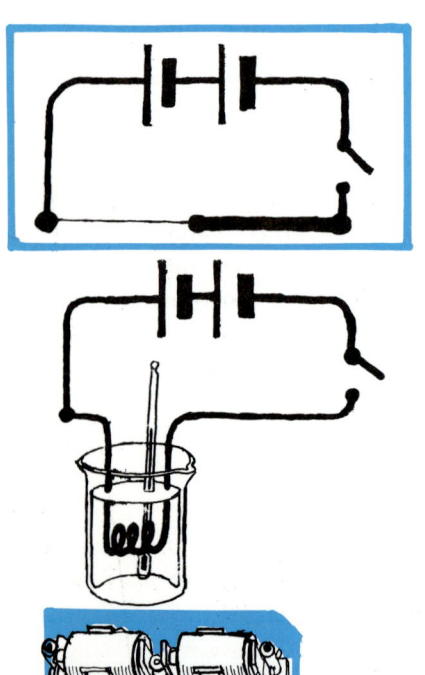

In this circuit there are two wires in a line; one thick and one thin. Build the circuit, putting a switch in the correct place. Switch on to allow the movement of electrons. Which wire becomes hotter? Which wire has the greater resistance? When a wire hinders the movement of electrons, what happens to the energy of the electrons? How is this idea used at home?

You can tell which wire becomes hotter. Try measuring this more exactly with a thermometer. Do not measure the temperature of the wires. Measure the temperature of water heated by the wires. How much water should you use? What lengths of wire should you use? Plan your work carefully and discuss it with your teacher. What electrical devices use this idea?

Build a series circuit with a bulb, 2 cells and a controller. When the circuit is working, turn the control knob. What happens to the brightness of the bulb? Why? What do you think is inside the controller?

Electric controllers are called rheostats. What devices do you use which have rheostats?

140

Electricity 3

Resisting the push

Some materials, the conductors, allow electrons to pass through easily. Others, the insulators, allow very few electrons to pass through.

When electrons are hindered

Even the best conductor resists an electric current. That means it hinders the passage of electrons through it. Resistance to the moving electrons depends on many things. It depends on the material the electrons are moving through. Nichrome resists an electric current more than copper. Resistance depends on the thickness of the material. A thin wire resists moving electrons more than a thick wire. Resistance depends on the length of the path. A long wire resists more than a shorter wire if the wires are the same material and the same thickness.

They give energy to the circuit materials

How many electrons actually get through depends on how hard they are pushed and on how much the material resists the push. More than that happens. Some of the energy of the moving electrons is passed to the particles of the wire. The greater the push and the greater the resistance, the more energy is transferred to the particles of the conductor. These particles cannot move even though they are given more energy. They begin to push against each other. The wire expands and as more energy is added the wire gets hotter and finally melts. No more energy can be added because no more electrons can pass. The circuit is broken.

We use this

We can, and do, use all of this. At the centre of most wire is a conducting material, copper. Wrapped round the copper is an insulator, plastic. Electrons can pass along the copper but not through the plastic. A fuse is another safety device. Fuse wire resists the passage of too many electrons. It melts when too many are pushed through. That prevents damage to other parts of that circuit. The wire at the centre of a light bulb resists the electric current too. It does not melt, however. It becomes hotter and hotter until it is white-hot.

Electricity 3

Patience

Have you ever thought about the light bulbs you use. Someone invented these. That someone was Thomas Edison, the wizard of electricity.

In the 1870s many public buildings were brightly lit with electrical lamps. These lamps gave a dazzling light which was very suitable for lighthouses. They did not give the cosy glow a family wanted in their home. These arc lamps were too big, too bright. What was wanted were little lights. They could be supplied with electricity in the same way a house is supplied with gas or water. Edison set about inventing one of these little lights.

The idea he started with was not new. A current of electricity was passed through a resistance wire. The wire glowed white-hot. It also combined with the oxygen in the air and burnt up. To prevent this from happening the wire was enclosed in a vacuum, which was simply a glass ball with the air pumped out.

Even so, the wire kept melting, which is fine in a fuse, but useless in a light bulb. One day Edison was thinking about this in his laboratory and playing about with a piece of tar and fine carbon powder. He kept rolling this sticky mass about. As he did this, he made a long thin thread. Suddenly, he looked at what he had made and got an idea. He made another thread, fitted it into a bulb and passed some current through. The light it gave was bright and beautiful but burned quickly. That was the answer though: some kind of carbon material.

The material he needed had to be tougher, so he used cotton thread which had been burned completely. This was tied into the bulb. To get one perfect piece of burned cotton thread and tie it into the bulb took three days. But the idea worked. Current was passed through that very delicate carbon wire for 45 hours. Edison said that if his lamp could burn that length of time it could burn longer.

Electricity 3

However, to tie that piece of carbon was a nightmare. He needed another kind of material. 'Somewhere in God's mighty workshop,' Edison said, 'there is a closely packed wood. The fibres in that wood are almost parallel. It has no soft centre and long strands can be cut from it.' He was right but he had to test thousands of materials to find the one he wanted. This turned out to be a strip of bamboo and he found it in a Japanese fan.

On New Year's Eve, 1880, Edison strung 50 bulbs in and around his laboratory at Menlo Park and invited the public to look. Thousands came to see the dawn of the Age of Electricity. The dawn had no real sun. Instead there was a tiny, man-made sun, shining in a man-made glass bulb.

Electricity 4

Counting electrons

Light bulbs show clearly that electrons are passing in a circuit. They do not show clearly how many electrons pass, or how hard they push. Meters do that.

Ammeters

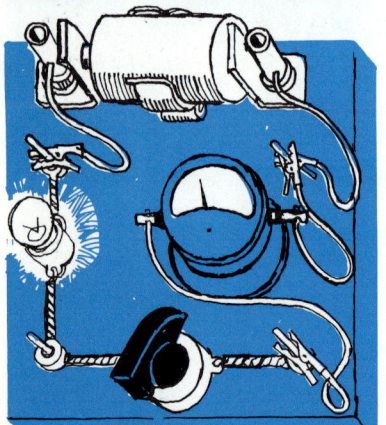

Build a circuit with a bulb, a cell, a rheostat, and a wire. Set the rheostat so that the bulb does not light. Write a sentence saying: What the cell does. What the bulb shows. Why the bulb will not light.

To measure the current flowing in that circuit an ammeter is used. Ammeters measure the number of electrons passing in a circuit. The unit of electric current is an amp. The currents you will use are measured in milliamps, which are thousandths of an amp.

Ammeters are connected into circuits with crocodile clips. Take the two meter plugs and put the plugs into the meter sockets. At the opposite ends of these wires are crocodile clips.
Ammeters take the place of part of the circuit. That means they are built in series into the circuit. Take out the wire the ammeter will replace. Ammeters are connected in a special order. Find the negative terminal of the meter. Find the negative terminal of the cell. Connect these two, then get your teacher to check. Then the two positive terminals can be connected.

Look at the bulb. Does it appear that any current is flowing through? Look at the ammeter. How much current is flowing through? Turn the rheostat so that the resistance decreases. What happens to the bulb? What happens to the current reading on the ammeter? What was the largest current to pass through?

Electricity 4

Voltmeters

Voltmeters measure the push of electrons through a circuit. Electrical push is measured in volts V.

Build a circuit with a cell, a bulb, and wires.

Voltmeters do not replace any part of a circuit. They are added to the circuit in parallel. The negative terminal of a voltmeter is joined to the part of the circuit nearest the negative terminal of the cell. Voltmeters are connected using crocodile clips.

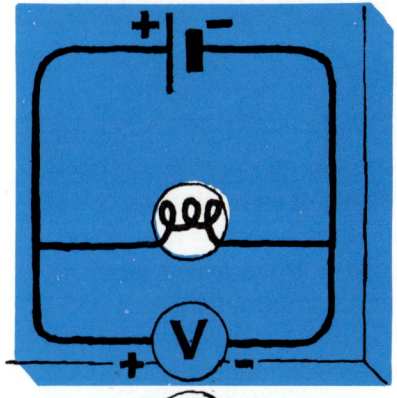

Connect the voltmeter correctly across the bulb. What is the reading on the voltmeter?

Electrons are pushed out from cells. Look at the cell and read the voltage marked on the cell.

Make a series circuit with three cells and a bulb. Connect the voltmeter correctly to measure the voltage across the cells.

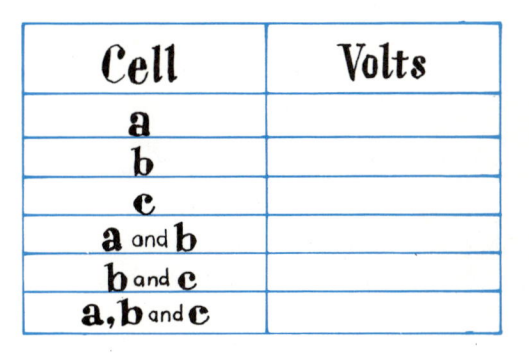

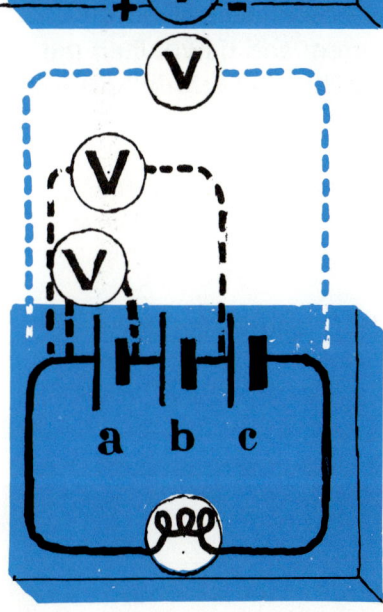

Cell	Volts
a	
b	
c	
a and b	
b and c	
a, b and c	

What happens to the voltage as you add more cells in series to a circuit?

Write one or two sentences to say what happens to the electrical push when three cells are joined in series.

145

Electricity 4

Measuring in different circuits

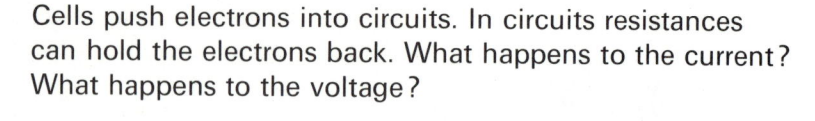

Cells push electrons into circuits. In circuits resistances can hold the electrons back. What happens to the current? What happens to the voltage?

Build a circuit with three cells in series. Put three light bulbs into the circuit, also in series. You will now measure the current and voltage at different parts of the circuit.

Put an ammeter in correctly to measure the current at position A. Then do this for positions B, C, and D. Is there any difference in the current readings at any of these positions? What does this tell you about the number of electrons passing through the bulbs?

Position	Voltage	Current
A		
B		
C		
D		

Put a voltmeter in correctly to measure the push of electrons at different positions. Measure the voltage across A and B, then B and C, then C and D. Add up these voltages. Measure the electron push between A and D. How does this compare with the voltages of the three cells? How does this compare with the voltages you measured?

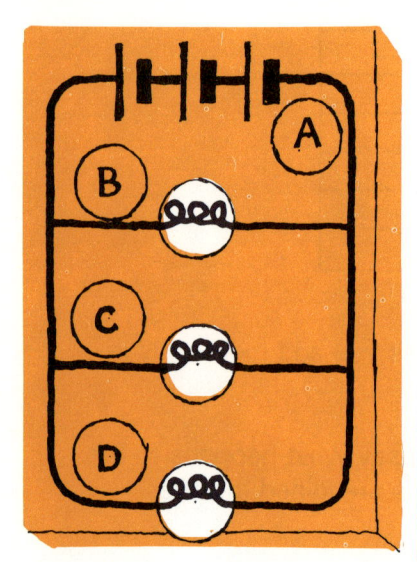

You will now measure electric current and push when the resistances are arranged in parallel. Keep the three cells in a line. Arrange the bulbs in parallel.

Measure the current at positions B, C, and D. Add the three readings together. Measure the current at A. What do you find?

Measure the voltages across A, B, C, and D. Do the electrons lose any push?

Position	Voltage	Current
A		
B		
C		
D		

Measuring electrons

Electrical measurements appear to be tricky because we sense electricity poorly. To make measurements we need instruments.

Ammeters measure electric current

How many electrons are passing through this part of the circuit? That is a question about electric current. You can answer it poorly using a light bulb. You can answer it more precisely using an ammeter. Ammeters are instruments used to measure the amount of electric current. The unit of current in electricity is called an ampere. Since electricians never use a long word where a short one will do, the unit is written as amp. The light bulbs at home use less than 0.5 amp of current. An even smaller current of electrons flowing through your body can kill you.

Voltmeters measure electric pressure

How great a push is there through the circuit? That is a question about electric pressure. We call electric pressure voltage. To measure voltage a voltmeter is used and it measures electric pressure in volts. The small cells you used gave a push of 1.5 volts. A car battery will give a voltage of 12 volts, and the voltage for homes is usually 240 volts.

These instruments show what happens in circuits

You used these instruments to check on what was happening in two kinds of circuits. In the first circuit the resistances were bulbs which were arranged in series. The current was the same at all points. Across the bulbs the voltage dropped. When all these voltages were added up you saw they were the same as the voltage of the cells pushing out electrons. When the bulbs were arranged in parallel the pressure of electrons stayed the same. Using the ammeters to measure the current you saw that the total current of electrons is greater.

Electricity 4

Communicating machines

Voltmeters and ammeters are electrical instruments which help our senses. Using them we can sense electricity better. Here are more instruments and their chief inventors. Using these we can communicate longer, further, and faster.

Alexander Bell and his telephone Take patterns of sound energy. Turn these into patterns of electrons. Push the electrons through a wire. Turn the electron patterns back into sound patterns. A message has been sent and received by telephone.

Samuel Morse and his telegraph Push some electrons through a wire. Push electrons through in definite patterns. Decode the patterns. A message has been sent and received by telegraph.

William Marconi and his radio Take patterns of moving electrons. Get the electrons to set up patterns of radio waves in the atmosphere. Collect the radio waves. Turn them back into patterns of electrons. Translate the electron pattern. A message has been sent and received by radio.

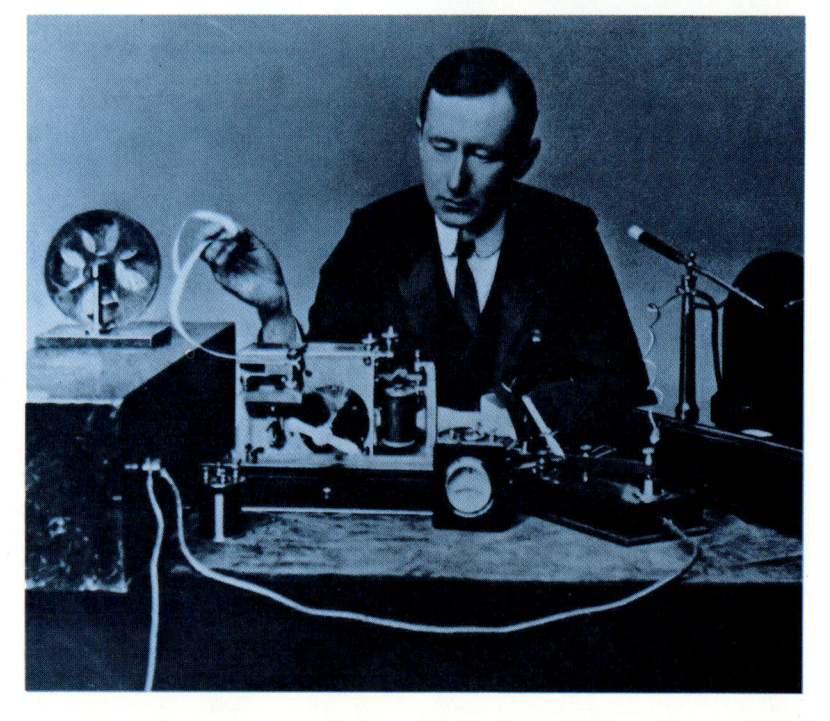

Electricity 4

Tape recorder Take a pattern of sound energy. Turn this into patterns of electrons. Change the patterns of electrons into patterns of magnetism. Put the magnetic patterns on to a tape. A message has been sent and memorized on a tape.

John Baird and his television Take an object. Use a camera to take a picture of a pattern of chemical dots. Turn this pattern into a pattern of electrons. Get the electrons to make a pattern of radio waves. Use a receiver to make a picture. A message has been sent and received by television.

Computer Take a pattern of words. Turn these into a pattern of two numbers: 0 and 1. Turn these number patterns into patterns of electrons moving in circuits. A message has been given to a computer.

The Future Tele-touching? Three-dimensional TV?

149

Electricity 5

Electrons working

We use electricity in the home to do more and more work. We must know about this kind of energy to use it safely and to use it well.

Dissecting plugs

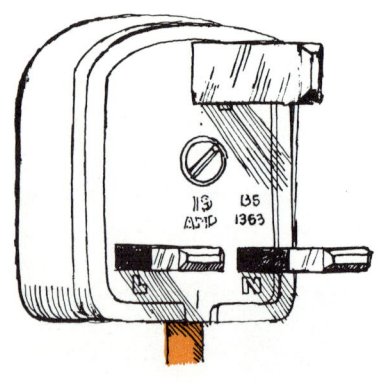

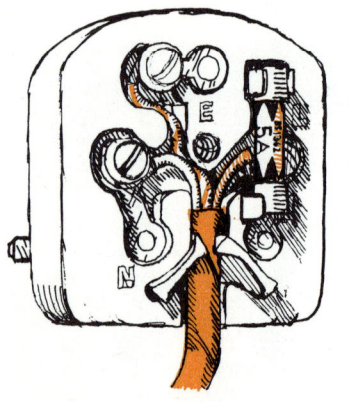

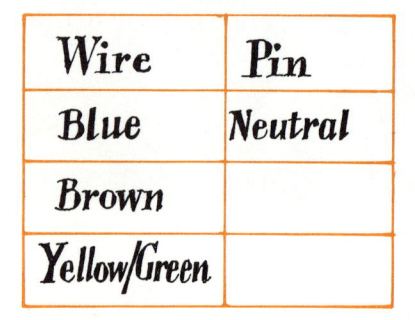

To use electrical machines at home we must connect them into the main circuit. We do this at power points. We do this using plugs.

Examine the plug. What material is the case made of? Why has this material been used? What material is used for the pins? Why?
Pull the cable coming from the plug. This cable should stay in place. Why?

Open the case. How many wires are there inside? What colour is each wire? Make a drawing to show where each wire goes. Disconnect these wires. Beside the brown wire there is a cartridge. What job does this cartridge do? Take it out and read what is printed on it. What do you think this means? If the plug is put together without this cartridge will the circuit be complete?

Release the cable from the plug. Why were you unable to pull the cable out earlier?

Check on the casing of the plug for the letters L, N, and E. These letters stand for Live, Neutral, and Earth. Which colour wire was connected to the Live pin? Which pin is connected to the yellow and green wire? Complete the table for the three wires and pins.

You will now put the plug together in the correct way, which is the only safe way. Attach the three wires to the correct pins. Put the cable in so that it cannot be pulled out. Replace the fuse.

Get your teacher to check your work. Then screw on the case. Do **not** practise this at home. Why?

Wire	Pin
Blue	Neutral
Brown	
Yellow/Green	

Electricity 5

Devising switches

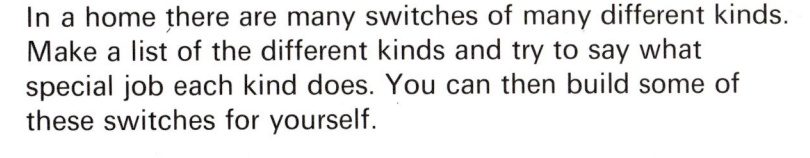

In a home there are many switches of many different kinds. Make a list of the different kinds and try to say what special job each kind does. You can then build some of these switches for yourself.

You will first make an automatic switch. To do this use a special metal strip. Clamp this strip into a stand. With a burner heat the free end of the strip. What happens? This strip can be built into a circuit. It can be put in so that when it is heated the circuit is complete. When the circuit is complete electric current will flow. The current can be used to ring a bell. The ringing bell tells you that the strip is being heated. What could this switch be used for? Using the wires, cells, and bell fit up a circuit so an automatic switch is made.

A fuse is a safety switch. Take a $4\frac{1}{2}$ volt battery with copper terminals. Put a strand of steel wool between these terminals. What happens? How can this be used as a safety switch?
Make a circuit with a power pack, wires, bulb, and a strand of steel wool. If more and more electrons are pushed from the pack into the bulb alone what will happen? Now slowly increase the voltage through the circuit. What happens? Did the steel wool act as a safety switch?

Press a door bell switch and the bell rings. Stop pressing and the bell stops. Look at the door bell switch. Use the materials you have been given to build your own electric door bell.

Hall lights can be switched on in one place and switched off in another. How does this work? Make up the circuit from the diagram to find out.

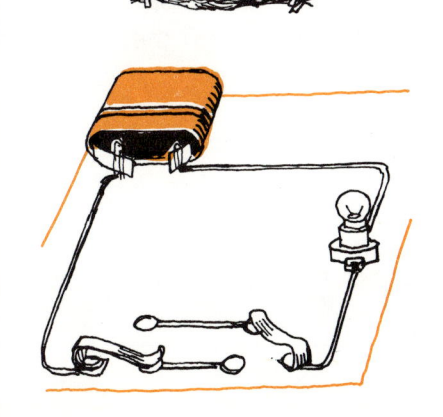

Switch puzzle A burglar alarm needs a switch that will switch on when someone opens a window or door. Plan a switch which works that way.

151

Electricity 5

Constructing motors

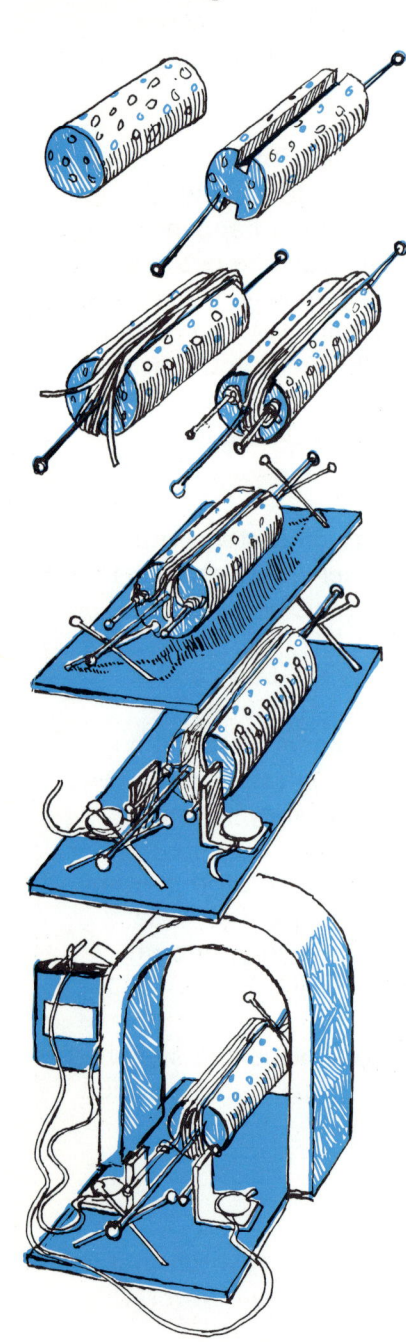

Many household machines use motors whose energy supply is electricity. How is the electrical energy turned into work? Build your own motor and find out.

To build the motor you will need:
a board   two sets of crossed pins at the ends of the board.

For the motor itself you will need:
a cork   thin insulated wire   two long pins
two drawing pins   two short pins
two rectangles of tin or copper foil.

For the energy conversion you will need:
a cell   connecting wires   a horseshoe magnet.

Carefully cut two grooves in the cork.
Wind the thin insulated wire round the grooves to make the coil.
Firmly stick the two longer pins in at the ends of the cork to make the motor axle.
Stick the two shorter pins in the same end of the cork.
Bare the two ends of the insulated wire and wrap one end round each of the short pins.
Support the axle and coil by the long pins on the crossed pins on the board.

Take the two pieces of metal foil. Bend them so they are in an L shape. Stick these pieces to the board with the drawing pins so that each touches a pin when the coil turns.

Place the horseshoe magnet over the coil and connect the drawing pins to the cell.

What happens? How can you use this?

Electricity 5

Electrons for you

In many ways electricity has freed men and women from drudgery. We can hold on to this freedom only by understanding electricity and the way we get it.

The past

Before we had electricity men and women lived hard lives. In homes women used their own energy to do their work. They cleaned their homes and their clothes by hand. They cooked their food over open fires. The fuel burned in the fire also gave light and heat. At work the same was true for men. Of course this was not true for all women and men. Some used the energy of other people. They used the energy of servants—even slaves.

The present

Today we can all be the possessors of billions of slaves. These slaves can be available at the touch of a switch. These slaves can be positioned in any house, in all places of work. They can be placed there, where we wish, ready to do as we wish. We can use these slaves to clean, to light, to communicate, to heat. These slaves are the electrons which drive our machines.

The future

But electrons are not free. They are not even cheap. Everyone of course pays for the electricity he or she uses. But there is a price we must all pay which is not seen in any electricity bill. Electricity is transformed from other energy sources. Have we enough of these energy resources to supply all the electricity we are using? Do we need quite as much electricity? Should each one of us use less? When we answer these questions honestly we shall begin to pay the right price.

Electricity 5

Making and transmitting electricity

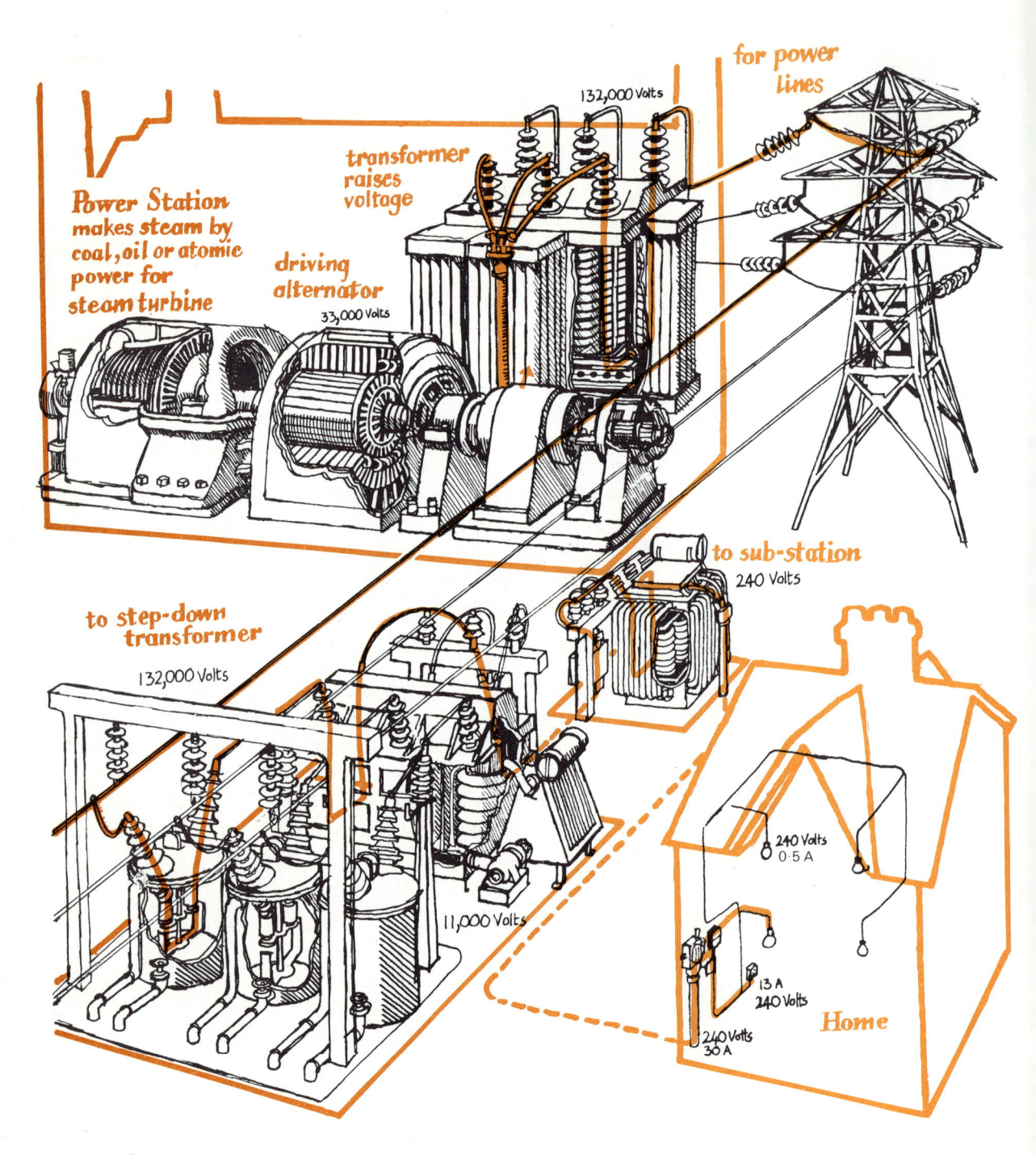

Power Station makes steam by coal, oil or atomic power for steam turbine

driving alternator 33,000 Volts

transformer raises voltage 132,000 Volts

for power lines

to step-down transformer 132,000 Volts

11,000 Volts

to sub-station 240 Volts

240 Volts 0.5 A

13 A 240 Volts

240 Volts 30 A

Home

The biggest blackout

We use electricity more and more in our lives. So when the electricity supply fails a lot of funny things happen.

On any evening at 5.26 in New York City millions of people are busy. They are not busy working. They are busy making their way home from work. From the skyscraper offices they pour out and pack into lifts taking them to the ground below. From the factories they crowd out and collect in queues at the stations and bus terminals. From the shops they pass into the streets and push their way through. This is the New York rush hour and that is how it was at 5.26 on the evening of November 9, 1965.

But at 5.27 on that evening the rush hour stopped. One minute millions were moving home. The next minute millions had stopped. They could do nothing else. In the corridors and on the subway platforms there was immediate darkness as all the lights went out. In the streets all traffic clogged in huge jams when all the traffic lights failed. In or between stations, at or between floors, the trains and lifts—with their passengers—stopped. At 5.27 exactly all electric clocks in the city stopped. They marked the beginning of the biggest power cut in history. It spread over much of the north-eastern coast of North America. It lasted 12 hours. 30 000 000 people were affected.

In the subway system of New York 800 000 travellers were trapped. When they realized what was going on they settled down to a long, cold night. But it was not a lonely night. People began to talk to their neighbours, and that does not happen during the rush hour. The normal rush hour that is. Those caught out in the streets tried the restaurants for a meal. The restaurants were serving, but they were not cooking. Many went to hotels to book a bed for the night. Soon the hotels were filled up. Then the managers started to break the rules to allow people to sleep in the lobbies.

The most unfortunate group were those trapped in a lift between the 24th and 25th floors of the Empire State Building. The staff took 5 hours to break through a heavy concrete wall to release them. The most surprised man was the captain of a plane flying into New York. As he started the run into New York he announced to the passengers 'And on your left you will see the fabulous lights of the city of New York...' Then he looked out of the window himself. The most worried people were those who phoned the police stations to blame themselves for causing all this damage. They said it was the way they switched on the heater. Or it was the way they had connected the plug. They were worried, but also a little proud. After all it is not everyone who can black out the whole of New York.

An ocean of air 1

Three gases

There is no easy way to tell the gases nitrogen, oxygen, and carbon dioxide apart. They have no colour or smell. To identify these gases scientists use special tests.

Practising tests

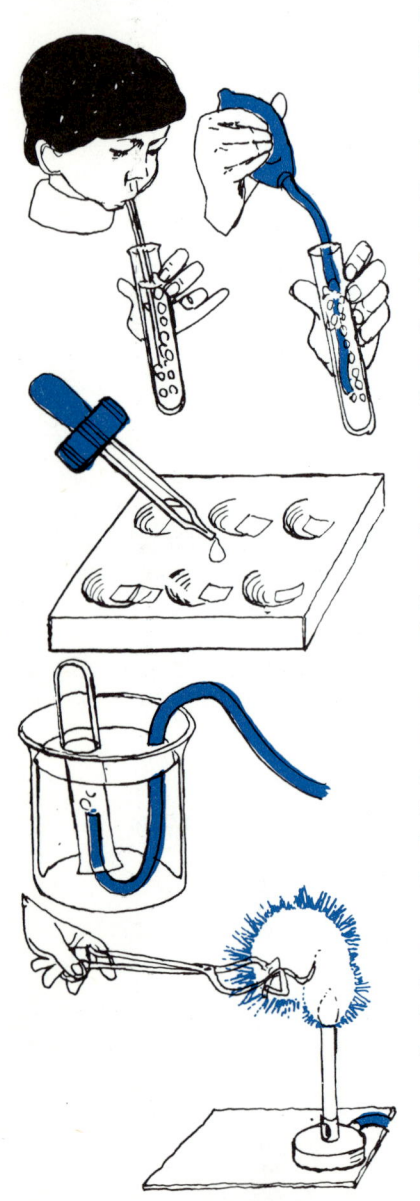

Put 2 ml lime water in two test-tubes. Blow gently into the liquid in one tube. Using hand bellows, gently blow air through the liquid in the other tube. What happens to the lime water in the two test-tubes?

The small piece of paper you have been given is called pH paper. You have also been given a pH colour chart. Match the colour of your piece of paper with a colour on the chart. What is the pH number for this colour? There are 5 different solutions. Use one piece of paper for each solution. Put one drop of solution on the pH paper. Match the colour of the wet paper with a colour on the chart. What is the pH number for each solution?

Light a wooden splint. Blow the flame out. Watch the glow. Does the splint go out right away? Use a stop clock to time how long the glow lasts.
Light a wooden splint. Watch the flame. Does the flame ever get brighter? Put this splint into an empty test-tube. What happens to the flame?

Put a test-tube of air upside down in a beaker of water. Use a clean piece of rubber tubing to suck a little of the air out. What happens to the water level? Put a test-tube of air upside down in a beaker of water and shake the test-tube gently. Imagine some of the gas particles dissolved in the water. What would happen to the water level?

Magnesium can be a very dangerous metal when burned. A piece of magnesium will be burned for you. It burns with a very hot and very bright flame. Partly close your eyes to look at the flame.

An ocean of air 1

Testing the tests

You know how to do the tests. Now use them with samples of the gases oxygen, nitrogen, and carbon dioxide. Use them to decide which test is best for each gas.

With each test follow the instructions on the next page.
Take a test-tube of one of the gases and carry out the test.
Try the same test on the other two gases.
Use a new sample of gas for each test.
Put your results in the results table immediately.

	Nitrogen	Oxygen	Carbon dioxide
lime water			
pH paper			
glowing splint			
burning splint			
solubility			
burning Magnesium			

A good test is one which works for one substance and only one substance. A good test is very clear. A good test works quickly.

When you have all your results you will choose the best test for each gas. You will decide:
Which test works with carbon dioxide and only carbon dioxide.
Which test works with oxygen and only oxygen.

Is there a test for nitrogen that works only with nitrogen?

157

An ocean of air 1

Testing the tests

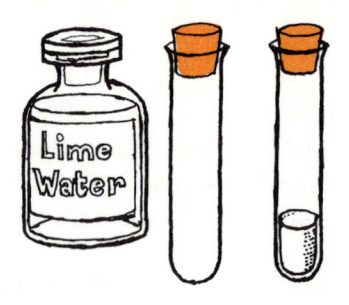

Lime water Add 2 ml lime water to the gas in the test-tube. Replace the stopper. Shake to mix the gas and the lime water. What happens to the lime water?

pH paper Add one drop of water to a piece of pH paper. Put the moist pH paper in the tube of gas. Watch the colour of the paper. Record the pH number.

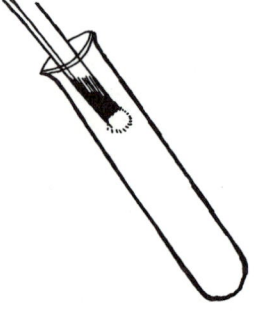

Glowing splint Dip a glowing splint into a sample of gas. What happens to the glow of the splint?

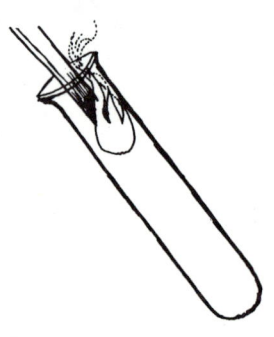

Burning splint Dip a burning splint into a sample of gas. Does the splint stay alight? Does it go out? Does it burn brighter?

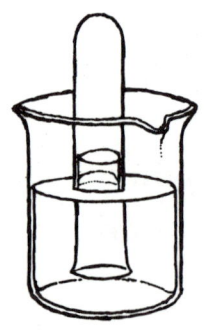

Solubility in water Put a tube of gas upside down in a beaker of water. Shake the tube gently. Watch the water level closely. If the level rises, the gas is soluble in water.

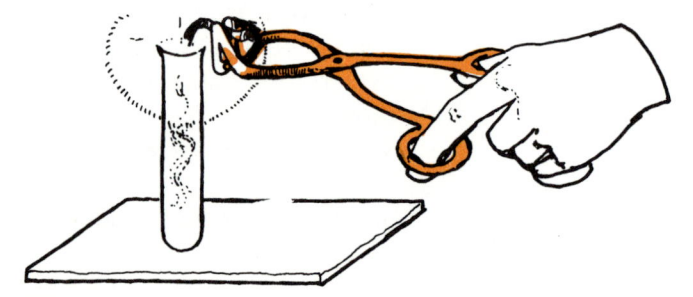

Burning magnesium This test will be done by your teacher. A piece of burning magnesium will be put into a sample of gas. Does the magnesium burn in the gas?

An ocean of air 1

Telling gases apart

Three very common gases are nitrogen, oxygen, and carbon dioxide. You cannot feel, or smell, or see any difference between them. To tell them apart these gas tests are used.

Carbon dioxide

A sample of each gas was put into three separate test-tubes. You knew which test-tube contained which gas. The first test you tried was the lime water test. A little lime water was put into each test-tube. The tube was stoppered and shaken. In the tubes with oxygen and nitrogen the lime water stayed clear. In the tube with carbon dioxide the lime water turned milky.
That is the test for carbon dioxide.

Oxygen

You set fire to a small piece of wood, then blew the flame out. The wood did not stop burning right away. It continued to glow. The glowing splint was put into the test-tubes with carbon dioxide and nitrogen. In each of these gases the splint quickly went out. In the test-tube with oxygen the splint also stopped glowing. But it did not go out. In oxygen the glowing splint burst into flames again. That is the test for oxygen.

Nitrogen

There are good tests for oxygen and carbon dioxide. There is no good test for nitrogen which is as simple as these two. That does not matter when you are working with these gases only. Then the test for nitrogen is that it does not relight a glowing splint and does not turn lime water milky. But that test works only when you know that the gas you are testing is nitrogen, or oxygen, or carbon dioxide.

An ocean of air 1

Nitrogen and its compounds

The symbol for nitrogen is N. Nitrogen is element number 7. Atoms of this element do not easily join with atoms of other elements. Nitrogen is normally a gas. It turns to liquid at −196 °C.

Nitrogen does not react easily with other materials. These materials remain unchanged for a long time if they are surrounded by nitrogen. Because of this and because nitrogen gas has no smell or taste, it is very useful for storing food materials.

Liquid nitrogen is very cold. It can be used to freeze-dry foods. Freeze-dried foods can be stored for a long time.

Nitrogen combines with other atoms to make very important compounds.

Nitrogen and oxygen can make the gas nitrous oxide. You may have breathed this gas. It can be used as an anaesthetic gas by dentists. You may have heard of its other name—laughing gas. After breathing this gas, some people laugh.

Nitrogen, hydrogen, and chlorine can combine to make ammonium chloride. This is one of the substances in the paste inside a dry cell battery.

160

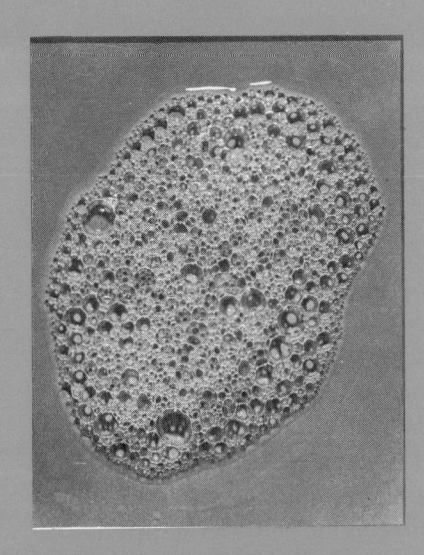

An ocean of air 1

Nitrogen, hydrogen, and oxygen can combine to give nitric acid. You will see this in your laboratory. Nitric acid, like ammonia, is a very important compound in industry.

One of the many compounds of nitrogen, hydrogen, oxygen, and carbon is nitroglycerine. This substance, when mixed with other materials, is dynamite. This was invented by a scientist called Alfred Nobel.

Nitrogen, oxygen, and potassium can give potassium nitrate. This is one of the substances in gunpowder. Nitrate compounds are very important fertilizers.

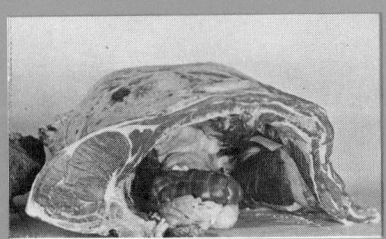

Other substances made by combining nitrogen, hydrogen, oxygen, and carbon are proteins. There are many different kinds of proteins. You eat proteins every day. You then make them into your own kinds of protein.

You have different proteins from your neighbour. That makes you different. The kind of proteins you have depends on another group of nitrogen compounds, the nucleic acids. Nucleic acids are the chemicals which make up the plans for all the cells in our bodies.

An ocean of air 2

What's in the air?

We live at the bottom of an ocean of air. What substances are around us in this complicated mixture?

Is air there?

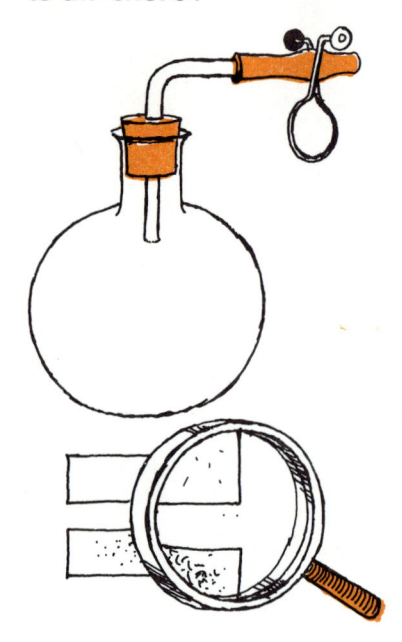

You cannot see gases; they are invisible. How do you know there are gases in air?
Weigh the flask and stopper. Attach the flask to a vacuum pump for one minute. Close the clip on the flask before switching off the pump. Reweigh the flask. What has happened to the weight of the flask? What did the vacuum pump do to cause this difference?
You started with an empty flask. Was the flask really empty? What would happen if you opened the clip on the flask? What will happen to the weight of the flask and stopper when you open the clip? Why will this happen? Open the clip and see if you are correct.

Two pieces of sellotape were left on the outside of the window. Piece 1 was left uncovered, sticky side up. Piece 2 was left covered, sticky side up. Use a hand lens to look at both these sticky surfaces.
What do you see on the uncovered piece?
Are gases the only things in the air?

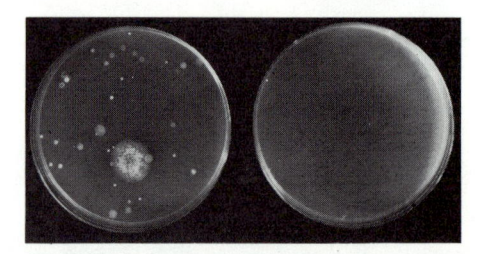

Two petri dishes containing jelly were set up 2 days ago. Petri dish 1 was opened to the air for 5 minutes. Petri dish 2 remained sealed. What has grown on the jelly? Where has this come from?

Mix some ice and salt in a beaker. Carefully dry the outside of the beaker.
What collects on the outside of the beaker? Where does this come from?

Which gases are in the air?

Bubble carbon dioxide gas through lime water. How quickly does the lime water go milky?

The flask at the sink contains lime water. It is attached to a pump which bubbles air through the lime water. This works when the water tap is turned on.
Bubble air through the lime water. Does the lime water turn milky quickly or slowly? Why is so much air needed to change the lime water?

Put a glowing splint in a sample of pure oxygen. What happens?
Hold a glowing splint in the air. Does it light up?
Does it go out immediately? Is there any oxygen in the air? Does the air contain only oxygen?

Put a glowing splint in a sample of pure nitrogen. What happens?
Hold a glowing splint in the air. Is there enough carbon dioxide in the air to affect the splint?
Which gas prevents the glowing splint from bursting into flame?

Put a layer of sand in a crucible. Place 3 cm magnesium ribbon on the sand. Cover the magnesium with more sand. Put on the lid. Heat the crucible for 3 minutes. What do you expect to happen to the magnesium?
Let the crucible cool for 5 minutes. Tip the sand on to a mat. Has anything happened to the magnesium? What is your explanation?
Put the piece of magnesium in the crucible without any sand. Heat the crucible. What happens to the magnesium this time? How does this happen?

A splint burns when there is oxygen present. When magnesium burns a new substance is formed. It seems likely that when magnesium burns it combines with oxygen. If that is true the new substance is a compound of magnesium and oxygen atoms. The compound is called magnesium oxide.

magnesium + oxygen → magnesium oxide

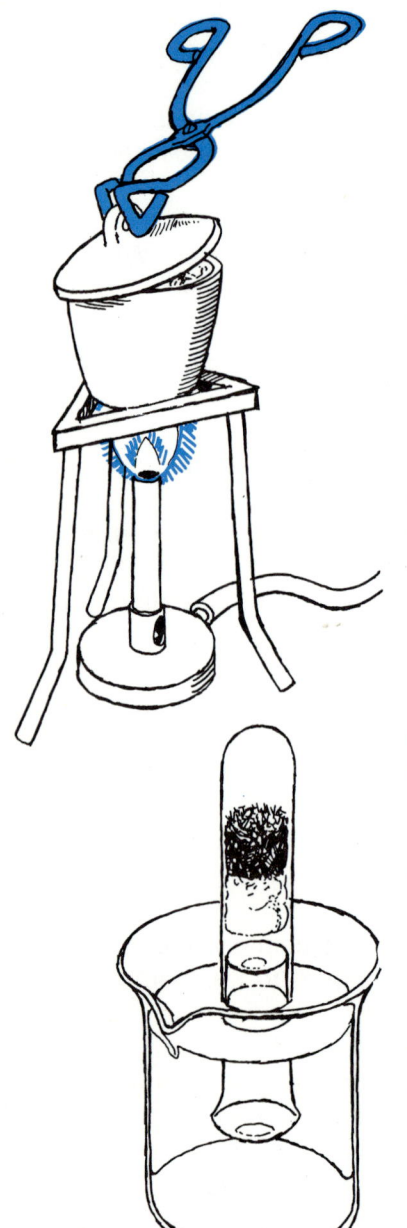

You started with atoms of magnesium. You finished with a compound in which the magnesium atoms have joined with oxygen atoms. Will the compound be heavier or lighter than the magnesium you started with?

Put 5 cm magnesium ribbon in a crucible. Weigh this with the crucible lid. Heat the crucible. Hold the lid partly open, using tongs to let air in. After the magnesium has burned, let the crucible and lid cool. Reweigh them.
What has happened to the weight? Is the new compound heavier than the magnesium? Can the magnesium have combined with oxygen to make magnesium oxide?

By using quick-burning magnesium we can see there is oxygen in the air. By using iron we can find out how much oxygen is present. The iron joins slowly with the oxygen to form iron oxide. You call that substance rust.

Put some iron powder in a test-tube. Put cotton wool loosely in the test-tube. Turn the tube upside down in a beaker of water. This traps a sample of air. The iron will rust, forming iron oxide. Leave the apparatus for at least a week.

Why has the water risen? How far has the water risen? How much air has been removed? How much of the air is oxygen?

There is gas left in the tube. Can you test it to make certain the gas is nitrogen? How much of the air is nitrogen?

A complicated mixture

Air is a very complicated mixture. Trying to say what, and when, and why, and where substances are present is even more complicated.

Nitrogen and oxygen

The most common substance in air is the gas nitrogen. Out of every 100 parts of air, 78 parts are nitrogen. Oxygen is the second most common substance. Out of every 100 parts 21 are oxygen. So almost all the air, 99 parts out of every 100, is nitrogen and oxygen.

Other gases

Other substances are present in small quantities but are still important. Argon is the most common of these substances. Argon belongs to the family of noble gases. The other gases of this family: helium, neon, krypton, xenon, and radon, are also in the air.
Carbon dioxide is also present in small amounts, about 3 parts in every 10 000.

Water

Often what is found in the air depends on when and where the analysis is made. Water is a good example of this. Over the Sahara desert the air contains little water. The water there is gas. Over the polar deserts there is also little water. The water there is present as ice crystals. Over the oceans there is much water. It may be present as solid—snow, hail or sleet; liquid—rain; or gas—water vapour.

Many other substances

The amounts of the less common substances vary from place to place and time to time. There is more carbon dioxide in a classroom of pupils than in an empty classroom. There are more microbes in a cinema than on a mountain top. There are more pollen grains in summer than in winter. There are more smoke particles near a chimney. More particles are being added by exhaust from planes and cars. Air is indeed a complicated mixture.

Our resources: air

Air polluters have two very odd ideas. They think: 'The air belongs to everyone, so I have a right to use it as a rubbish dump.' They think: 'There is so much air it does not matter what I put in it.' They are wrong, as you can see.

Pollution costs money Many of the substances causing pollution are valuable. We lose money by scattering them—we could collect these substances. We lose money because they are scattered—they cause damage. We lose money both ways.

Industry causes pollution Many factory chimneys pour out the gas sulphur dioxide. In the atmosphere this can react with water to make a new compound, sulphuric acid. This acid, like all acids, but even more than most, is corrosive. It reacts with metals. It destroys metal structures.

Cars cause pollution Exhaust fumes are a complex mixture of gases. Many of these are highly poisonous, especially carbon monoxide. Out in open streets carbon monoxide does not kill. But it does make people feel tired and stupid if they work in that kind of atmosphere.

Homes cause pollution Coal fires make much dust and grit. This collects on clothes. They must be washed more often. The dust and grit collects on buildings. The buildings must be cleaned.

An ocean of air 2

Towns cause pollution Often rubbish is burned in incinerators. Burning makes more rubbish. This rubbish is smoke. Smoke reduces visibility so we cannot see so far. Smoke cuts out sunlight so we cannot see for so long.

Farms cause pollution If the soil is not held together by the roots of plants, it can blow away. Great dust storms may result. This is terrible pollution. Both the land and the atmosphere are destroyed.

Armies cause pollution For many years nuclear bombs were exploded in the atmosphere. The dust from these bombs is very dangerous to our health. It lasts a long time. It spreads throughout the atmosphere.

All these things cause pollution Each kind of pollution is unpleasant enough on its own. But of course each kind is not on its own. In the atmosphere everything is spread out and mixed. You breathe that mixture in. What do you breathe out?

We can prevent pollution.

An ocean of air 3

Taking a breath

You breathe all your life. When you breathe, you take in air. How does the air get in? Where does it go? Why do you breathe?

Taking breaths

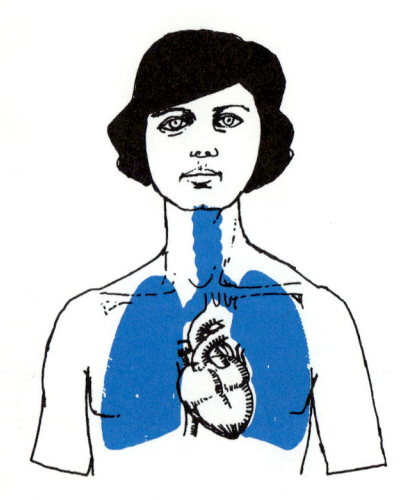

The next activities are on breathing. Do what you are asked once. Write what you notice and think. Repeat the activity to check. Repeat the activity and think.

Breathe in and out normally. Think about everything that you have to do to breathe.
Take a deep breath. What do you have to do to take this breath?
Breathe in and out slowly. How do you control this?

Breathe in and out normally again. What can you feel at your nose? Mouth? Throat? Chest? Stomach region?

At the back of your throat are two tubes. One goes down to the lungs. The other goes to the stomach.
Try to swallow and breathe in at the same time. Can you do it? Why is this important?

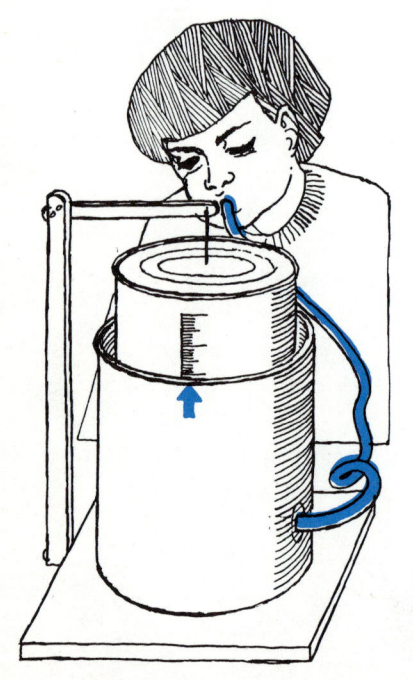

How many breaths do you normally take in a minute?
How few breaths can you take in one minute?
How long can you hold your breath without strain?
How long does it take to breathe in one breath?
How long does it take to breathe out one breath?

Use the special apparatus to find the volume of one normal breath. Many people have to use it, so keep the apparatus clean.
How much air is there in a normal breath? In a big breath?

An ocean of air 3

Looking at lungs

We can learn a lot about breathing by breathing. But there is a limit to what we can find out this way. Now we must look at the breathing system from the inside.

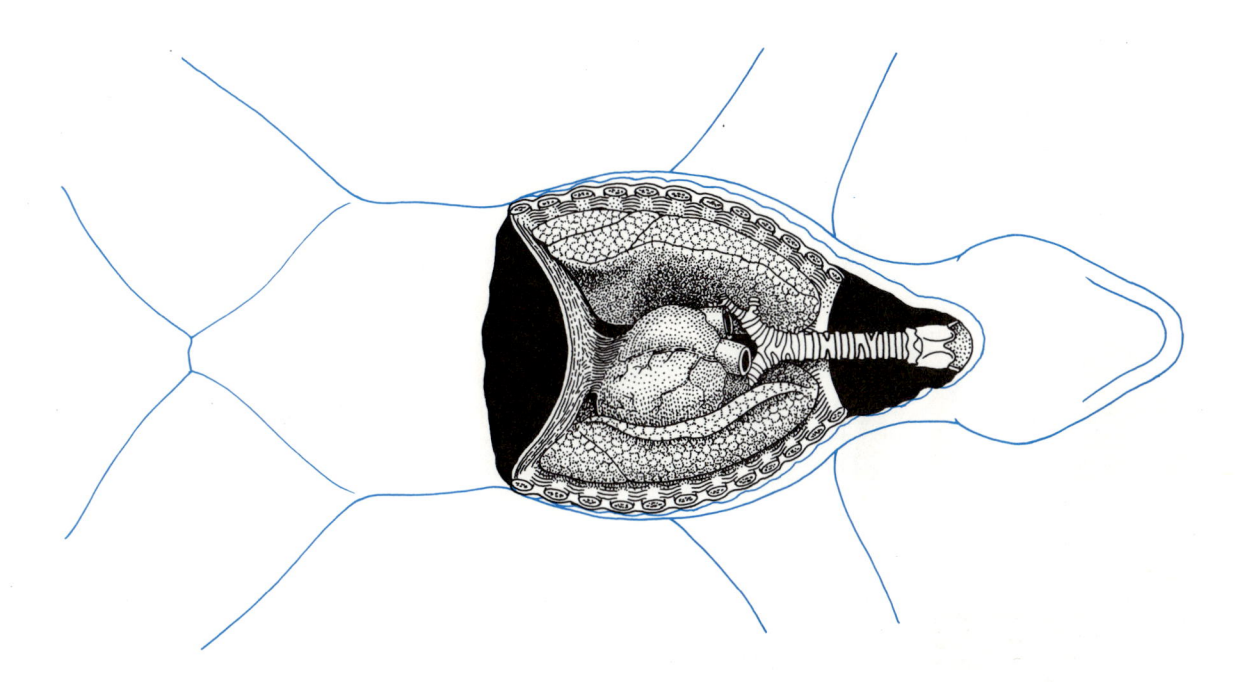

Look at the dissection of the animal. Find the:
lungs   heart   main breathing tubes   ribs
diaphragm muscle   rib muscles   voice box

Look at the main breathing tube. Why are there firm rings round this tube? Feel for these rings on your own neck.

Look at a slice of lung with a hand lens. Draw what you see.
Look at a piece of plastic foam. In what way is this material built like the lung?

Use a microscope to examine a very thin slice of lung. This will tell you how much of the lung consists of cells and how much is air space.

An ocean of air 3

Breathing

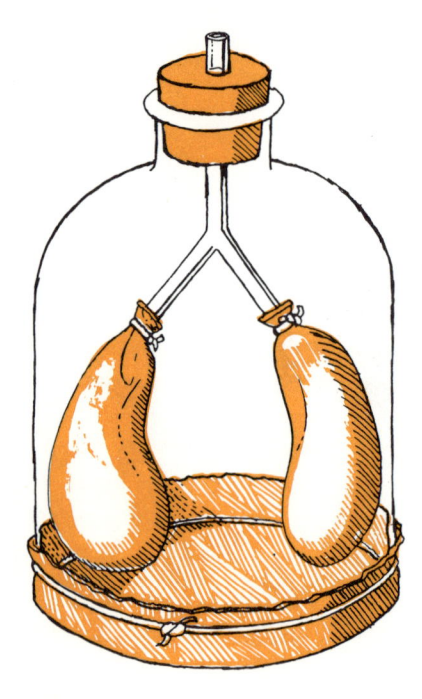

Examining our own breathing and looking at animal lungs does not tell us how we get air in and out of our lungs. To find out how we breathe you will work with models.

Here is a list of parts of the breathing system. Match them with the different parts of the breathing model:
lungs   big breathing tube   rib cage
diaphragm muscle
Pull down the plastic sheet. What happens to the balloons?
Push up the plastic sheet. What happens to the balloons?
Now try to explain how the diaphragm muscle works to bring air into the lungs.

The model helps us understand how the diaphragm muscle works in breathing, but it does not tell us the whole story of breathing. The model is not built like our body. What does it not show?

Rib muscles also help bring air into our lungs. Place your hands across your chest. Let the middle fingers touch at the bottom of your breast-bone.
Breathe in very deeply. Are your middle fingers still touching?
How do your rib muscles move your rib cage?
The diaphragm muscle works with the rib muscles to move air in and out of the lungs. Both work at the same time. These two sets of muscles make the space inside the lungs larger and smaller.

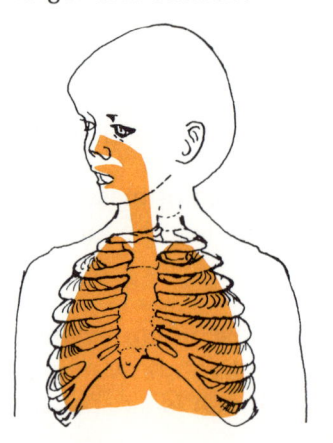

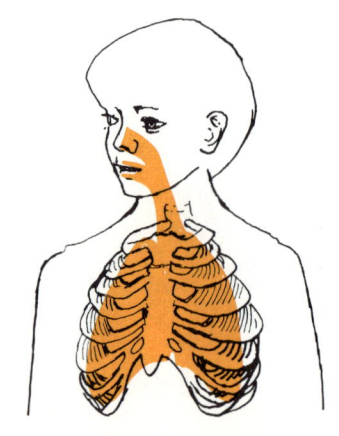

In and out

When we breathe, air is taken into our lungs. In the lungs there is an exchange of gases between our body and this air.

The upper breathing tubes

We take in air through our mouth and nose. We also take food in through our mouth. In the throat, the mouth and nose passages meet. There are two tubes coming from the throat. The front tube is the air passage, the soft tube behind is for food. Food can go into the breathing tube, but not often. There is a flap which fits over the air tube. When you swallow, this flap automatically closes the air tube.

The lower breathing tubes

The big breathing tubes are held open by firm rings. The main tube divides into two tubes and one tube goes to each lung. In the lungs these tubes divide again and again forming smaller and smaller tubes. At the ends of the smallest tubes are tiny rounded air sacs. This is where some gases go into the body and some gases come out of the body.

Diaphragm and rib muscles

Breathing is the job of two sets of muscles, the diaphragm muscles and the rib muscles.
To breathe in, the diaphragm muscle comes down and the rib muscles pull the rib cage up and out. This makes more space inside the chest. The lungs expand to fill this space and air flows in through the mouth and nose to fill this extra space in the lungs.
There is a short pause and air is pushed out again. But it is not quite the same as the air that came in.

An ocean of air 3

Different breathing systems

All living things need to breathe in one way or another. We use lungs for breathing. Other organisms have different breathing systems.

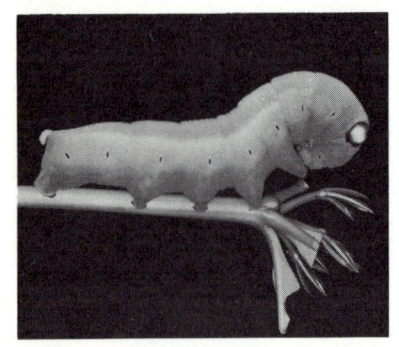

Insects have many openings to their breathing tubes.

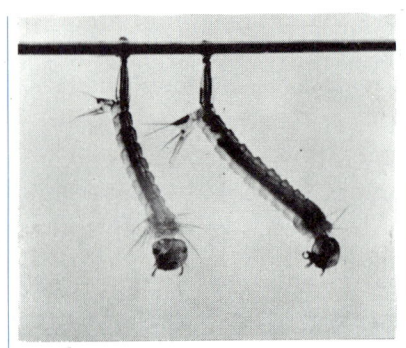

This insect grub breathes through a snorkel tube.

This diving beetle carries an air bubble aqualung.

Fish breathe in water by using gills.

This African lungfish has lungs. It breathes air.

This shrimp breathes with gills of another kind.

This woodlouse breathes through its legs.

This hydra breathes through its whole body.

And how do plants breathe?

Plenty of air, but not enough muscle

When Elizabeth Twistington Higgins was 14 she visited the ballet at Sadler's Wells. She decided to become a ballet dancer. After years of hard work and determination she succeeded and became a ballet dancer and a ballet teacher. Then in 1953, disaster.

One Saturday, Elizabeth felt ill. Her temperature was 39 °C. On Monday, she felt worse. She had a stabbing pain in her head. Her neck was stiff. She was taken to hospital. On Wednesday, she realized that she could not move her left arm. She felt exhausted, just lying there in bed. On Thursday, she could not breathe normally—she could only manage half breaths. Then the thought flashed into her mind, 'I've got polio and I'll never dance again.' She did have polio.

By now Elizabeth was desperately short of air. She was frightened of going into an iron lung, but the doctors quickly had to put her in one. The motor was switched on. That motor took the place of her paralysed muscles. She could breathe again... or so she thought. She was taken out of the iron lung that evening. But she could not breathe at all. Her muscles were paralysed from the neck down. From now on, that motor would take the place of her breathing muscles. She went back into the iron lung.

Elizabeth could not move, but she was determined not to lie there forever. To live a useful life, she had to learn to breathe without the machine. She had to train her neck muscles to do her breathing. Her doctor would switch off the machine and she would try to breathe. At first it was hopeless. She became blue within seconds. After three months of effort she could breathe for a minute and a half on her own. After seven months she could breathe for 15 minutes. Her progress seemed desperately slow, but it was progress.

She was able in time to leave hospital for short spells. Although she was still paralysed from the neck down, she learned to paint. She painted, holding the paint brush in her mouth. At first it was very awkward but she improved. She completed a picture. She was excited at the thought of being able to do something useful and creative again. She worked hard at her art studies. Her pictures were put in an exhibition where many were sold.

Although Elizabeth still sleeps in an iron lung, she has become very independent. What is she doing now? That is obvious, surely. She is back at her old job. She is a ballet teacher again. She cannot move, but she teaches others to move.

An ocean of air 4

What happens in the lungs?

When you breathe in, air is taken into the lungs. What happens there? To answer this, you must compare the air breathed in with the air breathed out.

Sampling and testing

It is easy to get a sample of the air you breathe in. Just take a sample of the air all around you.

It is easy to get a sample of the air you breathe out. Use the equipment shown to collect samples of breathed-out air so that it is not mixed with unbreathed air.

When you have invented a way of collecting samples of breathed-in and breathed-out air, test them. Test for oxygen and carbon dioxide.

Fill in the results table using the words 'more' or 'less'.

Testing for	Unbreathed air	Breathed air
Oxygen		
Carbon dioxide		

Fill a beaker with cold water. Dry the outside carefully. Breathe on the outside of this beaker. What collects there? Where did this substance come from?

Take the temperature of the air. Then breathe on the thermometer. Is there any temperature change?

From your results fill in the table. Use the words 'more' or 'less' for the amount of water vapour and 'higher' or 'lower' for the temperature.

Testing for	Unbreathed air	Breathed air
Water Vapour		
Temperature		

174

An ocean of air 4

Why the differences?

You can easily explain the water vapour and temperature differences you found on the previous page.
Use this information to make your explanations:

The breathing tubes and the lungs are covered with a watery liquid.
Your body temperature is higher than the temperature of the air around you.

The differences between the amounts of oxygen and carbon dioxide are not so easily explained.

There is more carbon dioxide in breathed air than in unbreathed air. Your body makes carbon dioxide. How can carbon dioxide be made?
Your teacher will show you how to carefully burn a sample of carbon in a test-tube of oxygen. After burning, try the lime water test. What happens? Now write out the equation:

    carbon + oxygen →

There is less oxygen in breathed air than in unbreathed air. What can be happening in your body to the oxygen?

We do not eat carbon, so where do we get the carbon to make carbon dioxide?
Carefully burn samples of food in oxygen. After burning, test for carbon dioxide. Put your results in a table.

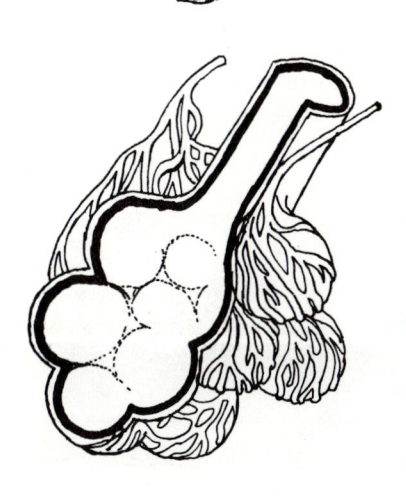

Food burnt	Carbon dioxide test

You can now make an explanation of how carbon dioxide is made in your body and how oxygen is used up. Start your explanation with: 'Some foodstuffs contain...'

175

An ocean of air 4

But why do we breathe?

When the food was burned in oxygen, what forms of energy were released?

Breathe on the bulb of a thermometer. What happens? Why does this happen?

Touch your toes 30 times.
What happens to your breathing rate?
What happens to your temperature?
How are these connected?

If you were to touch your toes 30 000 times, what would happen to your breathing rate?
How is this connected to the amount of oxygen you take in?
How would this exercise affect the amount of food you eat?

How are the oxygen and food intakes connected?

When the food was burned in oxygen, chemical energy was changed into other kinds of energy.
When you touch your toes what is the chemical energy changed into?

You now know a lot more about your breathing. You have connected together food, oxygen, carbon dioxide, energy, and changes of energy.
Now write a few sentences connecting all these words.
Start your first sentence with: 'When I breathe in, I take in…'

Respiration

You breathe in. There is a pause. You breathe out. What happens during this pause?

In the lungs gases are exchanged

The air going into our lungs contains more oxygen than the air leaving our lungs. Some of the oxygen has been removed. It has passed into the blood that surrounds the air passages in the lungs.
The air leaving the lungs has more carbon dioxide in it than the air entering the lungs. Carbon dioxide has been added to the air in the lungs. The carbon dioxide has come from the blood. Oxygen particles going into the blood have been exchanged for carbon dioxide particles.

In cells oxygen combines with food...

The heart pumps blood to every part of the body. The oxygen that passes from the lungs into the blood is carried to every part of the body. Every cell of the body gets its share of oxygen from the blood. Every cell also gets its share of food from the blood. In the cell oxygen combines with food particles. The new compounds made are carbon dioxide and water and energy is released.

...and energy is released

The energy in the food is changed from stored to working energy. It can work to keep us warm, to keep us moving, to grow, to think. The energy is used to keep us alive. This whole process is called respiration. We need to breathe to get oxygen for respiration. We need to breathe to get rid of the unwanted carbon dioxide.

An ocean of air 4

Keeping warm in the cold

Respiration provides energy for all living activities. Mammals and birds use energy to keep a constant body temperature of about 40 °C. Some mammals and birds are able to live in very cold places because they have special ways of keeping warm.

Insulation

Fur Ten centimetres of fur to trap warm air.

Fat Ten centimetres of fat to slow down heat loss.

Feathers Eider down keeps the duck warm—and us too.

Behaviour

Huddling together gives less surface area for heat loss.

Burrowing and insulating the burrow.

Nests insulate the young from the cold.

Shape

Noses and *feet* are kept cool so they do not lose heat.

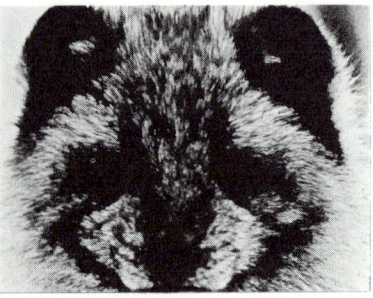

Ears lose less heat if they are small.

Temperature puzzle

Keeping cool in the heat
This is also a problem. How do animals overcome it in the desert?

178

How cold it can be

For the little warships there was another enemy. This enemy was more dangerous and more treacherous. This enemy was — the cold. The temperature had long since sunk below freezing point and the mercury was still shrinking down.

The cold was now intense. Ice formed in cabins and mess decks. Fresh water systems froze solid. Metal contracted. Hatch covers jammed. Door hinges froze, which locked the doors. The oil in the searchlight controls became gummy and made the lights useless.

To keep watch on the bridge was torture. The first shock of that bitter wind seared the lungs. It left a man fighting for breath. A man might forget to put on his gloves. First the silk gloves. Then the woollen mittens. Lastly the sheepskin gauntlets. He might forget to do all this and then touch a handrail. Then the skin on his palms would stick to the rail. His palms would be burned as if he had touched white-hot metal. On the bridge a man might forget to duck when the bows of the ship smashed down into a wave. The flying spray would solidify within a second into slivers of ice. A man might forget to duck and these pieces of ice would cut his face and forehead to the bone. Men did not forget.

On watch, hands froze. The very marrow of the bone was numb. The deadly chill crept upwards from the feet to calves and thighs. Nose and chin turned white from frostbite and demanded immediate attention. And worst of all, the end of the watch, the return below deck. This meant the excruciating agony of returning circulation.

Almost to a man the crew slept—or tried to sleep—with their heads pillowed on inflated lifebelts. Blown up, bent double, then tied with tape, these lifebelts were quite good pillows. This was what the lifebelts were used for. Orders were that these lifebelts were to be worn at all times in enemy waters. These orders were completely ignored. There was no point in wearing lifebelts in these waters.

There was enough air trapped between a man's clothes to keep him afloat for at least three minutes. If he wasn't picked up in that time he was dead anyway. It was shock that killed. The tremendous shock of a body at 37 °C being plunged into a liquid whose temperature was 40 degrees lower. For in arctic waters the temperature often falls below freezing point. Climbing out of the sea on to a raft was worse still. The wind temperature was much further below zero. This wind stabbed like a thousand daggers through the sodden clothing. The heart was faced with an almost instantaneous massive temperature change. It just stopped beating. But it was a quick death, men said— quick and kind and merciful.

An ocean of air 5

How do plants breathe?

Animals respire to keep alive. For their respiration they need food and oxygen. Plants are alive. Do they respire? Do they need food and oxygen?

Plants and breathing

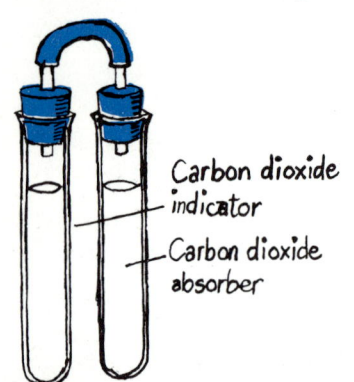

When testing for small amounts of carbon dioxide, a different test solution, bicarbonate indicator, is used. Pass carbon dioxide through bicarbonate indicator. Note the colour change. Use the special apparatus to remove carbon dioxide from the air above the indicator. Note the colour change. The bicarbonate indicator can be used to show when:

Amount of Carbon dioxide	Colour change
increases	
decreases	

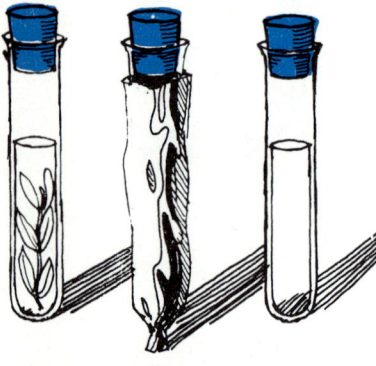

Put 10 ml bicarbonate indicator into three test-tubes. Put equal sized pieces of the water plant, *Elodea,* in two of them. Wrap foil round one tube with *Elodea* so no light gets in. Stopper all the tubes and put them in bright light for 45 minutes. Compare the colour in each tube.

Tube	Colour at start	Colour at finish
No plant		
Plant in dark		
Plant in light		

What do the colour changes tell you about:
The plant in the dark and carbon dioxide?
The plant in the light and carbon dioxide?

Take three 10 ml syringes. Put equal sized pieces of *Elodea* in two syringes. Cover one syringe with foil. Fill all three with water. Put all three in bright light for 2 days. In which syringe has a gas collected? Test to see if the gas is oxygen. When does the plant give out oxygen?

An ocean of air 5

Plants and respiration

Starch is one of our foods. We get starch from plants. You know how to test for starch in food. This is how to test for starch in the leaves of plants.

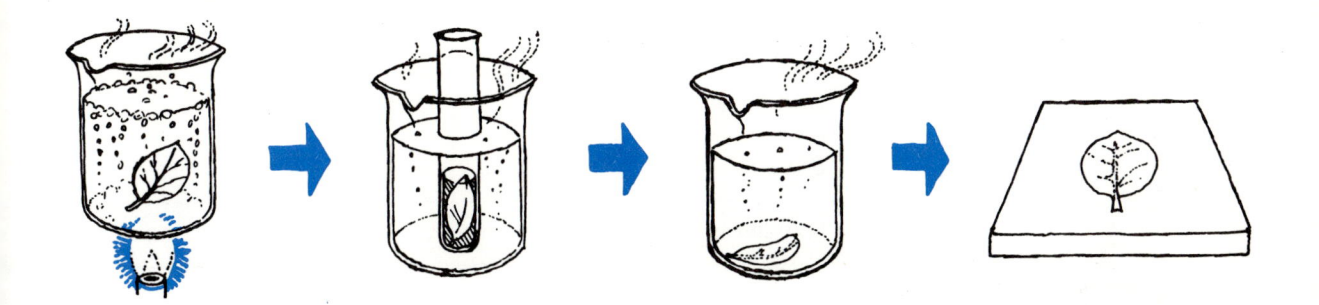

Boil a leaf in water for 2 minutes. This kills the leaf cells and softens the leaf.

Turn off the burner. Place the leaf carefully at the bottom of a test-tube. Add 2 ml ethanol. Put the test-tube in the beaker of hot water.
What does the ethanol do to the colour of the leaf?

When the leaf has lost most of its colour, lift it gently into the hot water to remove the ethanol. Then spread the leaf out on a white tile.

Add a few drops of iodine solution to the leaf.
Is there a colour change? Is there starch in the leaf?

Take a leaf from a geranium plant which has been kept in the dark for 2 days.
Carefully repeat the steps with this leaf to test for starch.
Is there starch present?

With no light, what happens to the starch in a plant?
With no light, what gas does a plant give out?
When these two things happen in animals, what name do we give to the process?
In the absence of light, what does a plant do?

Plants and food

We know how animals feed simply by watching them. We cannot see plants feeding, but they must get food to live. How do they get food? To answer this, collect your results together.

No light	Light
Carbon dioxide is	Carbon dioxide is
Starch is	Starch is
Oxygen is	Oxygen is

In the absence of light, plants respire. They give out carbon dioxide, and use up their food, starch. But what can plants do in the presence of light?

Take a leaf from a plant which has been grown without carbon dioxide in the air around it.
Carefully do the starch test with this leaf.
Can a leaf make starch without carbon dioxide?

You now know two things a plant needs to make its food. What are they?

Take a leaf from a plant whose leaves have two colours: green and another colour. Draw the leaf to show its colour pattern.
Test this leaf for starch.
Which parts of the leaf have starch?
Does the leaf have starch where there is no green colour?

Now you know three things a plant needs to make food. What are they?

Plants need one more thing to make their food. Without this they die. What is it?

Photosynthesis

Plants do not eat food, although they need the energy in food. They do not eat food because they make their own food.

Plants photosynthesize

Plants make food when the sun is shining. They use the energy of sunlight to join carbon dioxide particles with water particles. It is the job of the green stuff in plants to bring these three things together. In this process two things happen. New compounds are made, usually different kinds of sugar and starch. Making these new compounds is a way of storing the energy which comes from the sun. This process of making new compounds and storing energy is called photosynthesis.

And they respire

The food that is made in this way can be stored, or it can be used. It can be stored in many places, in many ways. It can be used to make new compounds, and these substances are needed for growth and development. Growth and development need energy. This food provides the energy in the process of respiration. In plants, as in animals and microbes, respiration takes place in all cells all the time. Photosynthesis takes place only in green cells and only in sunlight.

Animals respire only

We cannot make our food. Like all animals we must get our food from other organisms. So if the food we eat is traced back it always ends with plants. To respire that food we need oxygen. If the oxygen is traced back it too ends with plants. For when plants photosynthesize they give out oxygen. Without plants to trap the energy in sunlight, to produce oxygen, we cannot live. Plants need animals too. Can you see why?

An ocean of air 5

Scientists working with plants

Farmer Prepares soil. Decides when to sow seeds. Looks after growing plants. Harvests. Always looking for better ways of growing crops for a better yield.

Forester A tree farmer. Plants seeds. Looks after growing plants. Helps farmer by planting shelter belts to protect his crops.

Plant pathologist Studies plant diseases. What causes them? What can prevent them? Adviser to farmer and forester.

An ocean of air 5

Geneticist Breeds new varieties of plants which are resistant to disease and give better yields.

Plant hunter Searches wild places for new, useful plants. Works closely with geneticist, pathologist, and taxonomist.

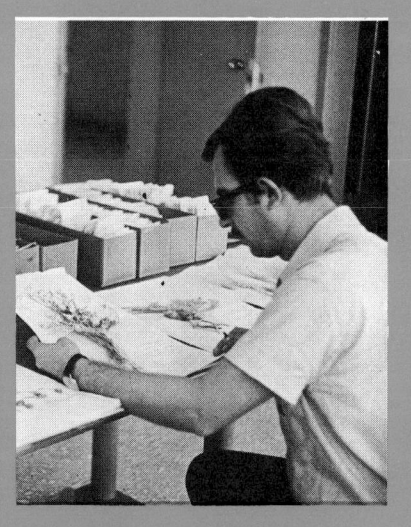

Taxonomist Describes and names plants. Is this a new variety of an old plant? Is it a completely new plant? Has a very important job.

Food engineer Gets food from farmer. Works out ways of preserving and processing this food.

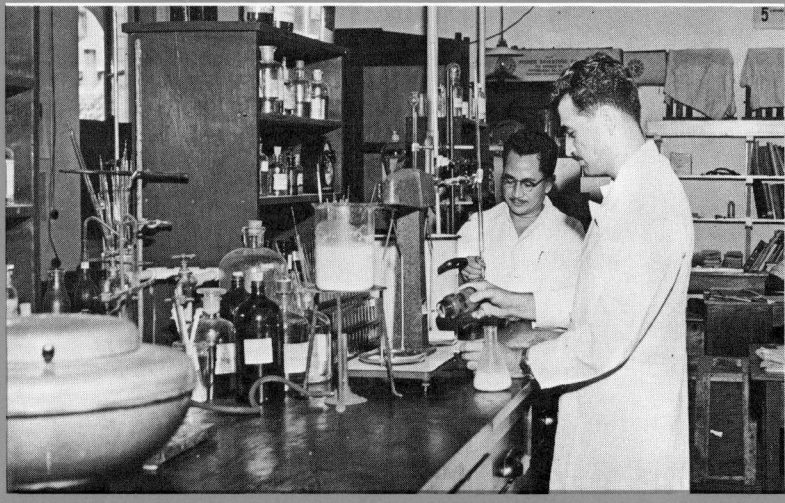

Biochemist Checks on the chemical make-up of plants. Looks for ways of extracting medicines and other chemicals from plants.

Puzzles and problems

Things to think out

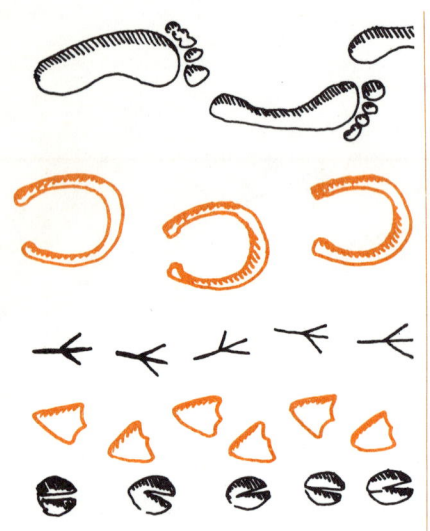

1 Which way were these animals going?

2 Which of these gear wheel systems will work?

3 Which of these bulbs will light?

4 Imagine a go-cart with two sizes of tyre. Which ones will wear down faster: the big ones or the small ones?

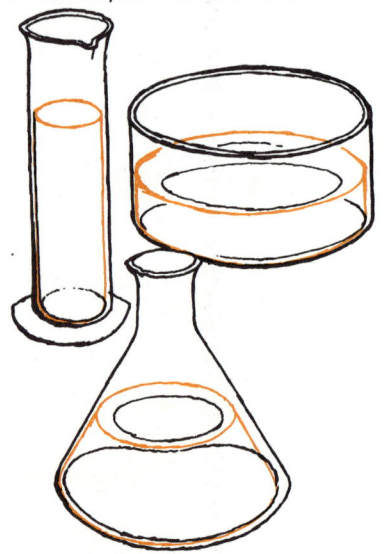

5 Each jar contains the same amount of water. In what order will they dry up?

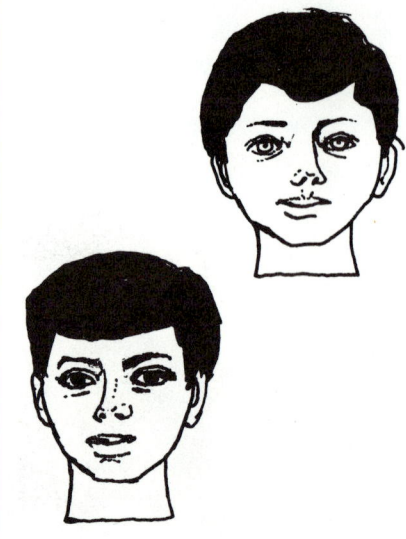

6 Most people's noses bend a little to one side of their faces. Are there more left hand noses than right hand ones? Do right hand noses go with right handed people?

Puzzles and problems

Things to do

1 Make a pop-up man. Use an egg shell, plasticine, match sticks, and a cork. Why does he pop up?

2 Put an ice cube in a glass. Fill the glass to the brim. Watch to see if the water spills as the ice melts.

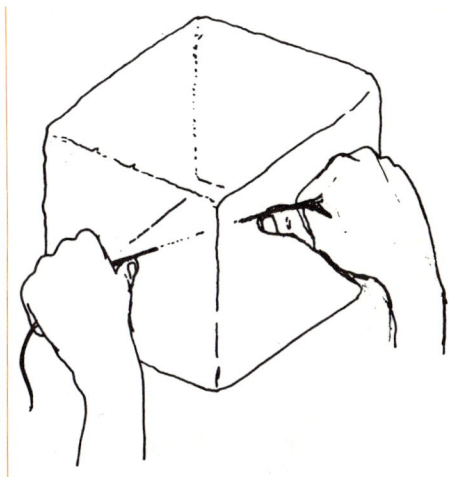

3 Can you cut a block of ice in two with a wire so that you still have only one block of ice?

4 Balance a brush on your hand for as long as you can. Then try to balance it the other way round. Which way is easier: holding the bristles or holding the handle?

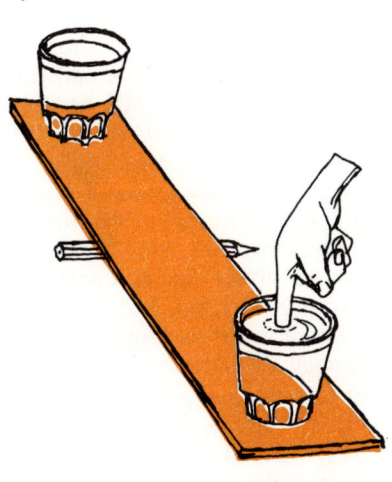

5 Balance two jars of water using a piece of wood and a six-sided pencil. What would happen if you put your finger into the water in one of the jars? Would they still balance?

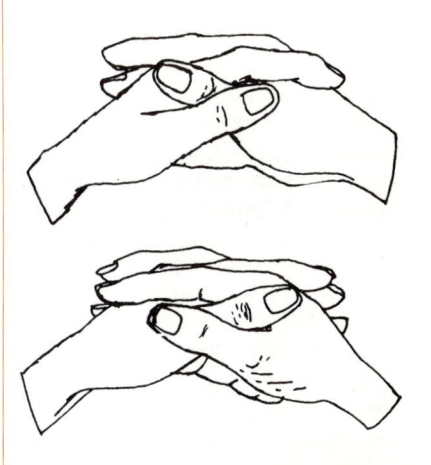

6 Clasp your hands together. Are you left thumbed or right thumbed? If you are left handed, are you also left thumbed? Find out how left and right handedness fits in with left and right thumbedness.

Acknowledgements

The authors are grateful for permission to reprint the following copyright works:

Extract 'Yellow fever' from *The microbe hunters* by Paul de Kruif, 1966. Reprinted by permission of Jonathan Cape Ltd. and Harcourt Brace & Jovanovich Inc, New York. Extract 'Ball lightning' from *Lightning* by Martin A. Uman, 1969. Reprinted by permission of McGraw Hill Book Company. Extract 'How cold it can be' from *HMS Ulysses* by Alistair Maclean, 1956. Reprinted by permission of Collins Publishers. Extract 'How the Bushmen get their water' from *The lost world of Kalahari* by Laurens van der Post, 1972. Reprinted by permission of the Hogarth Press Ltd. Extract 'Mr. Tanimoto's Story' from *Hiroshima* by John Hersey, 1946. Reprinted by permission of Hamish Hamilton Ltd. Adaptation 'Jumping into the oven' from *The Thunderstorm* by Louis J. Battan. Copyright © 1964 by Louis J. Battan. By arrangement with the New American Library Inc, New York, N.Y.

The publishers would like to thank the following for permission to reproduce photographs:

Anglo-American Corporation of South Africa, p. 84 bottom; Ardea Photographics, pp. 28 top centre, 105 top right, centre right, 178 top right, bottom centre; BBC, pp. 91, 124 bottom, 125 bottom left; Barnaby's Picture Library, p. 125 bottom right; Bell Laboratories, p. 131; Bolton Metropolitan Borough, p. 166 bottom left, bottom right; British Rail, p. 125 top left; Camera Press, pp. 13, 78, 79, 116 bottom right, 117 top right, top left, bottom right, 136 bottom right, bottom left, 166 top left, 167; Camera Talks, p. 116 bottom left; J. Allan Cash, p. 46 bottom centre; Central Electricity Generating Board, p. 137 top; Central Press Photos Ltd, pp. 41, 98 top left; Cinema International, p. 15 bottom left, bottom right; Bruce Coleman Ltd, pp. 22, 23 except centre left, 26 top, 27 centre, 28 top, top centre, centre, bottom, 105 centre left, centre, centre right, bottom centre, bottom right, 108, 172 top left, centre, bottom centre, 178 top left, centre top, centre left, bottom left; Columbia-Warner, p. 14 bottom left, bottom right; Euan Duff, pp. 98 bottom left, 99 top right, bottom left; M. C. Esher, p. 11; Mary Evans Picture Library, p. 123; FAO, pp. 84, 85; Forestry Commission, p. 184 top right; Gas Council, p. 46 bottom left; General Foods Corporation, p. 160 top; Henry Grant, pp. 89 bottom right, 109; HM the Queen (by gracious permission), p. 9 bottom; HMSO (Crown Copyright reserved), p. 72 centre; John Halas, p. 14 top; Philip Harris Ltd, p. 128 top right; Philip Harris Biological Ltd, pp. 101, 162; John Hillelson Agency Ltd, pp. 110, 111; ICI, p. 66; IMI, p. 161 top left; Keystone Press Agency, p. 166 top right; Frank W. Lane, pp. 20, 130; MCA, p. 15 top left; Mansell Collection, pp. 8, 9 top, 84 centre, 122, 143 bottom, 148 bottom, 161 top right; Meat and Livestock Commission, p. 161 top centre, bottom centre; Microcolour Ltd, p. 100; Bill Miller, p. 27 top; G. Munker, p. 124 top; NASA, p. 6 bottom right; National Coal Board, p. 46 centre left; National Publicity Studios New Zealand, p. 105 top centre; L. Hugh Newman, pp. 23 centre left, 28 bottom centre, 105 top left, 172 top centre, centre right, bottom left; Northern Electric Research Laboratories, p. 136 bottom centre; Novosti Press Agency, p. 149 bottom; Oxfam, p. 47; Pace, p. 136 top centre, top right; Paul Popper Ltd, pp. 161 bottom left, 172 centre left; Radio Times Hulton Picture Library, pp. 117 bottom left, 143 top, 148 top right, 149 top left; Ronan Picture Library, pp. 142; 148 top left, 160 bottom; Royal College of Surgeons, p. 116 top right; Shell, p. 46 top; Sony, p. 149 top right; J. R. Tabberner, pp. 27, 125 top right, bottom left, 137 except top, 172 bottom right; Twentieth Century Fox, p. 15 top right; UNESCO, pp. 72 left, right, 73; USIS, p. 167 centre; United Kingdom Atomic Energy Authority, p. 46 bottom right; John Walmsley, pp. 98 top centre, top right, centre left, centre right, bottom right, 99; Wellcome Museum, pp. 6 centre right, 116 top left.